Webs of Influence

Webs of Influence

Rahul Dev

Webs of Influence

ISBN 978-93-5111-249-5

Published in 2014 in India by

RANDOM PUBLICATIONS

4376-A/4B, Gali Murari Lal, Ansari Road
New Delhi-110 002
Phone : +91-11-43580356, +91-11-23289044
e-mail: randomexports@gmail.com, sales@randompublications.com, info@randompublications.com

Type Setting by : Keystoneprintads, Delhi-110051
Printed at Thomson Press (India) Ltd

Preface

Public Relations has been flirting with neuroscience for some time now, but although the attractions are obvious, it often seems that the relationship is still at the giggling and coy glances stage.

For PR, the factors that prevent full on courtship include shame and lack of self confidence. Some in PR go to great lengths to promote their good intentions as communicators and information providers, and go all squeamish if it is suggested they might be trying to manipulate the way people think and behave. Studying the science of how people make decisions and learning psychological techniques to trigger certain behaviours is somehow cheating.... and bad PR for a discipline that is so sensitive to mentions of propaganda and spin.

As we all know that Webs is one of the most important topics in today's world. Many books have been written in this topic. This modest effort is another pearl in the sequence. This book has been designed in mind the mentality of the general reader's language which is easy to understandable. The aim of this book is to provide students and lectures with a clear concise and comprehensive introduction to the theory and practice of advertising management.

The book is well organized easy to read and coves the syllabi of numerous universities by covering the entire scale of the subject and providing the students and practitioners with a thorough understanding of web of influence concerns in the financial services industry enabling them to evaluate the overall organizational impact and gain a better understanding.

We hope that the discussion made in this book will help the readers to understand and learnt about the different aspects of "Webs of Influence" in a most comprehensive way to face the present and future challenges which are occurred in this field.

I thank all members of my team who have helped in the preparation of the book. My special thanks go to "Random Publications" who have published the book.

– Rahul Dev

Contents

1

Influence of Online Store Characteristics on Consumer Impulsive Decision-making

INTRODUCTION

Consumers increasingly engage in impulsive online decision-making. Triggered by an easy access to products, instant ordering, lack of social pressures, and absence of delivery efforts, impulse purchases are assumed to account for about 40% of all online expenditures. As insight into consumer buying behavior is vital for e-commerce practitioners, it becomes important to understand the nature of online impulse decision-making and address the role of online store characteristics therein. Despite the relevance of impulsive decision-making, there is remarkably little research into the influence of online store characteristics on impulsive buying behavior.

The vast majority of online consumer research views purchase decision-making as a rational process, based on cognitive problem solving and information processing. From this perspective, decision-making usually is seen as sequence of belief formation, attitude formation, intention formation, and actual purchase behavior. Captured into models such as the theory of reasoned action and the technology acceptance model, researchers applied this sequence of effects to study the influence of online store beliefs such as online store merchandise, website style, ease of use and enjoyment on rational buying behavior. While these studies add to our knowledge on the impact of the online store on rational buying, they fail to provide insight into situations where decision-making is spontaneous, unreflective, dominated by emotions, and immediate, that is, in impulse buying situations.

We construct and empirically test a model relating the online store characteristics merchandise, ease of use, enjoyment, and website style to consumer impulse buying. By introducing the model, we intend to make four contributions. First, we aim to enhance our understanding of the impulse buying process. Conceptual foundations are discussed and incorporated in the proposed model. Second, using traditional theory on impulsive buying behavior as backbone, we test the applicability of this theory in online buying settings. This contribution can be seen as contextual extension. Third, being a core element of impulsive decision-making, we explicitly address the role of emotions in online settings. Knowledge about the role of emotions in online environments is scarce.

Fourth we validate the influence of four common online store characteristics on online impulsive decision-making. As such, we assess the impact of the online store on consumer decision-making beyond rational buying settings. The rest of this paper is organized as follows. In section 2, we discuss the concept of impulsive decision-making and provide a review of available works on online impulse buying. In section 3, we develop hypotheses and introduce our research model. Section 4 describes our research methodology, while section 5 reports on the empirical results of this study. In section 6 we discuss our findings and arrive at conclusions. We close with limitations and recommendations in section 7.

THEORETICAL BACKGROUND

THE BUYING IMPULSE

Impulse buying occurs when people experience a sudden urge to buy a product, without engaging in extensive cognitive evaluation and prepurchase deliberation. The urge to buy is often irresistible, and consumers may therefore feel temporarily out of control and pay less attention to behavioral consequences. As affective rather than cognitive processes dominate impulse buying, the decisionmaking usually is short and rather spontaneous in nature. The affective nature of impulsive decision-making also implies that consumers may experience ambivalence towards the purchase, since immediate gratification and long term consequences may pull the consumers in two directions. Typically, impulsive buying occurs at the spot, that is, in the shopping environment.

The instantaneous nature of impulse buying implies that 'the only available information, aside from internal or memory-base information, is the external information available in the shopping environment'. Therefore, one might assume that in-store information plays a substantial role in consumer impulsive decision-making, and may even have more influence than in planned buying situations. In-store elements that have been associated with impulse buying include product selection, store atmospherics, product pricing, promotions, easy payments, and word-of-mouth. By adding to the affective state of consumers, these elements may trigger impulsive behavior. When comparing the impulse buying process to contemplative buying processes, two core elements characterize impulse buying. First, the impulse buying process is unplanned and lacks deliberation. Although not all unplanned purchases are impulsive; unplanned purchases might be rational and may be decided later on, possibly away from the store as stimulus; the vice versa is true, that is, the impulse buying process is unplanned. This implies that consumers do not engage in extensive deliberation and evaluation, nor do they apply cognitive processes to consider costs, benefits or consequences. As such, the impulse buying process is unintended and does not lead to the formation of cognitive-structured attitudes or intentions. Second, emotions dominate the impulse buying process.

By emotions we refer to "a mental state of readiness that arises from cognitive appraisals of events or thoughts; has a phenomenal tone; is accompanied by physiological processes; is often expressed physically; and may result in specific actions to affirm or cope with the emotion, depending in its nature and meaning for the person having it". Although impulsive buying does not completely preclude information processing, emotions play a key role in the impulse buying process and may directly lead to impulse buying action. While many conceptualizations on emotions exist, most conceptualizations distinguish emotions into positive and negative affect. Positive emotions such as pleasure and excitement may stimulate people rewarding themselves and have them fulfill their need for instant gratification by buying the product. Negative emotions, like feelings of depression or sadness, on the other hand, may also stimulate impulse buying since buying the product helps consumers to feel better. In line with the above conceptualization, and following the works of and, online impulse purchasing is defined in this study as 'A sudden and immediate online purchase with no pre-shopping intentions, which occurs after experiencing an urge to buy and tends to be spontaneous, driven by emotions, and without a lot of deliberation'. This definition excludes other types of unplanned purchases as well as reminder impulse buying, that is consumers remembering previous knowledge of experience, which triggers the impulse purchase.

RESEARCH ON CONSUMER ONLINE IMPULSE BUYING

A few empirical studies into online impulse buying exist. Next to providing insights into the online impulse buying process, these works seem to offer interesting opportunities for further refinements. Adelaar, Chang, Lancendorfer, Lee and Morimoto were among the first to study online impulse buying. Using a student sample, they tested the direct influence of media format and emotions on consumers' impulse buying intent for music CDs. Their results indicated a rather strong effect of arousal as emotional determinant of the impulse buying intent. No clear evidence was found for effects of media format on either emotions or impulse buying intent. As the authors conceptualized the impulse buying intent as rational purchase intention, and measured the construct accordingly, the applicability of their model for studying the online buying impulse may leave room for discussion. Zhang and his associates addressed the influence of consumers' general tendency to buy impulsively on consumers' intentions to buy online. Using a student sample, Zhang, Prybutok and Koh tested this relationship as part of a modified TAM model. The results indicated a small though significant direct effect. A follow up study of Zhang, Prybutok and Strutton confirmed this outcome for another TAM modification, validated on another student sample.

While both studies provide insight in the role of consumer impulsiveness in online purchase behavior, the applicability of the adopted TAM perspective may be subject to debate. In fact, this view contrasts with the main body of consumer behavior literature claiming that impulse buying is unintended in nature; driven by emotions; does not lead to the formation of cognitive-structured intentions, and is unlikely to be captured via traditional attitude/ intention models. Jeffrey and Hodge conducted an experiment with visitors of an online transaction site to study the influences of amount of money spend and provision of a reason to purchase on consumers' likelihood to buy an impulse product. The outcomes of a logistic regression analysis demonstrated a significant though small effect of amount of money spent prior to purchase on the likelihood of buying impulse items. Moreover, a t-test showed that consumers are more willing to buy an impulse item when a part of the spend money is donated to a charity foundation.

As the study conceptualized impulse buying as unintended purchase, a conceptual limitation may be that the spontaneous and sudden nature of impulse buying was left outside consideration. Furthermore, no particular attention was paid to emotions. Finally, we refer to the study of Parboteeah et al. who proposed an integrated model of visual appeal, information fit-to-task, usefulness, enjoyment and urge to buy impulsively. Visual appeal and information fit-to-task were postulated as website characteristics that both lead to cognitive and affective reactions. Furthermore, usefulness was hypothesized as enjoyment determinant while enjoyment was proposed in the model as direct determinant of the urge to buy impulsively. An experimental study with a student sample was then conducted to test the research model in an online shopping context.

The empirical results confirmed the entire model structure and show that the urge to buy is directly and strongly determined by enjoyment. A follow-up experiment in their study validated the outcomes. A possible area for improvement of the model concerns the explicit focus on positive affect. As there is relative consensus in the literature that impulse buying is subject to positive *and* negative emotions, this leaves room for extensions. The above demonstrates the progress made in the current research field. More important, it suggests that if we want to further our understanding on online impulse buying we need to exclude rational paradigms, include the sudden nature of the buying impulse, focus on emotions, and pay attention to positive and negative emotions. Here, we intend to incorporate these elements into a model relating online store characteristics to impulse buying behavior. In the next section, we introduce the model and elaborate on its conceptual foundations.

HYPOTHESES DEVELOPMENT

As discussed above, several studies have shown that impulse buying is influenced by the emotions that consumers experience. Other influences on impulse buying have also been suggested but the empirical evidence is scarce. For instance, it has been suggested that the urge to buy impulsively influences impulse buying but this influence is hardly empirically demonstrated, offline and online. Furthermore, it is also known that the urge to buy is influenced by positive affect, negative affect, and the browsing activity.

However, only have demonstrated this latter influence of browsing. In this study, we will consolidate these influences mentioned above in the online context. Furthermore, we research what the antecedents are of affective responses and what causes browsing behavior in an online context, influences that have not been researched so far. It is well known that when online users visit a website, they will have cognitive as well as affective reactions. Especially affective responses have been found to be of influence on the urge to buy impulsively. A considerable amount of research has been undertaken regarding the structure of affect and two dominant emotional dimensions of affect have consistently emerged: positive affect and negative affect. These two dimensions have been shown to be stable across cultures, gender and age groups. Positive affect and negative affect are considered as independent, i.e. orthogonal and to represent two independent dimensions. According to positive affect "reflects the extent to which a person feels enthusiastic, active, and alert". High positive affect is a state of high energy, pleasurable engagement and concentration. Negative affect is the dimension for general distress and includes emotions like anger, disgust, guilt and fear.

Several types of factors have found to be of influence on affect. In this paper, we focus on two types of store attributes that might influence affect, i.e., high taskrelevant cues and low task-relevant cues. High task-relevant cues are the site descriptors "that appear on the screen which facilitate and enable the consumer's shopping goal attainment", like merchandise and ease of use. Low taskrelevant cues refer to "site information that is relatively inconsequential to completion of the shopping task", like website enjoyment and website style. High and low task-relevant cues are suggested to influence consumer emotions. However, empirical research on these effects is scarce. show that these cues influence perceived enjoyment, but do not focus on positive affect in general or negative affect. Furthermore, they only focus on information fit-to-task as the high task-relevant cue and visual appeal as the low task-relevant cue. In this study we take a broader spectrum of cues into account.

THE INFLUENCE OF HIGH TASK-RELEVANT CUE ON AFFECT AND BROWSING

An important task-relevant cue is merchandise, which refers to aspects like the number of products on a site, interesting offers, value for money, and whether products are aligned to the consumer's interest. Merchandise has been suggested to influence affect. However, the link between products and emotions has only been empirically researched in the offline context. For instance, shows that products can create positive affect such as joy, pleasure and delight as well as negative effect like worry, irritation, and disappointment. In the online context, the link between special offerings and positive affect has been shown for auctions. In line with this research we argue that websites with products that are in line with the consumers' interests and with interesting offers may create positive feelings. Furthermore, we believe that good merchandise will produce less negative affect. Therefore, we hypothesize:

- There is a positive relationship between perceived online store merchandise and positive affect.
- There is a negative relationship between perceived online store merchandise and negative affect.

Ease of use is another important high task-relevant cue. Ease of use of the website allows the customer to easily access the products, there is an organized layout, consumers can easily navigate the site, and learn how to use the site.

Although the direct influence of ease of use on affect has not been researched, several related constructs indicate an influence. For instance, and found out that a positive evaluation of usability, including ease of use, has a positive impact on positive emotions and a negative impact on negative emotions. show in their study that system design plays a very important role in triggering emotional reactions such as pleasure and arousal that are significant determinants of the online buying impulse. And although not researched empirically yet, it is understandable that in case a site is more easy to use, consumers will experience less distress and will explore and consequently browse the site more. Therefore, we hypothesize:

- There is a positive relationship between perceived ease of use and positive affect.
- There is a negative relationship between perceived ease of use and negative affect.
- There is a positive relationship between perceived ease of use and browsing.

THE INFLUENCE OF LOW TASK-RELEVANT CUE ON AFFECT AND BROWSING

An important low task-relevant cue is enjoyment, which refers to a fun site, whether it is a great pleasure to browse through the site, and the attractiveness of the site. The influence of site enjoyment on affect has not been researched as such, but several related constructs have been found to influence affect. For instance, reveal in their study that cues like music in the background and visual effects have a significant effect on positive emotions and compared to the high task-related cues, are a stronger predictor of positive affect.

Also, show that a fun website may create positive affect. This is in line with the findings of that, in an offline context, individuals who enjoy shopping in the store more tend to experience more positive affect. Also, demonstrate that fun aspects on a website can offset negative effects. Applying this to our research, this may suggest that site enjoyment may decrease irritation and distress.

Finally, it is expected that site enjoyment will increase browsing behavior on a website. Beatty and Ferrell, in an offline context, expected but did not find that shopping enjoyment lead to more in-store browsing. However, they point out that this might be caused by the lack of a clear distinction between browsing and shopping. "True shoppers" may have not liked their definition of browsing – just looking around. Overall, it is understandable to expect that the enjoyment that consumers experience, while being on the website will positively influence their online browsing. Therefore, we hypothesize:

- There is a positive relationship between perceived shopping enjoyment and positive affect.
- There is a negative relationship between perceived shopping enjoyment and negative affect.
- There is a positive relationship between perceived shopping enjoyment and browsing.

Website style is another important low task-relevant cue. Website style refers to the fact whether a website is calm, friendly, and knowledgably. Like with the other cues, the effect of website style on affect has not been researched as such but several related constructs indicate its influence. For instance, in their research on the effects of multi-media website content on emotions and impulse buying found that a video format alone on a website was not enough to generate the positive feeling that was expected. However, showing the lyrics while playing the song created positive feelings. So, a mix of verbal and visual stimuli, i.e. more knowledge on the website, could strengthen emotional responses from the consumers.

In another research, show that the more interactive and the more vivid the online stimuli, the stronger is the pleasure and the higher the arousal felt by online customer. Finally, we believe that in case a site has a better style, consumers will experience less distress and irritation. Therefore, we hypothesize:

- There is a positive relationship between perceived website style and positive affect.
- There is a negative relationship between perceived website style and negative affect.

THE INFLUENCE OF EMOTIONS AND BROWSING ON URGE TO BUY AND IMPULSE BUYING

Several researchers identified affect as a variable that influences impulse purchasing. Also argue that when one is experiencing positive affect, one is more likely to engage in approach behavior than avoidance behavior. When negative affect is experienced one's urge to buy impulsively may be influenced negatively. Although they write about general affect, they specifically measure emotions. In addition, as well as show that the more of a positive emotion felt by the individual, the greater the likelihood of overspending and impulse buying. We, in line with argue that emotions influence impulse buying through a stronger urge to buy. Therefore, we hypothesize:

- There is a positive relationship between positive affect and urge to buy.
- There is a negative relationship between negative affect and urge to buy.

The effect of browsing on impulse buying has only been empirically researched by. They argue that browsing is a central component in the impulse buying process. As consumers browse longer, they will encounter more stimuli, which would increase the likelihood of experiencing impulse buying urges. And, obviously, as more urges are experienced, the likelihood of engaging in an impulse purchase increases. Although show these relationships in the offline context, we argue that the same effects may happen in the online context. While browsing online, consumer encounter desirable products and these encounters produce an urge to buy. This urge is difficult to resist as it is just one click to get the product in the online shopping cart. Therefore, we hypothesize:

- There is a positive relationship between browsing and urge to buy.
- There is a positive relationship between urge to buy and impulse buy.

RESEARCH METHOD

PROCEDURE

An online survey design was adopted to collect empirical data. The sample consisted of customers of an online store selling fashion items in the Netherlands. Our decision to focus on fashion products was supported by the fact that these products evoke affective reactions and support consumers' selfimages, two product characteristics that are assumed to trigger impulsive decisionmaking. As impulse buying is accompanied by an immediate desire to buy and usually occurs spontaneously, a pre-purchase survey was unlikely to grasp the instantaneous nature of the phenomenon. Therefore, we adopted the approach of and gathered information from buyers immediately *after* the overt buying behavior. Customers who completed an online transaction received an invitation to participate freely in the study, which was shown in the order confirmation that appeared on screen after the transaction closure. The invitation included a link that led to a webbased survey. The online survey addressed perceptions of the research constructs, and socio-demographics. As an incentive, respondents were asked to fill in their e-mail address to engage in the raffle of a book token of 50 Euro, and two clothing items together being worth 95 Euro. The questionnaire was constructed using standard translation and back translation. A member of the research team translated the questionnaire into Dutch. A second member of the research team compared this Dutch questionnaire to the original American English questionnaire. To investigate whether the Dutch draft questionnaire contained any faults in the wording that could result in comprehension difficulties a pretest was held. Six graduate students participated in the test. The participants were asked to evaluate the clarity and interpretability of the questionnaire. Following this pretest, the participants met with one member of the research team to discuss and suggest improvements. Some minor modifications were made.

MEASURES

We operationalized the constructs with multi-item scales. The items for the *merchandise* construct were derived from the online store studies of and. *Ease of use, enjoyment* and *website style* were adopted from. *Browsing, positive affect, negative affect* and *urge to buy* were modified from. The major modification included the change of wording of the positive affect and negative affect items to make them applicable for the online context. To measure *impulse buy* we applied established procedures on scale construction. First, the construct was conceptualized and defined. Then, a sample of six items was selected based on previous literature, each of the items tapping into the conceptual domain of the construct. To judge the representativeness of the items, a pretest was conducted with a panel of three IS researchers. To judge the interpretability and ambiguity of the items, a focus group interviews with 10 undergraduate students was held. Based on the pretest and the focus group interviews, some minor refinements were made. Finally, a pilot test was conducted using 85 undergraduate students following a course e-business. The subjects were asked to keep track of their online purchases during the period of the course, and fill in the test survey each time after completing an online purchase. This resulted in 64 viable responses that were then used to study the convergent validity, discriminant validity and reliability of the instrument. We removed one item. The remaining instrument was unidimensional and contained an acceptable alpha.

SAMPLE

The online survey yielded 532 responses. The sample characteristics. The demographics indicate that the majority of the respondents was between 15 and 34 years old, and mostly female. Most respondents considered themselves experienced in using the Internet, while a slight majority reported to have experience in buying at the online fashion store. The online store confirmed that the sample profile matched their own findings on the customer profile. Although a sample bias was noticed, the Internet shopper is assumed to be more balanced in gender and more diverse in age, it is likely to be representative for the kind of store under examination.

DATA ANALYSIS AND RESULTS

VALIDITY AND RELIABILITY OF MEASUREMENT

Confirmatory factor analysis (CFA) was applied to test the adequacy of the measurement model. The software package Amos 7 with maximum likelihood estimation (MLE) was used for the analysis. The initial fit indices demonstrated poor fit. Following model respecification procedures we focused on the pattern of residuals to assess whether items shared a high residual variance with items across constructs. Five items shared large residuals with other items.

We deleted these items and reran the CFA. Overall, the respecified model demonstrated a satisfactory fit, suggesting unidimensionality, convergent validity and discriminant validity of the measures. We conducted additional study on convergent validity, and assessed measurement reliability by computation of Cronbach's alphas, composite reliabilities, minimum item-to-total correlations and Average Variance Extracted (AVE). The convergent validity of the measures was confirmed by the alphas, minimum itemto- total correlations, and AVE's. All scores exceeded accepted criteria.

Except for the two-item measure *browsing,* the alphas exceeded the value of 0.70. As all composite reliability scores exceeded the value of 0.70, and all AVEs surpassed the 0.50 guideline, acceptable reliability of all measures was demonstrated. Finally, we further tested for discriminant validity by comparing the square roots of average variance extracted of each construct with its squared correlations with other constructs. The results confirmed discriminant validity as all squared AVEs exceeded the values of the squared correlations.

Finally, as both dependent and independent variables were collected from the same respondents, we decided to test for common method bias by conducting Harmon's single-factor test. First, we loaded all measurement items into one exploratory factor analysis and assessed whether a) one single factor emerged or b) one factor emerged that accounted for the majority of the variance. As the factor solution demonstrated more than one factor, and the first factor accounted for 27.3% of the variance, no indication for common method bias was found. Second, we conducted a CFA to assess the fit of a single factor model and compared the outcomes with the fit indices of the nine-factor measurement model. The single-factor model showed very poor fit, which confirmed the absence of common method bias.

HYPOTHESIS TESTING

SEM was applied to estimate the structural model and test the hypotheses. The results indicated a good fit with the data. The path coefficients (ß) and *R*2 values of the structural model. Overall, the results confirm the predictive power of the model. The results indicate that nine hypotheses are accepted are rejected.

2

The Internet and Surveillance

INTRODUCTION

Surveillance has notably increased in the last decades of modern society. Surveillance studies scholars like David Lyon or Clive Norris and Gary Armstrong stress that we live in a surveillance society. Although there are a lot of other features in contemporary society, such as information, neoliberalism, globalization, or capitalism, surveillance in general and Internet surveillance in particular are crucial phenomena. For instance, web 2.0 activities, such as creating profiles and sharing ideas on Facebook, announcing personal messages on Twitter, uploading or watching videos on YouTube, and writing personal entries on Blogger, enables the collection, analyzes, and sale of personal data by commercial web platforms. The overall aim of this chapter is to clarify how we can theorize and systemize such phenomena. Lyon accentuates that economic surveillance on the Internet such as monitoring consumers or the workplace, are central aspects of modern surveillance societies. The approach that is advanced in this chapter recognizes the importance of the role of the economy in contemporary surveillance societies. For doing so, the following thematically grouped research questions are subject to this contribution:

- Foundations of Internet surveillance studies:
  - How is Internet surveillance defined in the existing literature?
  - What are commonalties and differences of various notions of Internet surveillance?
  - What are advantages and disadvantages of such definitions?
- Critical Internet surveillance studies:
  - Which theory provides a typology in order to systemize Internet surveillance in the modern economy?
  - What are examples of Internet surveillance in the spheres of production, circulation, and consumption?

This paper wants to undertake a systematic analysis of surveillance in general and Internet surveillance in particular in the modern economy and wants to study the field of surveillance critically. It deals with surveillance in the modern economy and is a critical contribution to surveillance studies insofar as it is based on the foundations of a critical political economy approach. The term Internet refers to the global system of computer networks that use the Internet Protocol Suite. Emerged in the 1970s, the Internet is a network of networks which includes systems such as the world wide web and the infrastructure of electronic mail. According to The Oxford Dictionary of English, the term surveillance originated from the French sur- "over" + veiller "watch" and from the Latin vigilare "keep watch" in the early 19th century.

The term modern economy refers to the capitalistic economy of modern societies. Modern society is the historical period, which has begun with the Enlightenment and lasts up to today. This contribution constructs theoretically founded typologies in order to systemize the existing literature of Internet surveillance studies and to analyze examples of surveillance. Therefore, it mainly is a theoretical approach combined with illustrative examples, advancing from the abstract to the concrete level. Based on the research questions and the described methodology, the following structure can be outlined. Section two analyzes how Internet surveillance is defined in the existing literature, what commonalties and differences of various notions of online surveillance exist, and what advantages and disadvantages such definitions have.

Furthermore, section two describes how different notions deal with economic surveillance on the Internet and makes clear if there is a gap in the existing literature in order to study Internet surveillance in the modern economy. The specific economic mode of Internet surveillance is studied in section three. Based on the foundations of a critical political economy approach and the distinction of surveillance in the economy into the spheres of production, circulation, and consumption, a typology of online surveillance in the economy can be constructed. Constructing a theoretically founded typology of economic surveillance is important in order to undertake a systematic analysis of surveillance in the modern economy. Economic surveillance on the Internet in the spheres of production, circulation, and consumption will be outlined. Section four concludes with a summary and makes some political recommendations in order to overcome Internet surveillance in the modern economy.

FOUNDATIONS OF INTERNET SURVEILLANCE STUDIES

Since Michel Foucault has published his book Surveiller et punir in French in 1975 and in English in 1977, the amount of literature on surveillance has increased enormously and represents a diffuse and complex field of research. Lyon stresses: "Michel Foucault's celebrated, and contentious, historical studies of surveillance and discipline had appeared that mainstream social theorists began to take surveillance seriously in its own right". David

Murakami Wood emphasizes that "for Surveillance Studies, Foucault is a foundational thinker and his work on the development of the modern subject, in particular Surveillir et Punir, remains a touchstone for this nascent transdisciplinary field". According to Google Scholar, Foucault's book Discipline and Punish is cited more than 17 thousand times. According to the Encyclopedia of Philosophy and to the Routledge Encyclopedia of Philosophy, Foucault is one of the most important historians and philosophers of the 20th century with wide influence in different disciplines.

The overall aim of this section is to elucidate how Internet surveillance is defined in the existing literature, what commonalties and differences of various notions of online surveillance exist, and what advantages and disadvantages such definitions have. For doing so, Foucault's understanding of surveillance and the idea of the panopticon are introduced. Based on these findings, subsections two and three of this section contain a systematic discussion of the state of the art of Internet surveillance by establishing a typology of the existing literature and discussing commonalties and differences. For analyzing the existing literature on a more abstract level and identifying advantages and disadvantages, it is essential to discuss commonalties and differences and to find certain typologies. Finally, subsection four gives a summary, discusses how different notions deal with Internet surveillance in the modern economy and makes clear if there is a gap in the existing literature.

FOUCAULT'S NOTION OF SURVEILLANCE AND THE PANOPTICON

Foucault analyzes surveillance in the context of the emergence of disciplinary societies. He stresses an evolution from feudal societies of torture, to reformed societies of punishment, and on to modern disciplinary societies. In the age of torture, arbitrary penalties and public spectacles of the scaffold took place in order to exterminate bodies. Afterwards, in the age of punishment, defendants were punished and exterminated. In the age of disciplines, direct violence has been replaced with softer forms of power in order to discipline, control, and normalize people in respect of drilling docile bodies and "political puppets".

For Foucault, Jeremy Bentham's panopticon is a symbol for modern disciplinary society. "On the whole, therefore, one can speak of the formation of a disciplinary society in this movement that stretches from the enclosed disciplines, a sort of social 'quarantine', to an indefinitely generalizable mechanism of 'panopticism'". The panopticon is an ideal architectural figure of modern disciplinary power. It exists of an annular building divided in different cells and a huge tower with windows in the middle. Prisoners, workers, pupils, as well as patients stay in the cells and a supervisor occupies the middle tower. The architecture allows the supervisor to observe all individuals in the cells without being seen. Not every inmate is observed at every moment, but no one knows if she or he is monitored. Observation is possible anytime. As a result, everyone acts as if kept under surveillance all the time – individuals discipline themselves out of fear of surveillance. The panopticon creates a consciousness of permanent visibility as a form of power, where no bars, chains, and heavy locks are necessary for domination any more.

Foucault finally asks: "Is it surprising that prisons resemble factories, schools, barracks, hospitals, which all resemble prisons?" In summary, Foucault analyzes surveillance in the context of the emergence of modern disciplinary societies. He understands disciplines as forms of operational power relations and technologies of domination in order to discipline, control, and normalize people. For Foucault, the panopticon is an ideal symbol of modern surveillance societies. Foucault's understanding of surveillance and the panopticon allows to distinguish panoptic and non-panoptic approaches of defining Internet surveillance that can be used for constructing a typology of existing surveillance literature and for discussing commonalties and differences of definitions of Internet surveillance: The task of the following two subsections is to give a representative, but still eclectic overview about different definitions of online surveillance.

NON-PANOPTIC NOTIONS OF INTERNET SURVEILLANCE

Lyon understands the "world wide web of surveillance" as a neutral concept that identifies positive consequences such as protection and security as well as negative consequences such as control. Computerization of surveillance makes bureaucratic administration easier and surveillance in cyberspace permits "greater efficiency and speed, and may well result in increased benefits for citizens and consumers, who experience them as enhancing their comfort, convenience, and safety". Nevertheless, Lyon says that the nation-state and the capitalist workplace are the main sites of surveillance on the Internet and argues that surveillance technologies such as the Internet reinforce asymmetrical power relations on an extensive and intensive level. "So surveillance spreads, becoming constantly more routine, more intensive and extensive, driven by economic, bureaucratic and now technological forces".

The Internet has become a multi-billion dollar industry, because it is primarily corporations that are interested in collecting, analyzing and assessing a huge amount of personal consumer data in order to target personalized advertisement. Similarly to Lyon's notion of Internet surveillance that assumes there are enabling and constraining effects, Seumas Miller and John Weckert articulate advantages and disadvantages of being monitored. Their paper examines monitoring at the workplace in general and observing of email and the Internet usage in particular. Although the authors claim that privacy is a moral right and criticize existing approaches that stress benefits of workplace monitoring for both employers and employees, they argue that "surveillance and monitoring can be justified in some circumstances"and reason: "The proposition must be rejected that the extent and nature of the enjoyment of rights to individual privacy is something to be determined by the most powerful forces of the day, be they market or bureaucratic forces." For Anders Albrechtslund, positive aspects of being under surveillance are worth mentioning and he argues that online surveillance also empowers the users, constructs subjectivity, and is playful. Internet surveillance as social and participatory act involves mutuality and sharing.

Hille Koskela emphasizes individuals' active role in the context of surveillance in general and online surveillance in particular. For instance, reality shows are based on viewer participation, mobile phones with cameras create an active subject, and home webcams generate new subjectivities. Koskela wants to analyze "the other side of surveillance", which has resistant and liberating elements. "Webcams can also be argued to contribute to the 'democratization' of surveillance". In addition, Koskela argues that webcams have an empowering role and that the active role of individuals with surveillance equipment shows that the lines of control are blurred. In conclusion, non-panoptic notions of Internet surveillance either use a neutral concept that assumes there are enabling effects such as protection and security as well as constraining effects such as control or a positive concept that identifies comical, playful, amusing, and even enjoyable characteristics of surveillance and where everyone has the opportunity to surveil.

In addition, these approaches tend to reject the proposition that surveillance mechanisms are dominated by political and economic actors and see monitoring not necessarily as annoying and disturbing. In nonpanoptic notions, Internet surveillance is understood as a useful and effective management tool and as fair methods and procedures of monitoring individuals online. Now, we move on to panoptic notions of Internet surveillance.

PANOPTIC NOTIONS OF INTERNET SURVEILLANCE

Based on a diagrammatic understanding of panoptic surveillance, Greg Elmer predominantly understands the Internet as a powerful space of economic surveillance. "The Internet is first mapped, through indexical search engines, and then diagnosed, via 'spiders' and 'cookies', to actively monitor, survey, solicit and subsequently profile users' online behavior". Corporations map consumer profiles including demographic and psychographic data in order to target advertising and to accumulate profit. Likewise, in The Internet Galaxy, Manuel Castells describes the Internet not only as a space full of opportunities, but also as a technology of control, which has primarily emerged from the interests of economic and political actors such as corporations and state institutions. He argues that these institutions make use of such technologies in order to locate individual users. State institutions such as governments and corporations like Microsoft and Google use special surveillance technologies that allow the monitoring of online behaviour in one central database.

- Surveillance technologies... often rely on identification technologies to be able to locate the individual user ... These technologies operate their controls under two basic conditions. First, the controllers know the codes of the network, the controlled do not. Software is confidential, and proprietary, and cannot be modified except by its owner. Once on the network, the average user is the prisoner of an architecture he or she does not know. Secondly, controls are exercised on the basis of a space de fined on the network, for instance, the network around an Internet service provider, or the intra-network in a company, a university, or a government agency.

Castells understands the rise of the Internet as an emergence of a powerful electronic surveillance system and concludes: "If this system of surveillance and control of the Internet develops fully, we will not be able to do as we please. We may have no liberty, and no place to hide". Castells considers, just like Foucault, surveillance to be negative and centralized and being connected to control and power.

Hence, although Castells does not refer to the concept of the panopticon directly, his contribution to online surveillance can be considered as being a panoptic notion of Internet surveillance. Michael Levi and David Wall emphasize the new politics of surveillance in a post 9/11 European information society and the increase of the panoptic power of the EU member states mediated through surveillance techniques such as identity/entitlement cards, asylum seekers' smartcards, data sharing schemes, and smart passports in order to create a suspect population.

Wall analyzes the growth of surveillant Internet technologies in the information society. He draws on Foucault's understanding of panoptic power relations and distinguishes between personal and mass surveillance. For Wall, the Internet as a multidirectional information flow has brought new opportunities for individuals in the context of surveillance. Techniques such as spyware, spam spider bots, and cookies allow a synoptic effect where the surveilled can surveil the surveillers.

The Internet is not simply a 'super', 'virtual' or 'electronic' Panopticon: an extension of Foucault's conceptualization of Bentham's prison design – 'seeing without being seen', as has become the conventional wisdom. It is important to emphasize that Internet information flows are simultaneously panoptic and synoptic – not only can the few watch the many, but the many can watch the few. Wall argues that the balance between personal surveillance on the one hand and mass surveillance on the other hand is "rarely even" and lists powerful corporations such as DoubleClick and Engage that are able to undertake largescale surveillance. In addition, he emphasizes the growth of surveillance and privacy threats as tradeable commodities in information capitalism and presents an empirical case study of the spam industry such as e-mail list compilation and unsolicited bulk e-mails. Joseph Turow speaks about marketing and consumer surveillance in the digital age of media.

He stresses that online media are interested in collecting data about their audience in order to sell these data to advertisers. In a next step, the advertisers use these data in order to increase the efficiency of marketing. Furthermore, customer relationship management constructs audiences and produces a surveillance-driven culture, where consumers understand surveillance as a cost-benefit calculation and willing to the data collection of media and advertisers. Turow's understanding of surveillance can be seen in the context of Foucault's notion of panoptic surveillance. He considers, just like Foucault, surveillance to be negative and centralized and being connected to discipline, control, and power.

Similarly to Foucault, Turow stresses that surveillance is predominately undertaken by powerful institutions such as corporations. Also interesting in this context is the national survey of Internet privacy and institutional trust by Joseph Turow and Michael Hennessy. In 2003, they undertook 1200 quantitative telephone interviews in the United States with adults (18 years and older), who go online at home. The authors tried to analyze what US citizens think about institutional surveillance and conclude "that a substantial percentage of Internet users believe that major corporate or government institutions will both help them to protect information privacy and take that privacy away by disclosing information to other parties without permission". Mark Andrejevic wants to offer an alternative approach of online privacy in the era of new media.

Andrejevic studies the economic surveillance of interactive media such as interactive TV and Google's business model of free wireless Internet access and analyzes interactive surveillance in the digital enclosure: "the model of enclosure traces the relationship between a material, spatial process – the construction of networked, interactive environments – and the private expropriation of information".

The author argues that Foucault's approach of the panopticon is suitable in order to study surveillance and hierarchical power asymmetries in the online economy and speaks about a "digital form of disciplinary panopticism". Andrejevic argues that just like workplace surveillance rationalized production in the era of scientific management, online surveillance rationalizes and stimulates consumption, produces customized commodities and the crucial capital of the economy. "Viewers are monitored so advertisers can be ensured that this work is being done as fiefciently as possible.

Ratings, in this context, are informational commodities that generate value because they help to rationalize the viewing process". Also in the context of economic surveillance, John Edward Campbell and Matt Carlson revisit Foucault's idea of the panopticon as well as Gandy's notion of the panoptic sort. They apply these notions to online surveillance and the commodification of privacy on the Internet:

- The Panopticon was seen as a way of organizing social institutions to ensure a more orderly society by producing disciplined and 'rational' citizens. With Internet ad servers, the goal is to provide marketers with the personal information necessary to determine if an individual constitutes an economically viable consumer. The enhanced consumer profiling offered by these third-party ad servers increases the effectiveness and efficiency of advertisers' efforts, reducing the uncertainty faced by producers introducing their goods and services into the marketplace.

Summing up, panoptic notions of Internet surveillance argue that power, control, and surveillance have increased in the era of the Internet. Furthermore, the rise of the Internet has brought a space of electronic surveillance, where the powerful will appropriate the Internet as a technology of control for their own instrumental advantage. These approaches consider online surveillance to be negative and being connected to coercion, repression, discipline, power, and domination. For these authors, power is primarily centralized and society tends to be repressive and controlled.

CRITICAL INTERNET SURVEILLANCE STUDIES

The overall aim of this section is to analyze the specific economic mode of Internet surveillance. Based on the foundations of a political economy approach, the distinction of production, circulation, and consumption within the economy is introduced in order to establish a typology of online surveillance in the economy and to study Internet surveillance in the spheres of production, circulation, and consumption.

THE SPHERES OF THE ECONOMY

In the Introduction to a Contribution to the Critique of Political Economy, Karl Marx distinguishes between (a) production, (b) circulation (distribution and exchange), and (c) consumption as dialectically mediated spheres of the capitalistic economy (a).

The sphere of production appears as the point of departure. In the capitalist mode of production, entrepreneurs consume purchased commodities (means of production and labour power) in order to produce new commodities and surplus value. (b) Circulation is the "mediation between production and consumption". In the process of circulation, consumers purchase commodities for daily life and proprietors sell the produced commodities to realize profit. (c) In the sphere of consumption as the final point of the process, "the product drops out of this social movement, becomes the direct object and servant of an individual need, which its use satisfies". While in production the person receives an objective aspect, in consumption the object receives a subjective aspect. The "consumption, as the concluding act, ... reacts on the point of departure thus once again initiating the whole process". Although production, circulation, and consumption are separated spheres, they correlate in an interconnected relationship:

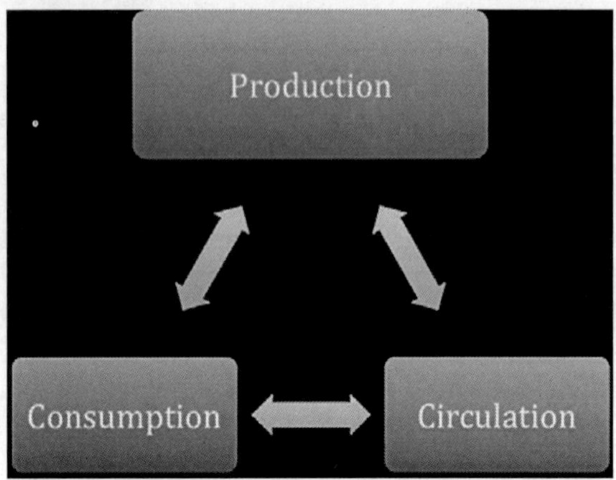

Fig. Production, circulation, and consumption as dialectically mediated spheres of the modern economy

In the sphere of production, means of production are consumed and in the sphere of consumption, labour power is (re)produced. "Production is consumption; consumption is production. Consumptive production. Productive consumption". Production is not possible without demand and consumption does not take place without material. "No consumption without production; no production without consumption". Moreover, the process of production is determined by circulation of labour power as well as means of production, whereas circulation itself is a product of production. Production, circulation, and consumption are not "identical, but that they are all elements of a totality, differences within a unity ... There is an interaction between the different moments". Nevertheless, production, circulation, and consumption are not equal spheres in the economy; production is rather "the dominant moment, both with regard to itself in the contradictory determination of production and with regard to the other moments. The process always starts afresh with production ... A definite production thus determines a definite consumption, distribution, exchange and definite relations of these different moments to one another. Production in its one-sided form, however, is in its turn also determined by the other moments". Based on the distinction of production, circulation, and consumption, a typology of surveillance in the economy can be constructed. Such a typology will be outlined in the next subsection.

INTERNET SURVEILLANCE IN THE SPHERES OF THE ECONOMY

Illustrative examples of economic online surveillance in the spheres of production, circulation, and consumption will be presented. The following three parts are therefore structured according to this distinction.

Internet Surveillance in the Sphere of Production

The Electronic Monitoring and Surveillance Survey offers interesting examples of Internet surveillance in the sphere of production: according to the American Management Association and the ePolicy Institute that undertake an annual quantitative survey about electronic monitoring and surveillance with approximately 300 US companies, "more than one fourth of employers have fired workers for misusing e-mail and nearly one third have fired employees for misusing the Internet". More than 40% of the studied companies monitor e-mail traffic of their workers, and 66% of the corporations monitor Internet connections. In addition, most companies use software to block non-work related websites such as sexual or pornographic sites, game sites, social networking sites, entertainment sites, shopping sites, and sport sites. The American Management Association and the ePolicy Institute also stress that companies track "content, keystrokes, and time spent at the keyboard... store and review computer files... monitor the blogosphere to see what is being written about the company, and... monitor social networking sites". Furthermore, about 30% of the companies were also firing employees for non-work related email and Internet usage such as "inappropriate or offensive language" and "viewing, downloading, or uploading inappropriate/ offensive content".

Internet Surveillance in the Sphere of Circulation

An interesting phenomenon of surveillance in the sphere of circulation is applicant surveillance: Rosalind Searle states in this context that "checking procedures are increasingly utilised to authenticate candidates' data. In several countries financial services authorities have sanctioned formal vetting, often outsourcing it to external contractors ... such as Kroll and Carratu International". The corporate investigation company Carratu International is headquartered in London. The company operates around the world with national and multi-national corporations, insurance companies, law firms, and financial institutions, which are primarily found in the Fortune 500 and the Financial Times Top 100 rankings. Carratu International argues that pre-employment screening is crucial, because up to 80% of new job candidates give incorrect information about themselves.

According to Carratu International, the only opportunity to "know that the information provided is complete and honest" is to undertake a systematic off- and online check of information such as personal data and information on civil litigation, credit history, bankruptcy, employment history, educational achievements, professional qualifications, and professional or occupational licensing. In addition, Carratu International provides three levels of off- and online pre-employment screening at different prices: the basic service includes data analyzes of items such as address, educational qualification, and employment history. The intermediate service includes the basic service plus searches of the media, ownership records, company directorship and judicial data. Finally, the professional level includes an investigation of "all details contained on the application document, carry out all checks as detailed in Level Two validations, together with additional relevant research and investigations to confirm the probity and standing of the applicant".

Internet Surveillance in the Sphere of Consumption

For Internet surveillance in the sphere of consumption, the example of Google and DoubleClick can be outlined: According to the top sites of the web by Alexa Internet, Google has the most visits on the Internet. Google uses a wide range of methods in order to collect data on its users, namely click tracking (to log clicks of users), log files (to store server requests), JavaScript and web bugs (to check users visits), as well as cookies (to record individual actions). DoubleClick is one of the main projects of Google. It is a global leader in ad serving and has developed sophisticated methods in order to collect, analyze, and assess huge amounts of users' data on the Internet. Google acquired DoubleClick in 2008 for US$ 3.1 billion. DoubleClick is headquartered in New York City.

It was found in 1996 and works for leading digital publishers, marketers, and agencies around the world such as About, Durex, Ford, Friendster, Optimedia, Scripps, and MTV. Ad serving companies such as DoubleClick use methods by placing advertisements on websites and analyzing their efficiency. DoubleClick develops and provides Internet ad serving services that are sold primarily to advertisers and publishers. DoubleClick collects personal data on many websites, sells this data, and supports targeted advertising. DoubleClick's main product is known as DART (Dynamic Advertising, Reporting, and Targeting). DART is an ad serving programme working with a complex algorithm and is primarily developed for publishers and advertisers in order to "ensure you get the right message, to the right person, at the right time, on the right device" (DoubleClick). In this section, Internet surveillance in the context of the economy was analyzed. Based on the foundations of a critical political economy approach, the distinction of production, circulation, and consumption in the economy was introduced in order to establish a typology of Internet surveillance in the economy. Illustrative examples of economic online surveillance in the spheres of production, circulation, and consumption were presented.

CONCLUSION

The overall aim of Critical Internet Surveillance Studies and Economic Surveillance was to clarify how we can theorize and systemize Internet surveillance in the modern economy. The chapter constructed theoretically founded typologies in order to systemize the existing literature of Internet surveillance studies and to analyze examples of surveillance.

Therefore, it mainly was a theoretical approach combined with illustrative examples, advanced from the abstract to the concrete level. Foundations of Internet surveillance studies were discussed in the second section. In the third section, a critical contribution to Internet surveillance studies was drawn in order to distinguish Internet surveillance into the spheres of production, circulation, and consumption. Based on these findings, we were able to systemize illustrative examples of Internet surveillance in the modern economy such as the Electronic Monitoring and Surveillance Survey, Carratu International, and DoubleClick into the spheres of production, circulation, and consumption. As shown in this chapter, economical actors such as corporations undertake surveillance and exercise violence in order to control a certain behaviour of people and in most cases people do not know that they are surveilled. Corporations control the economic behaviour of people and coerce individuals in order to produce or buy specific commodities for guaranteeing the production of surplus value and for accumulating profit. Therefore, one can assume that Internet surveillance is a negative phenomenon of modern societies, which should be questioned and struggled against. Based on Gandy, Castells, Parenti, Ogura, Lyon and Fuchs, some political recommendations can be drawn in order to overcome economic online surveillance:

- The first recommendation is that support is needed for critical privacy movements on the Internet in order to develop counter-hegemonic power and advance critical awareness of surveillance.
- "Such public awareness of surveillance issues could further be raised through professional groups and organizations, especially those directly concerned with computing, information management, and so on."
- Furthermore, Lyon states the importance of political activism by critical citizens: "Films, consumer groups, Internet campaigns and international watchdogs are just some of the ways that ongoing surveillance practices are brought to the surface of our consciousness, and thus overtly into the realm of ethical evaluation and political response."
- According to Fuchs, "critical citizens, critical citizens' initiatives, consumer groups, social movement groups, critical scholars, unions, data protection specialists/groups, consumer protection specialists/groups, critical politicians, critical political parties observe closely the relationship of surveillance and corporations and document instances where corporations and politicians take measures that threaten privacy or increase the surveillance of citizens".
- In addition, it is recommended to support cyber activism and

"counter-surveillance" in order to surveil corporate surveillants or rather to watch the watchers.

- Parenti suggests civil disobedience, rebellion, and protest: "It will compel regulators to tell corporations, police, schools, hospitals, and other institutions that there are limits. As a society, we want to say: Here you may not go. Here you may not record. Here you may not track and identify people. Here you may not trade and analyze information and build dossiers".
- A further recommendation is to create non-profit, non-commercial social networking platforms on the Internet such as Kaioo. Kaioo is owned by the non-profit organization OpenNetworX, has been available since 2007, and has currently about 30.000 users. Kaioo's privacy terms are created in common and can be edited online by every user. In addition, the data belong to their users. OpenNetworX can do so, because they are not interested in targeting advertising and they do not need to produce surplus value and to accumulate profit.
- "To try to advance critical awareness and to surveil corporate and political surveillers are important political moves for guaranteeing civil rights, but they will ultimately fail if they do not recognize that electronic surveillance is not a technological issue that can be solved by technological means or by different individual behaviours, but only by bringing about changes of society". Therefore, Internet surveillance has to be put into the larger context of societal problems in public discourse. "We should look at the whole macro picture."
- Finally, Internet surveillance is caused by economical and political issues and is inherent in modern society. It is neither just a technical issue, nor an individual problem, but a societal problem. Internet surveillance is a crucial phenomena, but there are a lot of other features in contemporary society such as information, neoliberalism, globalization, and capital.

3

Internet Technology and Social Work

From a base of unintended consequences, this article illustrates how the Internet's original purposes have been employed by social work professionals, especially those in academic settings and professional associations. It first reviews the military roots of the Internet and its salient features which on the surface appear contrary to traditional social work values. It then reviews how social work professionals have employed the Internet, offers guidelines, and makes recommendations to other professionals. Due to space restrictions, Internet history and its use by social work professionals outside of the USA is not addressed.

The Internet is often described as "organized chaos." We can use the same words to describe the history of the internet in tracing linkage among: the military agenda, astounding engineering feats, online social interaction action, and social work education and practice. Within the context of "chaos," one must appreciate that if it were not for the distinct possibility of complete nuclear annihilation during the cold war, there may have been no Internet! American paranoia of Communism reached its zenith immediately following the success of Sputnik. The Eisenhower Administration pursued a fail-safe communications system (which led to what is known now as the Internet). During a nuclear holocaust, military experts knew that communications systems would be wiped out. Military experts needed a communications system that could evoke the delivery of nuclear warheads and defend against the entry of warheads.

UNINTENDED CONSEQUENCES OF MILITARY REQUIREMENTS

Although this history has many streams of thought, our focus must be on the U.S. Department of Defense's funding of ARPANET. ARPA is an acronym for Advanced Research Projects Agency. NET, of course, is short for "network." Beginning their work in 1969, ARPANET's teams of hardware and software engineers configured four computers as an experimental network. Bolt, Beranek, and Newman Inc. coordinated the experiment and was awarded several contracts by the DoD. BBN built the first Interface Message Processors. The IMP is the mother of the often heard Internet jargon, "File Transfer

Protocol." On September 2, 1969, IMPs were first used with intermittent success to transfer information among these major research institutions. On October 1972 in Washington, DC, the first International Conference on Computers and Communities was convened. Here, over 1,000 attendees witnessed the first public display of ARPANET. Tolhurst et al. described the demonstration as flawless, but the behind the scenes preparations bordered on comical.

The network was not operational until seconds prior to the presentation. Yet, every observer was profoundly impressed with the demonstration. Some thought it has been fully functional for years! "The flawless demonstration so impressed the attendees that they returned to their research centers with a vision of the promise of greater things to come". Tolhurst et al. is accurate, but the science behind the development of the Internet was sloppy! Yet, any professor of research methods knows that the mother of cutting edge research is unleashed and sometimes undisciplined creativity.

Three technical advances created the evolution of ARPANET to the Internet. First was the development of the Transmission Control Protocol/Internet Protocol. TCP/IP was more user-friendly than its predecessor. Second, Xerox completed a long series of experiments that led to the development of the EtherNet. Third, in an effort to maximize the use of the network among institutions of higher education, DARPA established a contract with BBN and the University of California at Berkeley to invent a low-cost TCP/IP. Berkeley is credited with the all-familiar File Transfer Protocol and c-mail. By 1975, engineers and computer scientists were beginning to learn the practical applications of the network-and the problems.

INCREASING TRAFFIC, REGULATION AND ONLINE SOCIAL INTERACTION

By the early 80s, the network traffic increased to the point of becoming sluggish. As a result, in 1983 ARPANET was split. MILNET was used for military sites and ARPANET was used for non-military traffic. However, it did not take long for growth to go beyond control a second time. To deal with the unceasing growth, standardized protocols were required by the Secretary of Defense.

Unknown at the time, these standardizations laid the ground work for the successful commercialization of the Internet. Utilizing these standards, the National Science Foundation funded or partially funded six supercomputer centers known as NSFNET. These centers merged into a backbone of the Internet. NSFNET permitted an easier access in order for researchers to share their ideas in a more user-friendly environment. Time could be spent developing scientific ideas rather than spending countless hours figuring out the network. A key innovation occurred with Paul Mockapetris's November 1983 memo entitled "Domain Name System." To compensate for the unexpected increase of addresses, he proposed an international system which includes seven "top-level domains":

- com (commercial)
- edu (educational)
- gov (government)
- mil (military)
- net (networking organizations)
- org (non-commercial organizations)
- int (international organizations, like the United Nations).

Three-letter county codes were added later. This was a complex political task, not an engineering problem. By 1992, the Internet had continued to grow without any controls. No single entity could claim authority. The real success of the Internet is not attributed to the various technical consortia but consistently is attributed to "cooperation" among the users. When one person or a group violates the boundary of reasonableness, users work together to establish a position.

Observances of Internet activity are an irreplaceable social psychology laboratory. Two extremely different behavioral forces on the Internet set the tone for legislative control. First, Stoll's (1989) The Cuckoo's Egg discusses the most cited and most exciting problem that emerged from the Internet. Stoll describes how he stumbled into a ring of eastern block spies.

The process of his discovery and cooperation has inspired the Internet community. On the other extreme and dark side of the Internet, we have the case of the Internet worm. Burstyn (1990) outlines the actions and consequences of Robert Morris, son of a scientist of the National Security Agency's Computer Security Council, and a Cornell graduate student. He developed a computer program that could have clogged the entire Internet. Although he claimed his action was an accident and that he had no ill intentions, he received a three-year sentence.

No physical damage was inflicted nor was any information lost, but many human and computer hours were spent in a network clean-up. Schmidt and Darby state that the effect of the worm was devastating while Burstyn (1990) estimates that approximately 10% of computers connected to the Internet were affected. The most serious problem was the interruption of the Army's Ballistic Research Laboratory which stayed off the Internet for a week. The most important outcome was federal legislation concerning criminal acts on the Internet.

Congress wanted to send a message to pranksters and saboteurs. Thus, Morris's action induced a precedent for legal control of the Internet, while Stoll's experiences encouraged lawmakers to refrain from over-involvement. Congress faced a paradox. They realized the need for legislation for damage control, but desired the rich contributions made in an atmosphere of organized chaos. The above discussion illustrates that the history of the Internet is a history of rapid technological improvements wed to an environment of human cooperation. The technological advances and social linkages occurred in three general categories that are not necessarily mutually exclusive. They include:

- Communication
  - E-Mail
  - InterNIC
  - Listserv
  - Chat
- Information Acquisition
  - Archie
  - Bulletin Board
  - Gopher
  - Hytelnet
  - UseNet NewsGroups
  - Veronica
  - WAIS
  - World Wide Web
- Other
  - File Transfer Protocol
  - Telnet

Perhaps the most exciting of the above list is the World Wide Web. WWW has gained more national and international attention than all the other Internet services combined.

The WWW is a network of Internet sites that use a common site identification system and common language for displaying information organized by Web pages. In 1989, the first Web page was developed under the sponsorship of the European Laboratory for Particle Research (the combined resources of 18 countries).

The first Web navigation software was far from user-friendly. It was run on UNIX-based computers and little thought was given to PC-based machines. As soon as Mosaic was written in 1993 by students at the National Center for Supercomputing Applications (University of Illinois at Urbana-Champaign), a new computer milestone emerged.

The WWW exploded into popularity because Mosaic is a user-friendly and intuitive software that could be adapted for non-UNIX computers. In 1994, Mosaic dominated the use of the Web by personal computers. However, by 1996, Rafter (1996) notes that Mosaic's popularity dropped rapidly when Netscape appeared on the market. Mosaic was a "hassle to install," slow, and lacked an integrative e-mail function.

However, Mann (1996) predicts that with all the improvements in Microsoft's Explorer, Netscape may soon follow the path of Mosaic. Since January 1994, Pitkow has been involved in surveying the Web. To date, at least seven comprehensive surveys have been completed.

THE INTERNET AND SOCIAL WORK: A PERSONAL PERSPECTIVE

A vast array of social work Web sites have sprung up. The first systematic social work invasion of Web service was in educational institutions. Michael McMurray (Colorado State University) was the first, most notable effort. A long-lived and well-managed example is the University of South Carolina's SWAN (Social Work Access Network). At the time of this writing well over 25% of all accredited social work academic programs have Web sites. Clearly, Web pages that are owned and operated by large institutions are the most reliable. Nevertheless, I believe the future power of the Web lies elsewhere.

Although psychotherapy on the Internet existed prior to the popularity of the Web, employing the Web as a medium of psychotherapy has mushroomed. During a recent survey, well over 1,000 psychotherapists were capitalizing on the Web. Each time Marson and Brackin study psychotherapy on the Web, the number of therapists increases. NASW News is chronicling efforts of private practitioners in this arena. Clearly, the Web will have a profound effect on future strategies for psychotherapy and other forms of social work practice. For example, Schein-Levi and Pollack (1997) demonstrate how social workers can employ the Web for enhancing parenting skills. According to Anderson et al. (1 995), the most widespread use of the Internet among the general public is not browsing the Web, but email and listservs. Marson (1997) confirms this finding among social workers.

A personal history will help explain the importance of these two uses. When I first learned of access to the Internet, I also learned about listservs and immediately searched for a listserv that addressed social work issues. In my search, I discovered the Social Work discussion list. SOCWORK started as an idea for introducing students at the School of Social Work, University of Toronto, to computer communication technology. Bellamy (1987), and Bellamy and Mielniczuk (1988) offer historical details of how and why the list became operational on February 3, 1988. It began with 11 students and four faculty and staff. Within four months there were 20 members. By May 1989 there were approximately 75 members and a new management under the watchful eye of Harry Chaiklin at the University of Maryland. It was about this time that I discovered SOCWORK and joined the list when there were fewer than 80 subscribers.

During Harry's tenure, two major developments occurred. First, after much prodding among various members of the listserv, the Council on Social Work Education subscribed to SOCWORK. Second, staff from the National Association of Social Workers WASW] subscribed. Participation by our two major professional organizations established an aura of legitimacy and personal subscriptions to SOCWORK surged. Later, when the subscribers grew to approximately 700 in the spring of 1995, Cindy Jones from the University of Arkansas inherited SOCWORK. Soon SOCWORK had over 1,000 subscribers and many thought the listserv was out of control. As a result, in the fall of 1996, Ogden Rogers from the University of Wisconsin at River Falls became the new manager. The number of subscribers shrank to less than 300, but SOCWORK became more manageable. Listservs are now flourishing and are being systematically evaluated for their contribution to the profession. Berman (1996) provides an excellent example of such research in his analysis of two listservs. Noticing the congressional proposals to decentralize social services, the Consortium of State SOCWORK Listservs was founded in 1993 by Steve Marson at the University of North Carolina at Pembroke.

With decentralization, each state has gained greater control over social service resources. The direction of the services may greatly depend on the ability of state social workers to spread knowledge to grassroot organizations and to lobby the state house in a favorable direction. State social work listservs should prove to be vital for the speedy dissemination of needed information. Social workers have a long history of technology avoidance. This avoidance was first noted by Richmond (1911) when she had to encourage turn-of-the-century social workers to exploit the telephone as a tool for practice. Toward the end of this century and with the inaugural issue of a newsletter entitled Computer Use in Social Services Network (CUSSN), Dick Schoech (1981) took Richmond's place as the nurturer of technology.

Schoech's newsletter evolved into a journal entitled Computers in Human Services which continues to lay the ground work for integrating and advancing computer technology in social work. For example, it served as a platform for Hanna (1995) to report on early efforts to combine and link many existing electronic networks through the Internet. Prior to this effort, electronic and political barriers prohibited members of one network from sending email or conference with members from other human services networks.

INTERNET AND KEY SOCIAL WORK ORGANIZATIONAL EVENTS

Four happenings in recent history have had an influence on social work and the Internet. In the late 80s, CSWE board members and NASW staffs became active on the Internet. A CSWE staff member coordinated a meeting of two Internet enthusiasts. Although they communicated often over the Internet, they first met face to face at the CSWE 1990 Annual Program Meeting. Here, they gave birth to the Baccalaureate Program Directors Association's Committee on Information Technology and Social Work Education. In 1992, the unofficial committee offered its first workshop at the BPD annual conference. At the 1995 APM, the committee became an important part of BPD's table of organization as a standing committee. The most stirring moment in the short history of technology and social work professional organizations was at the 1992 APM. Marshall Smith requested the floor in an open meeting of CSWE's Accreditation Board. In a very eloquent, short, but powerfully moving speech, Marshall expressed the importance of the Internet for the accreditation process. He made a plea that board members consider accepting self-studies via the Internet. Marshall was ahead of his time. Now we are wagering on which school will take the bold step to be the first the submit a self-study via electronic means. One positive intermediate step was taken to achieve this goal.

Through the advocacy of BPD's Committee on Information Technology and Social Work Education, CSWE's Directory of Colleges and Universities with Accredited Social Work Degree Programs included e-mail addresses. Soon web page locations will be published in the Directory. These actions lay the ground work for the electronic transmission of self-studies and a more efficient means of educational research. Technical and confidentiality problems related to document transfer are on the verge of being resolved. Third, in early 1995, Rita Vandivort, of the NASW national office, established a listserv for technologically capable social workers to plan an Internet symposium at the upcoming NASW conference. As a staff member of NASW, she was able to acquire funds to put together an impressive Internet demonstration facility at the Philadelphia conference. Members of the technology committee involved in the planning were overwhelmed and profoundly impressed with the Internet resources that Rita was able to pull together. It was a success beyond anyone's imagination.

Since the Philadelphia conference, the use of an Internet lab continues to be an important feature of the NASW annual conference. Perhaps more than any single event in the history of social work and the Internet, the lab at the NASW conference has had the greatest influence on the utilization of the Internet among seasoned social work practitioners. Fourth, in the fall of 1992, Ogden Rogers proposed that SOCWORK subscribers who were also CSWE members meet face-to-face. Ogden dubbed the group "OffLine." Subscribers/CSWE members had been communicating with each other on a wide variety of levels. Close friendships were established, accreditation consultation support was given, and in some cases enemies were made! Steve Marson organized this group's first "get-together" during the 1993 APM in New York. The second get-together in 1994 in Atlanta was also a great success. During a SOCWORK discussion, subscribers decided to formalize OffLine in order to avoid scheduling conflicts. Since the formalization of Offline, the "social" get-togethers have been well attended and led to more serious academic conferences.

RECOMMENDATIONS

The profound influence of the Internet and technologies that the Internet will spawn in the future is undisputed. Social work and the entire social welfare system will not escape utilizing the Internet anymore than social workers were able to escape the use of the telephone during Richmond's era.

As a result, we have an ethical obligation to systematically encourage others to employ the Internet in their daily activities. Competence and comfort with the Internet leads to and enhances one's creativity in using the Internet, which in turn leads to improved human services. Such statements are grandiose and easy to state. How does one operationalize this?

Reading and recalling recent history is a good place to start. Our short history and experience offers some simple guidelines:

- Like Richmond, professors and field instructors must shepherd their students (particularly non-traditional students) into feeling comfortable with the Internet.
- Leaders both in education and practice must share their ideas by writing, presenting papers at conferences, and offering workshops about technology. Tom Hannah, Dick Schoech and Rita Vandivort are good conternporary role models for the rest of us.
- Leaders of professional organizations must be nurtured into accepting that computer technology and the Internet have vast implications for their organization's benefit. This can only be accomplished by a one-by-one strategy and face-to-face interaction. In addition, technologically competent professionals must organize themselves to vote for leaders who recognize the importance of the Internet. Actions like Marshall Smith's speech is a good illustration. Members of CIFTSWE make efforts to support candidates that have a history of supporting technology.
- Leaders of professional organizations should be shown that technology committees made up of volunteers are a cost effective manner of spreading the advantages that the Internet and computers have for human services. The development and actions of CIFTSWE provide an excellent example.
- Workshops must be freely offered in a nonintimidating manner to those professionals and educators who are technophobic. CIFTSWE's annual workshops are good illustrations of an effective strategy.
- Technophobic professionals must be approached in the same manner as Richmond approached social workers at the turn of the century. They must be nurtured, reassured, and shown that such technology is not dehumanizing but improves the quality of care. Vandivort's coordination of NASW's Internet lab at annual conferences represents an excellent example.
- Technologically competent professionals should meet socially (i.e., OffLine) and professionally (i.e., conferences). These meetings must be used to share ideas on effective methods of spreading the good news of technology and the Internet.
- Technologically capable human service professionals need to lead the way to make Internet technology user-friendly and practical. As

stated earlier, CIFTSWE is developing a structure for the confidential transmission of CSWE self studies and research via the Internet.

CONCLUSIONS

The key to advancing the Internet in social work is the theme found in the history of the development of the Internet. As a social worker, two aspects of Internet history are striking. The concept of "unintended consequcnces" is first apparent. The present use of the Internet is nothing like the original notion expected by its designers. A vast array of commercial and non-commercial applications for social work practice now exist. We are just witnessing the tip of the iceberg. Second, and closely related to the concept of unintended consequences, is social work values. The values to which most social workers cling are contrary to the values behind the original design of the Internet. Recall that the original intent of the Internet was to deliver weapons of mass destruction. Now, we see social workers employing it as a system to deliver social services. The success of the Internet must be attributed to the cooperative nature of it's users. I find that the massive level of cooperation found in the Internet is unprecedented in the twentieth century. In the end, social work success in employing the Internet will be limited only by the cooperative nature of those using it in practice and research.

4

The Impact of Internet Banking on Bank

INTRODUCTION

Internet technology holds the potential to fundamentally change banks and the banking industry. An extreme view speculates that the Internet will destroy old models of how bank services are developed and delivered. The widespread availability of Internet banking is expected to affect the mixture of financial services produced by banks, the manner in which banks produce these services and the resulting financial performances of these banks. Whether or not this extreme view proves correct and whether banks take advantage of this new technology will depend on their assessment of the profitability of such a delivery system for their services.

In addition, industry analysis outlining the potential impact of Internet banking on cost savings, revenue growth and risk profile of the banks have also generated considerable interest and speculation about the impact of the Internet on the banking industry. Banking through internet has emerged as a strategic resource for achieving higher efficiency, control of operations and reduction of cost by replacing paper based and labour intensive methods with automated processes thus leading to higher productivity and profitability.

However, to date researchers have produced little evidence regarding these potential changes. Nonetheless, recent empirical studies indicate that Internet banking is not having an independent effect on banking profitability, although these findings may change as the use of the Internet becomes more widespread. More recently in India too, a wider array of financial products and services have become available over the Internet, which has thus become an important distribution channel for a number of banks. Banks boost technology investment spending strongly to address revenue, cost and competitiveness concerns.

For some activities, banks hope to see a near-term impact on profitability. Other investments are motivated more by a desire to establish a competitive position or avoid falling behind the competition. The purpose of present study is to analyze such effects of Internet banking in India, where no rigorous attempts have been undertaken to understand this aspect of the banking business. The primary aim is to advance the understanding of how Internet banks are different from the non-Internet banks in terms of profitability, cost efficiency, asset quality and other characteristics by examining bank financial statements from year end 1998 to year end 2006. The present study tests not only whether the Internet delivery channel affected the financial performance of the commercial banks in our sample, but also how these changes happened.

The study examines a comprehensive set of 10 measures of financial performance that allow us to "look inside the black box" of bank performance. By developing a deeper understanding of these phenomena, we can draw more insightful inferences about the impact of the Internet on banking business strategies, production processes and financial performance. Increasing this type of knowledge is vital for both academic literature and also for bank marketers who cannot count on the initial success achieved by the Internet banking investment. The paper is organized as follows. The next section reports a brief review of the literature on Internet Banking, comparing and contrasting conclusions of previous research. Section 3 describes the data and current status of Internet banking in India. Section 4 explores whether there is a financial gap between the Internet and non-Internet banks in India by using univariate analysis on banks' balance-sheet data collected by various regulatory authorities. Section 5 explores whether Internet banking has had a noticeable impact on Indian Banks' performance and risk, using multivariate analysis. Section 6 concludes the paper.

REVIEW OF EXISTING LITERATURE

A few empirical studies exist in the literature, which have examined the relative performance of banks offering Internet banking services. Table summarizes the previous research done on the performance of Internet banks. The table also includes the studies which have examined the financial performance of Internetonly banks that do not operate any physical branches. Egland was the first important study, which estimated the number of US banks offering Internet banking and analyzed the structure and performance characteristics of these banks.

It found no evidence of major differences in the performance of the group of banks offering Internet banking activities compared to those that do not offer such services in terms of profitability, efficiency or credit quality. However, transactional Internet banks differed from other banks primarily by size. In contrast to the results of Egland, Furst found that banks in all size categories offering Internet banking were generally more profitable and tended to rely less heavily on traditional banking activities in comparison to non-Internet banks. An exception to the superior performance of Internet banks was the de novo Internet banks, which were less profitable and less efficient than non-Internet de novos. The authors concluded that Internet banking was too small a factor to have affected banks' profitability. Sullivan found that click and mortar banks in the 10th Federal Reserve District incurred somewhat higher operating expenses but offset these expenses with somewhat higher fee income. On average, this study found no systematic evidence that banks were either helped or harmed by offering the Internet delivery channel. Similar to the results of Furst et al., this study also found that de novo click and mortar banks performed significantly worse than de novo brick and mortar banks. Using information drawn from banks in Italy, Hasan found that the Internet banking institutions were performing significantly better than the non- Internet groups. Additionally, the risk variables associated with the Internet group continued to be lower relative to the non-Internet group.

The asset-liability variables revealed that on average the banks in this Internet group were larger and had significantly higher trading and investment activities and less dependent on retail deposits (both demand and saving deposits) relative to the non-Internet group. The only category where the Internet group showed a lower performance was the noninterest expense category. It found a significant and positive link between offering of Internet banking activities and banks' profitability and a negative but marginally significant association between the adoption of Internet banking and bank risk levels particularly due to increased diversification. Hernando and Nieto examined the performance of multichannel banks in Spain between 1994 and 2002. The study found higher profitability for multichannel banks through increased commission income, increased brokerage fees and (eventual) reductions in staffing levels and concluded that the Internet channel was a complement to physical banking channels. In contrast to earlier studies, the multichannel banks in Spain relied more on typical banking business (lending, deposit taking and securities trading). The adoption of the Internet as a delivery channel had a positive impact on banks' profitability after one and a half years of adoption. It was explained by the lower overhead expenses and in particular, staff and IT costs after the same period.

Sathye investigated the impact of the introduction of transactional Internet banking on performance and risk profile of major credit unions in Australia. Similar to the results of Sullivan, the Internet banking variable didn't show a significant association with the performance as well as with operating risk variable. Thus, Internet banking didn't prove to be a performance enhancing tool in the context of major credit unions in Australia. It neither reduced nor enhanced risk profile. DeYoung observed the change in financial performance of Internet community banks in U.S. during 1999-2001. The results found that Internet adoption improved community banks' profitability, particularly through increased revenues from deposit service charges. Internet adoption was also associated with movements of deposits from checking accounts to money market deposit accounts, increased use of brokered deposits and higher average wage rates for bank employees. It found little evidence of changes in loan portfolio mix. The findings suggested that Internet adoption was associated with an economically and statistically significant improvement in bank profitability.

DeYoung analyzed systematically the financial performance of pure-play Internet banks in U.S. The study found relatively lower profits at the Internet-only institutions than the branching banks, caused in part by high labour costs, low fee based revenues and difficulty in generating deposit funding. However, consistent with the standard Internet banking model, the results indicated that Internet-only banks tended to grow faster than traditional branching banks. Internet-only banks have access to deeper scale economies than branching banks and because of this, they are likely to become more financially competitive over time as they grow larger. Delgado found similar results for Internet-only banks in the EU. Nevertheless, the magnitude of technology based scale economies found in Delgado was substantially larger than that estimated by DeYoung studies. The evidence of the impact of the adoption of Internet as a delivery channel on financial performance is mixed at both sides of the Atlantic. Nevertheless, the latest studies seem to find a positive relationship with profitability. It can be argued that as the intensity and experience in the usage of Internet increases, the financial performance of multichannel banks is likely to improve. In Indian context, many publications throw light over the importance of Internet banking and also its prospects for the Indian banking industry. However these studies don't depict any empirical relationship between banks' profitability and Internet banking. The purpose of this paper is to study the same correlation applicable in Indian context. This paper also proposes and tests the existence of financial gaps between Internet banks and non-Internet banks in India.

DATA AND PROFILE OF BANKS

DATA

The primary data set comes from the publicly available data source on bank's financial statements and income-expense reports sent to the regulators and banking associations. The Reserve Bank of India (RBI), provided the data. The data was matched with Indian Banking Associations data source, IBA Bulletin and Center for Monitoring Indian Economy (CMIE) data source PROWESS, for additional variables. The Internet related details were drawn from a survey of commercial banks' Websites during the period of June 2007. The banks whose home pages were not discovered despite of best efforts were assumed to be banks with no Website. The data set is limited to the banks that are operating as commercial banks as on March end 2006. In doing so, the banks that are acquired by other banks or have closed down their operations during the period are not included. Finally, a panel data of 85 commercial banks turned out to be the sample of the study over the period 1998-2006 which represented nearly 39 percent of total scheduled commercial banks in India.

As all the banks in sample are not observed in the entire period, the study has used an unbalanced panel data for the empirical work. The 85 banks consisted of 28 public sector banks (8 banks in State Bank of India (SBI) group) and 20 nationalized banks), 28 private sector banks (21 old and 7 new private sector banks) and 29 foreign banks. The sample includes 49 Internet banks and 36 non-Internet banks. Table reports the description of sample banks.

Table. Adoption Rates of internet banks

Bank	Number of Banks	Number of Banks With Websites	Number of Internet Banks	Internet banks as a percentage of banks in category
Private Sector Banks	28	27	17	60.7
New[1]	7	7	7	100.0
Old[2]	21	20	10	47.6
Public Sector Banks	28	28	26	92.8
SBI Group[3]	8	8	8	100.0
Nationalized[4]	20	20	18	90.0
Foreign Banks	29	29	6	20.7
All Banks	85	84	49	57.6

The survey results reveal that, during the period of June 2007, 84 banks in India had Web sites, of which 49 allowed transactions to be initiated through the Internet. However, the adoption rates across individual bank categories are not uniform. Adoption rates for transactional Web sites are highest in public sector and are lowest in foreign banks. Among the sub-categories, the adoption rates for transactional Web sites are highest in new private sector banks and SBI group.

INTERNET AND NON-INTERNET BANKS: COMPARISON OF PERFORMANCE

Evaluating bank performance is a complex process that involves assessing interaction between the environment, internal operations and external activities. In general, a number of financial ratios are usually used to assess the performance of banks. Financial performance has been studied under different yardsticks of performance i.e., size, profitability, financing pattern, economic efficiency, operational efficiency, asset quality, diversification and cost of operations. This section reports the results of univariate analysis to differentiate the Internet and non-Internet banks. The null hypothesis regarding the financial performance of Internet and non-Internet banks is: H1: The financial performance of banks adopting Internet banking is not different from those of banks choosing not to adopt Internet banking, in terms of size, profitability, operating capability, financing, asset quality, diversification and cost of operations. The decision to accept or reject null hypothesis is made on the basis of the value of the test statistic obtained from the data at hand. In the present study, the statistical significance of the means of various test statistics is determined by using the two independent samples t-statistic. For each pair of observations in a table, a probability (p) value is provided for the hypothesis that the means in the Internet and non-Internet samples are the same. A lower p-value indicates a greater likelihood that the two figures compared represent real differences between the two categories of banks (Internet vs. non-Internet, etc.). Tables show the univariate statistics for the Internet group as well as the non-Internet group across 10 financial performance measures. In these tables, the performance of an Internet group with non-Internet banking group and separately for public sector banks (SBI group and nationalized banks), private sector banks (new and old private sector banks) and foreign banks has been analyzed.

SIZE

Table shows the size variables for the Internet and non-Internet banking group. Internet banks are statistically and significantly larger than non-Internet banks in terms of total assets and employees. The results are similar to Furst et al., Hasan and Hernando and Nieto. Table shows that Internet banks are larger in almost every category of bank.

Table. Size of internet and Non-internet banks (1998-2006)

	Assets (Rs Crores)			Employees		
	Internet Banks (N_1)	Non-internet Banks (N_2)	Statistical Significance of the Difference Between the Two Means	Internet Banks (N_1)	Non-internet Banks (N_2)	Statistical Significance of the Difference Between the Two Means
	Mean	Mean	"t"-statistics	Mean	Mean	"t"-statistics
All Banks (N_1=143) (N_2=596)	50283.67	11829.13	5.65*** (.000)	17854	9091	2.63*** (.009)
Public Sector (N_1=58) (N_2=187)	87391.85	31787.80	3.84*** (.000)	38450	26563	1.58 (.116)
SBI Group (N_1=17) (N_2=55)	142023.121	30096.89	2.44** (.026)	68313	28963	1.75* (.094)
Nationalized (N_1=41) (N_2=132)	64739.85	32492.34	5.82*** (.000)	26068	26396	-.121 (.904)
Private Sector (N_1=58) (N_2=180)	26919.62	3916.89	3.99*** (.001)	4541	2174	3.85*** (.000)
New Private (N_1=35) (N_2=15)	37472.78	5264.75	3.52*** (.001)	4814	610	4.37*** (.000)
Old Private (N_1=23) (N_2=165)	10860.45	3794.36	5.35*** (.000)	4126	2316	4.47*** (.000)
Foreign Banks (N_1=27) (N_2=229)	20759.27	1750.23	7.25*** (.000)	2207	260	6.26*** (.000)

Sources: Statistical Tables relating to banks available at www.rbi.org.in and various Issues of IBA Bulletin

N1 = No. of observations for Internet banks

N2 = No. of observations for non-Internet banks

******* = Significant at the 1 percent or better level; ** = significant at the 5 percent level; and * = significant at the 10 percent level.

PROFITABILITY, OPERATING EFFICIENCY AND FINANCING

Table compares the profitability, operating efficiency and financing pattern of Internet banks with non-Internet banks. On an average, Internet banks are more profitable than non-Internet banks and are operating with lower cost as compared to non-Internet banks, thus, representing the efficiency of the Internet banks. Internet banks in public sector, particularly, in nationalized bank category are more profitable than non-Internet banks. Comparatively, both the categories of private sector Internet banks are less profitable than non-Internet banks but the difference is not statistically significant. The lower profitability of these banks may be due to higher operating expenses, both fixed cost as well as labour cost.

Table. Profitability, Operating Efficiency and financing pattern of internet and Non-internet banks (1998-2006)

	Profitability (Return on Assets) (%)			Operating Efficiency (Operating Cost) (%)			Financing Pattern (Deposits) (%)		
	Mean (N_1)	Mean (N_2)	"t"	Mean (N_1)	Mean (N_2)	"t"	Mean (N_1)	Mean (N_2)	"t"
All Banks (N_1=143) (N_2=596)	.898	.697	2.06** (0.039)	50.790	56.448	-3.07*** (.002)	77.441	71.144	4.17*** (.000)
Public Sector (N_1=58) (N_2=187)	.935	.647	4.65*** (.000)	48.766	59.764	-7.25*** (.000)	82.177	85.354	-2.00** (.050)
SBI Group (N_1=17) (N_2=55)	.870	.924	-.76 (.450)	47.885	51.680	-1.97* (.054)	80.419	79.863	.69 (.491)
Nationalized (N_1=41) (N_2=132)	.962	.531	5.35*** (.000)	49.132	63.132	-7.28*** (.000)	82.907	87.643	-2.15** (.037)
Private Sector (N_1=58) (N_2=180)	.714	.694	.162 (.871)	53.584	55.320	-.57 (.567)	79.095	86.182	-4.36*** (.000)
New Private (N_1=35) (N_2=15)	.806	.866	-.24 (.809)	51.772	44.859	1.17 (.247)	74.154	79.086	-1.81* (.076)
Old Private (N_1=23) (N_2=165)	.575	.678	-.56 (.575)	56.340	56.271	.01 (.988)	86.614	86.827	-.215 (.830)
Foreign Banks (N_1=27) (N_2=229)	1.212	.740	1.83* (.070)	49.136	54.626	-1.35 (.176)	63.714	47.720	5.03*** (.000)

Sources: Statistical Tables relating to banks available at www.rbi.org.in and various Issues of IBA Bulletin

N1 = No. of observations for Internet banks

N2 = No. of observations for non-Internet banks

*** = Significant at the 1 percent or better level; ** = significant at the 5 percent level; and * = significant at the 10 percent level.

Table also shows major financing characteristics of Internet and non-Internet banks. The Internet banks in India are able to generate more deposits or customer accounts than non-Internet banks. The results are consistent with Hernando and Nieto. Internet banks in India rely more on traditional source of financing i.e. deposits as compared to borrowing financing which is inconsistent with previous studies. As far as categories of the banks are concerned, the private sector Internet banks fund less of their assets from traditional sources, such as deposits. Internet banks in public sector, particularly in nationalized bank category have also shown the same preference. It appears as these banks have begun to view the addition of Internet banking as a way to offer products that will reduce their dependence on core deposits. On the other hand, foreign Internet banks rely more on generating deposits, consistent with overall results.

ASSET QUALITY AND DIVERSIFICATION

Asset quality indicators measure the changes in the bank's loan quality. The Internet banks show higher asset quality as compared to non-Internet banks. Internet banks are having lower net Non Performing Assets (NPAs) to net advances as compared to non- Internet banks. Differences in the business strategies of Internet and non-Internet banks also are evident in Table. The second column shows the ratio of non-interest income to total income, which is a rough proxy for the amount of revenue generated by "nontraditional" activities. Internet banks generated a lower proportion of their income from non-traditional activities compared to non-Internet banks. However, the difference is not statistically significant. Internet banks in public sector particularly nationalized banks and banks in private sector particularly new private sector rely more heavily on non-traditional sources of income.

Table. Asset Quality and diversification statistics for internet and Non-internet banks (1998-2006)

	Asset Quality (Net NPAs to Net Advances) (%)			Diversification (Non-Int Income/Total Income) (%)		
	Mean (N_1)	Mean (N_2)	"t"	Mean (N_1)	Mean (N_2)	"t"
All Banks **(N_1=143) (N_2=596)**	2.497	6.889	-9.64*** (.000)	18.747	18.902	-.19 (.848)
Public Sector **(N_1=58) (N_2=187)**	2.010	7.013	-9.70*** (.000)	15.985	14.249	2.81*** (.005)
SBI Group (N_1=17) (N_2=55)	2.136	5.920	-6.28*** (.000)	16.312	16.632	-.28 (.776)
Nationalized (N_1=41) (N_2=132)	1.957	7.468	-8.05*** (.000)	15.850	13.256	3.79*** (.000)
Private Sector **(N_1=58) (N_2=180)**	2.474	6.705	-9.91*** (.000)	19.163	15.254	3.89*** (.000)
New Private (N_1=35) (N_2=15)	1.899	4.238	-3.93*** (.000)	21.504	15.962	4.06*** (.000)
Old Private (N_1=23) (N_2=165)	3.349	6.929	-5.86*** (.000)	15.600	15.190	.27 (.786)
Foreign Banks **(N_1=27) (N_2=229)**	3.594	6.933	-2.22** (.031)	23.786	25.570	-.78 (.434)

Sources: Statistical Tables relating to banks available at www.rbi.org.in and various Issues of IBA Bulletin

N1 = No. of observations for Internet banks

N2 = No. of observations for non-Internet banks

*** = Significant at the 1 percent or better level; ** = significant at the 5 percent level; and * = significant at the 10 percent level

COST OF OPERATIONS

In addition to revenue enhancement, Internet banking may enable banks to reduce costs of operation, in particular, by allowing them to reduce expenditures on "brick and mortar." To the extent this may be so, Internet banking could be considered a causal factor in generating lower expenses related to maintaining physical branches. On the other hand, banks with relatively high expenses in maintaining their branch networks may be expected to have the incentive to adopt Internet banking. The adoption of Internet banking would thus be the effect of existing characteristics of banks. The data in Table shows that, consistent with the first hypothesis, overall Internet banks had lower expenses for building and equipment. While, nationalized Internet banks and Internet banks in private sector follow the second hypothesis. This difference may indicate that these banks with high costs of maintaining a branch network are motivated to adopt Internet banking by the prospect of future cost savings.

Table. cost of operations of internet and non-internet banks (1998-2006)

	Labour Cost (Salary exp/Employees) (Rs Crs)			Financing Cost (Cost of Funds =Interest expended/ Total Funds) (%)			Fixed Cost (Expenses on Fixed Assets/Fixed Asset) (%)		
	Mean (N_1)	Mean (N_2)	"t"	Mean (N_1)	Mean (N_2)	"t"	Mean (N_1)	Mean (N_2)	"t"
All Banks (N_1=143) (N_2=596)	0.0427	0.0461	-1.01 (.312)	5.153	8.003	-1.23 (.219)	106.04	155.79	-3.8*** (.001)
Public Sector (N_1=58) (N_2=187)	0.0324	0.0228	8.96*** (.000)	4.942	6.691	-11.29*** (.000)	98.926	93.409	.94 (.345)
SBI Group (N_1=17) (N_2=55)	0.0312	0.0211	6.77** (.000)	5.243	6.805	-4.84** (.000)	126.054	139.958	-1.47 (.146)
Nationalized (N_1=41) (N_2=132)	0.0329	0.0235	6.80*** (.000)	4.817	6.644	-10.54*** (.000)	87.678	74.014	2.35** (.021)
Private Sector (N_1=58) (N_2=180)	0.0339	0.0202	7.32*** (.000)	5.241	7.306	-8.04*** (.000)	78.716	64.238	2.82*** (.005)
New Private (N_1=35) (N_2=15)	0.0357	0.0198	3.62*** (.001)	5.048	7.773	-4.77*** (.000)	80.373	51.695	3.44*** (.001)
Old Private (N_1=23) (N_2=165)	0.0311	0.0202	6.87*** (.000)	5.534	7.264	-6.11*** (.000)	76.193	65.378	2.08** (.044)
Foreign Banks (N_1=27) (N_2=229)	0.0837	0.0853	-.18 (.855)	5.418	9.621	-.48 (.625)	180.009	278.689	-2.69 *** (.008)

Sources: Statistical Tables relating to banks available at www.rbi.org.in and various Issues of IBA Bulletin

N1 = No. of observations for Internet banks

N2 = No. of observations for non-Internet banks

*** = Significant at the 1 percent or better level; ** = significant at the 5 percent level; and * = significant at the 10 percent level

Table also shows that the Internet banks in public and private sector are generating higher labour cost. The results are expected as the Internet banks involve the higher salaries for computer professionals and other trained staff. The Internet banks enable themselves to lower the financing cost (low Interest paid on deposits and borrowings).

MULTIVARIATE ANALYSIS

Although, the univariate analyses depict a tremendously higher performance by banks in the Internet group(s) relative to non Internet bank group, however, it is hard to make any conclusive statement on the actual impact of the Internet adoptions on firm performance without a multivariate analysis. Here a multivariate regression model is estimated to investigate whether there is a link between offering Internet banking and bank's performance and risk.

The focus of the investigation is to see if Internet banking has an effect on bank performance and risk. A dummy variable (INTERNET) was created that takes a value of 1 if the bank has adopted Internet banking activities; otherwise it takes a value of zero. The coefficient associated with this Internet Adoption dummy will indicate the possible association between the Internet adoption by banks and their overall performance. The other variables affecting the banks' performance have been developed from the available literature on determinants of banks' performance and literature on Internet banking performance.

Return on Assets and Return on Equity are used as performance measures and Ratio of Net NPAs to net advances has been used as a measure of bank risk. In selecting potential factors associated with performance and risk, various bank characteristics are used as proxies for the banks' internal measures, e.g., size, capital, risk management and expenses management ratios and bank ownership dummies while macro-economic indicators are used to represent the external measures. A linear equation, relating the performance measures to a variety of financial indicators is specified. Following model has been used to examine the relationship between the performance of banks and adoption of Internet banking after controlling the other variables affecting the performance and risk.

$$Y_{it} @ c . d * INTERNET_{it} . \hat{1} e_i X_{it} . h_{it}$$

Where Y_{it} presents profitability and bank risk measures of bank i at time t, c is a constant term, the X_{it} are explanatory variables and h_{it} is the disturbance term.

The subscript i indexes bank level observations and the subscript t indexes time in years. INTERNET is a dummy variable equal to 1 for Internet banks and the coefficient á provides the main static test. A statistically significant value for á indicates a financial performance gap between the Internet banks and the non- Internet banks at the means of the data. The coefficients are estimated by employing OLS regressions on a sample of all banks as well as samples of different categories of banks. The explanatory variables with their labels and definitions that have been used to examine the relationship between the performance of banks and adoption of Internet banking are given in the Table

Table. Description of variables affecting the bank performance and risk

Label	Name	Definitions
Dependent Variables		
Y_1	ROA	The ratio of Average Net Profits to Average Assets
Y_2	ROE	The ratio of Average Net Profits to Average Equity
Y_3	NPA	The ratio of net NPAs to Net Advances
Independent Variables		
X_1	INTERNET	Dummy for the banks who have adopted Internet banking
X_2	SIZE	The natural log of the Total Assets.
X_3	EQUITY	The ratio of Equity Capital to Total Assets
X_4	LOANS	The ratio of Total Loans to Total Assets
X_5	OPCOST	The ratio of Non-interest Expense to Net Operating Revenue Where, Net Operating Revenue = Net Interest Income + Non-interest income
X_6	NIINCOME	The ratio of Non-interest income to total income
X_7	NPA	The ratio of net NPAs to Net Advances
X_8	DEMAND	The ratio of demand and saving deposits to total funds
X_9	SPREAD	The ratio of Net Interest Margin to NOR Where, Net Interest Margin = Total Interest Income minus Interest Expense
X_{10}	OWNPUB	Dummy for the Banks in Public sector
X_{11}	OWNPVT	Dummy for the Banks in private sector.
X_{12}	INF	The Annual Inflation Rate

CONCLUSIONS

The present study is an attempt to present the present status of Internet banking in India and its implications for Indian banking industry. A survey of the bank websites during the period of June, 2007 reveals that only 57 percent of the commercial banks operating in India as on March end 2006 offer Internet banking. Using data on the financial performance, the present study also analyzed the performance of an Internet group in comparison to non-Internet banking group and impact of Internet banking on banks' performance and risk.

A panel data of 85 banks was taken for the period of 1998-2006. The analysis indicates several significant differences in the profile of banks that offer Internet banking and banks that do not. Broadly speaking, on an average, Internet banks are larger, more profitable and are more operationally efficient than non-Internet banks.

Internet banks have higher asset quality and are better managed to lower the expenses for building and equipment. In contrast to developed countries Internet banks in India rely substantially on deposits, the traditional source of financing. Last, but not the least, attempt was made to see if there is any association between adoption of Internet banking and the banks' performance and risk.

The evidence reveals no significant association between adoption of Internet banking by banks and their performance. However, Internet banking has a negative and significant impact on profitability of private sector banks particularly new private sector banks. Thus, adoption of Internet banking was a reason behind the lower profitability of these banks, as Internet banks in new private sector were operating with higher cost of operations, including fixed cost and labour cost, thus affecting negatively the profitability of these banks. On the other hand, internet banking has a negative and significant impact on risk, which shows that, the adoption of Internet banking has not increased the risk profile of banks.

5

Internet and Web Publishing

INTRODUCTION TO THE INTERNET

WHAT IS THE INTERNET?

Strictly speaking, the Internet is a *communications protocol,* a language which computers use to talk to each other, called TCP/IP. This language is designed to enable computers to exchange data reliably and efficiently, though not necessarily quickly. More generally, the term is used to signify the network of computers connected using TCP/IP: the connecting wires and the equipment used to route the information and the computers themselves.

Even more generally, the Internet is often used to indicate the community of users and computers collectively. Though a very broad definition, this is perhaps the most useful and interesting — the Internet is really an information-based society.

PROTOCOLS CREATED BY THE COMMUNITY

The TCP/IP and related protocols that are used across the Internet are designed and agreed upon by the users and administrators of the individual parts of the Internet: anyone can contribute to the growth and direction of the Internet, though you do need to know a fair amount of technical detail to get involved. In this way, the Internet is not so much controlled by an organisation, as encouraged in a certain direction by its members. It's a kind of open, contributory democracy. Sometimes, companies will try to force the net to go the way they want, but usually there's enough resistance from the mass of contributors to only go that way if the idea or direction is good for the 'net as a whole. The influence each person has on the direction of the Internet is usually related to their technical knowledge and reputation, with widely respected techies holding the most power. It's perhaps more of a technocracy than a traditional democracy.

PROTOCOLS SERVING INFORMATION TO A COMMUNITY

The Internet, as a "network of networks", consists of many computers, called *servers* or *hosts,* which are linked by communication lines. The administrators of these hosts may make information or software stored on them publically available, so that others can view, download or use the data. At the last count, there were an estimated 489 million hosts connected to the Internet.

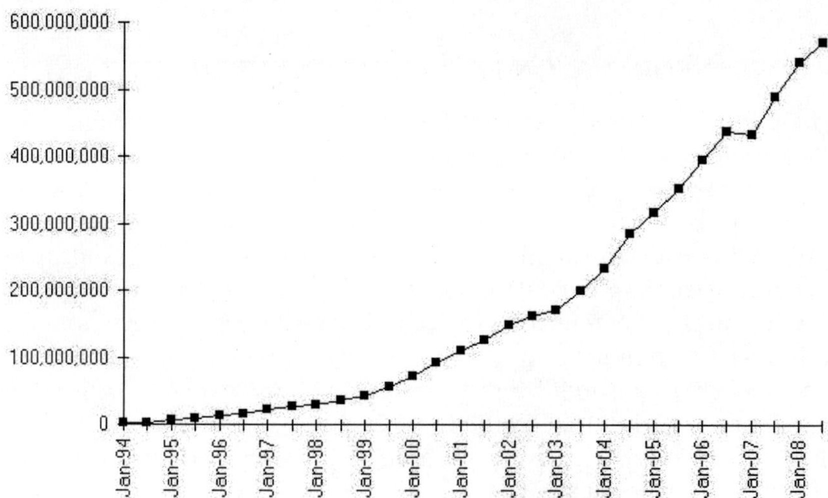

Fig. Growth in number of Internet hosts

However, most Internet-connected computers act only as *clients;* they access the data stored on other servers, but don't store or share any information themselves. It's hard to estimate how many client computers there are in cyberspace, because many connect dynamically or are hidden behind firewalls, but a conservative estimate would be more than 800 million, possibly much higher. According to Internet World Stats, nearly 1.5 billion people have some form of Internet access.

DYNAMIC AND PERMANENT CONNECTIONS

Clients may be permanently connected or may connect dynamically when needed. Permanent connections are most commonly made through a *local area network* (LAN) or a *digital subscriber line* (DSL or *ADSL*), and give instant 24/7 access. A temporary, dynamic connection such as that provided by a *modem* link needs to be connected each time the Internet is used, which can cause a delay. Modem links also tend to be slower than dedicated digital links, because they use normal voice telephone lines which are not designed to carry digital signals.

DSL connections also carry a digital signal across wiring designed for analogue signals, but do so by overlaying a very high frequency signal (well beyond human hearing) onto the normal connection. This means that not only can the same line carry voice and data simultaneously, but that for short distances, a much higher bandwidth can be carried. Dedicated wiring for Internet traffic is most commonly found in companies and other organisations, where a LAN is used to connect clients and hosts together. Usually, this forms an enclosed network which connects to the outside world through a single point, which can be controlled and protected against intrusion and viruses. Connection to this type of network is normally instantaneous and 'always-on'.

HOW DOES INFORMATION TRAVEL THROUGH THE INTERNET?

The Internet is based on *packet-switched* protocols. Information is carried in *packets*, which can be imagined as small parcels being passed from computer to computer. Large chunks of data are usually broken up into several smaller packets before being sent through the network. The delivery mechanism, or protocol, that is used to encode the packet ensures safe transit, and provides a way of reconstructing the data when it reaches its destination. The protocols used on the Internet are referred to as TCP/IP, standing for *Transmission Control Protocol/ Internet Protocol*.

As a *switched network*, the physical connections between computers do not matter as far as Internet traffic is concerned — the protocols ensure that guaranteed information delivery is more important than speed or use of a particular route. This means that a sequence of packets might arrive out of order, with some travelling through the net by a faster, shorter route than others. TCP/IP provides the means for your software to piece together those packets into meaningful data. The ability to take different routes through the network is a fundamental part of the original design of TCP/IP, as it allows the Internet to route around damaged areas of the network.

THE INTERNET IN THE ACADEMIC WORLD

The University has a permanent Internet connection, which connects it to the JANET (*Joint Academic NETwork*). JANET is maintained by UKERNA (*UK Education and Research Networking Association*), which in turn is part of JISC (the *Joint Information Services Committee*).

CONNECTING USING AN ISP

An ISP, or Internet Service Provider, is a company that provides you with a point of access to the Internet. When you connect to your ISP, your computer (or your own network) becomes an extension of the Internet itself whilst you remain connected.

HOW DOES THE CONNECTION WORK FROM HOME?

To connect from home you need several things. Apart from a computer (obviously!) you'll need a phone connection, a modem or ADSL router, and some Internet software. Things will be easier if you're using a relatively recent operation system, such as Windows Vista/XP or MacOSX, but it's possible to connect with older or more obscure systems. With a modem and the appropriate software, you can dial up another modem connected to another computer, and establish a network connection with it. Usually, this computer is linked into the Internet, and so you're online. With an ADSL modem or router, a similar procedure happens, but a filter splits the telephone line into voice and data (low and high frequencies) and your router negotiates a connection with the ADSL equipment in the telephone exchange.

CHOOSING AN ISP

Within the University, the computers are connected permanently to the Internet. If you want to connect from home, you'll need to connect temporarily to an Internet Service Provider, or ISP, each time you need to access Internet resources. Setting this up is a fairly painless process, though you need to choose your ISP carefully.

What to look for

The first decision to make is the type of connection you want. If you're a *very* occasional user, then getting a dialup connection is still often the cheapest and simplest. It's also useful if you travel around a lot, as it's not (usually) tied to a particular phone line/number. Most people, however, will want a broadband connection, because it gives a reliable, almost instant connection (or 'always-on' operation) at a high bandwidth.

You might also consider a wireless connection using data over a mobile phone network. These offer the ultimate mobile solution, but can be very expensive, often charging per megabyte of download.

CHOOSING A BROADBAND PROVIDER

For broadband ISPs, there are several important factors to check, including reliability, speed of connection, how many other customers share the total bandwidth (the Contention Ratio), and of course, cost. Most charge a set-up cost, and many have a minumum contract period, so be careful you don't get locked into a poor deal for many months!

There are now also variable packages, where you can control the amount of bandwidth available, paying extra for more capacity if you need it. For more recommendations and relatively independent advice I find ThinkBroadband useful.

A recent development is the capping of Internet connections by limiting the monthly downloads to, say, 10GB. This may seem reasonable at first, but if you wish to listen to Internet radio or download video clips from the BBC, for example, then you'll hit this limit sooner than you expect. Check whether your ISP offers an "unlimited" or "unmetered" service.

HOW FAST? HOW RELIABLE?

Another thing to look out for is the speed and reliability of the connection. This is partly dependent upon the speed of your modem and your computer but also depends on your ISPs facilities too. Again it's worth shopping around to see which service provides fastest access, and the quickest, most reliable connection. There are a number of websites that run independent tests and surveys on each of the major ISPs, so there's no shortage of advice! It's also worth shopping around for *extras,* such as webspace and email boxes, domain names, and even telephone deals.

Remember, though, that if you use your ISP's email facilities, your email address will change each time you change your ISP; it's often better to have a separate, permanent account from an independent email provider, such as Microsoft's hotmail or Google's gmail.

CONNECTING THROUGH THE UNIVERSITY

You can use the University as your ISP. Check the DialUp page for more details. If you live in University-run accommodation that has a built-in network connection, you can also connect to ResNet, the University's residential network. For a small(ish) fee, currently £70 per year, you get an always-on connection into the campus network. Note that this is only a limited service; you get full web and email access, but other services such as chat, filesharing or multimedia streaming may be limited. Whenever you connect to the campus network you're also bound by the University's rules and regulations, so don't do anything naughty - someone may be watching!

CONFIGURING YOUR COMPUTER

If you're using your own PC, you'll need to configure networking for your operating system (eg Windows XP). The easiest way to do this is to obtain a CD with the tools and settings combined— most ISPs give these away free. If you know all the details of the connection (usually obtainable from the ISP's tech-support website), you can set up the connection by hand, but this is often not for the faint-hearted!

There are some hints on configuring Windows for the University's dialup and ResNet services on the IT Services website.

MEASURING BANDWIDTH

Though the speed and quality of links are not the most important factors for Internet traffic, they will still affect your use of the net. In particular, you'll notice the difference (hopefully) between connecting on Campus, and connecting from home using a modem. Modems are described by their bandwidth; a typical analogue modem may have a bandwidth (or speed) of 56kb/s (kilobits per second), and a broadband modem anything between 256 to 2048 kb/s. This compares to the campus ethernet network, which has bandwidths of between 10 and 2000 Mb/s (megabits per second). Of course, on the campus ethernet, this bandwidth is often shared between many users (eg all computers in a single building) whereas the bandwidth of your analogue modem at home is exclusively yours. Broadband (DSL) connections often state how many others you'll be sharing your bandwidth with - this is called the Contention Ratio.

WHO GOVERNS/REGULATES/CONTROLS THE INTERNET?

This is a difficult question! The Internet grew as a collaborative network of researchers keen to share their discoveries in a simple, accessible way. Because of this, there was no real need to regulate or control the Internet; the information was already free and was of interest only to other researchers, so it didn't need protection. But as the Internet has grown, it has become a more commercial, public entity, and some who use it now wish it to be governed and policed to prevent certain types of abuse.

However, there are various bodies that govern parts of the Internet, which we'll look at in the next few paragraphs.

Domain names

One form of control that is necessary (and possible) is the name service, which allocates *Domain Names* on the Internet. These are unique names for subnetworks, which allow easier (human) access to Internet addresses. So, instead of having to remember that Exeter's (numeric) addresses all begin 144.173, you can just use.ex.ac.uk at the end of a name. (We'll explain more about addressing in the next lecture). In the UK, these domain names (all ending in.uk) are managed by an organisation called *Nominet.UK*. It delegates some UK addresses to other organisations, such as UKERNA (for.ac.uk and.gov.uk addresses), but manages most itself.

Internet Protocol Addresses

Every computer, server and other device that connects to the internet needs an address to be found, and these need to be unique across the whole of the network. Managing to keep these unique and ordered is the job of IANA, the *Internet Assigned Numbers Authority*.

Other bodies and institutions

On a global level, things are more complex. Since the Internet grew primarily out of the United States, the bodies that control the Internet worldwide are organised from there. The main body is *IANA*, and as previously mentioned, this has overall control for assigning numeric addresses. Recently, a new corporation, called ICANN, the *Internet Corporation for Assigned Names and Numbers*, was set up to oversee this role and other important aspects of Internet governance. All of these organisations, and many more governing and researching aspects of the Internet, are members of the Internet Society.

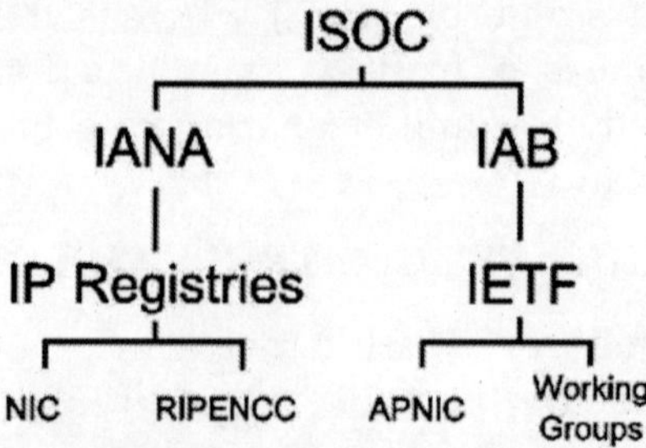

Fig. The internet society structure

WHO OWNS THE INTERNET?

This again is a difficult question. The individual networks and connections are owned by many individual companies and organisations, and each makes the chunks it owns available to be used to a greater or lesser extent creating the Internet as a whole. So, when you connect to your ISP from home, you are effectively leasing a connection to their part of the network. They in turn will lease connections to ISPs and network providers 'upstream', and so on. The core UK network providers own and maintain a backbone of connections criss-crossing the country. Other providers run connections to Europe and the United States, and so on. So when you send an email from your computer in Exeter to your Aunt in Peru or your best friend travelling the world and connecting in a cybercafe in Touva, the message is travelling via many networks owned by many people, companies and government bodies. What's remarkable is that you're not charged by each company en route, since they all cooperate and allow (almost) all traffic to pass through. Payment is made through the chain of ISPs by each ISP paying for its right to connect higher up the chain, and agreeing to pass traffic through its own network.

It's a model that works well, though it is becoming more complex as the commercial value of connectivity increases. The multiple ownership of the Internet also has implications for the security of your messages, as your text will pass through many networks and may be readable by any of them (unless you take steps to safeguard it).

THE WORLD WIDE WEB

WHAT IS THE WORLD WIDE WEB?

The Web consists of many millions of internet-connected computers, each with information on them that their owner has decided to share. These documents can be formed of anything from plain text to multimedia or even

3D objects. These computers, called servers, deliver this information over the Internet to client computers (such as your PC at home) using a protocol called HTTP (*HyperText Transfer Protocol*). The HTTP protocol is very simple; essentially it just provides a mechanism that allows a client to request a document, and a server to send that document.

As the web has become more and more popular, its capabilities have increased to include such things as graphics, animations, scripts and even complete computer programs, all embedded into the pages of the documents. Essentially, the web is the easiest to use of all the internet toolkit —this is partly why it has become so popular. Various mechanisms allow the viewer to move around (navigate) the document easily. Clicking on a hyperlink moves you to another part of the document, or to another document altogether.

The Web's unique features

The web has become the most predominant of the new digital media, and has provided the mechanism for many new forms of publishing. There are many reasons why this is so; a few of them are discussed in the following sections.

Universal readership

As the accessing of information stored on computers has become more widely accepted and used, the number of methods, and hence the number of computer applications needed, has multiplied. The web provides a way of integrating these methods and applications, using a common interface to allow easy access to any information stored on any computer provided you are authorised to read it, of course).

HTML or *HyperText Markup Language*, the language of the web, was specifically designed to be easy to learn, and was based around the concept of marking text functionally, to ensure a wide authorship. Thus, when the author wrote their document, they would be able to concentrate on its structure, and not worry about its presentation. As it has grown, the web has moved away from this concept, becoming more complex and more graphical than originally envisioned, which has led to many presentational features creeping into the HTML standard. Happily though, the core functions still lie beneath all the complexity, and allow more or less anyone to write their own web pages quickly and easily, with a minimal set of software tools.

Hypertext and Hypermedia

One of the most powerful features of the web is the ability to link documents together using *hyperlinks*. On clicking a hyperlink (usually underlined), the browser tries to access the linked document, providing an almost instantaneous cross-referencing system. This creates a non-linear form of text, known as *hypertext*. Web pages can also contain multimedia content that can also be hyperlinked, termed *hypermedia*. Many theorists believe that hyperlinks change the way we view and read texts, and certainly the element of choice that hyperlinks give the reader create a very different reading experience. The idea of hypertext has been around at least as long as books have contained footnotes or external references/bibliographies, but the computer and the Internet make following hyperlinks instantaneous.

Authoring for computers and humans

Though it may not seem so when you first see a raw web page, the language it is written in, *HTML*, is designed to be easily read by humans, as well as computers. It was developed to make sharing information easy, and to make it easy to write documents that would be displayed on many types of computer. HTML can be interpreted at different levels, even in text-only mode (try turning off the image-loading in your browser - you'll be surprised at how much faster everything loads, and how much information is preserved!). Now with devices such as mobile phones having Internet capabilities, the accessibility of web information is even more important.

Availability of information

The goal of a web server is to serve information to anyone who requests it; the web pages stored on the server are made publically available. It's possible to restrict access to certain parts of the Internet, or to those who have usernames and passwords, but it's not usual - most web sites are open for all to read their contents. The use of the web as a public space to provoke discussion or to provide otherwise difficult-to-publish information has been instrumental in its popularity. Examples of this range from the subversive (terrorists or political groups publishing propaganda) to the more mundane (businesses publishing time-critical data such as stock information or market prices).

Surface and deep web

With the rise of commerce on the Web, and the recognition of the market value that certain types of information can command, parts of the Web have been locked away, hidden behind corporate intranets and firewalls, passworded sites, and subscription services. A high proportion of this *Deep* or *Invisible Web* is hidden from view, whether from you and I, or from search engines. Estimates of the size of this deep Web vary, but most agree that it is many times the size of the *Surface Web*, i.e. the web that is open and accessible to the public.

Flexibility to adapt to new media

The HTTP protocol was specifically designed from the outset to be *media neutral*, in that the documents and data it transfers need not be in any particular format. As the document is transferred, it is accompanied by a header which specifies a MIME type (more about MIME in the section called "Using Email Attachments"), and this tells the browser viewing the item what needs to be done to display (or play) the data. Similarly, the HTML language is designed to use these media items by linking to them from within a web page. HTML has evolved over the years to allow all kinds of media to be embedded; from simple static images through video and animations, and even to 3D data.

How does the web work?

The backbone of the web is the network of *webservers* across the world. These are really just computers that have a particular type of software running on them - software that knows how to speak the HTTP protocol and knows which information stored on the computer should be made accessible through the web.

It's possible to turn almost any computer into a webserver by downloading and installing server software (the most popular is Apache, see http://www.apache.org/), though it's not recommended unless you know what you're doing!

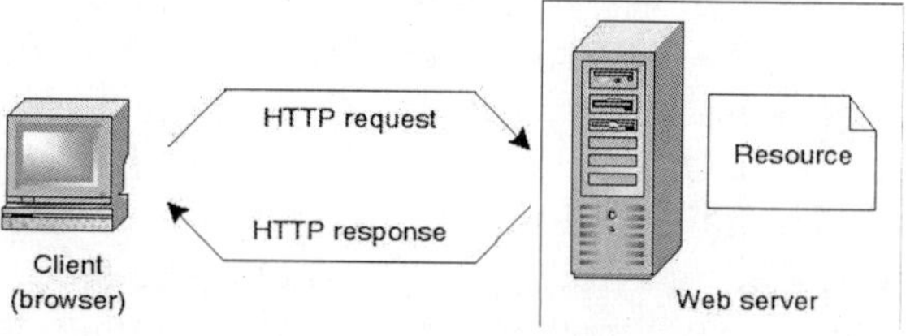

Fig. How HTTP works: retrieving a web page

The *HyperText Transfer Protocol* (HTTP) is actually quite simple. The web browser (or client) makes a request of a webpage to the server, and the webserver passes the page back to the browser

The web browser is also particularly clever in the way it displays what it retrieves. Web pages are written in HTML, and the browser knows how to display these correctly, whether you have a huge flat screen or a tiny screen on a handheld device or phone. The HTML language gives the browser hints on how to display things, and the browser decides the final layout itself.

WEB PUBLISHING

A website, also written as Web site, web site, or simply site, is a collection of related web pages containing images, videos or other digital assets. A website is hosted on at least one web server, accessible via a network such as the Internet or a private local area network through an Internet address known as a Uniform Resource Locator. All publicly accessible websites collectively constitute the World Wide Web. A web page is a document, typically written in plain text interspersed with formatting instructions of Hypertext Markup

Language (HTML, XHTML). A web page may incorporate elements from other websites with suitable markup anchors.

Web pages are accessed and transported with the Hypertext Transfer Protocol (HTTP), which may optionally employ encryption (HTTP Secure, HTTPS) to provide security and privacy for the user of the web page content. The user's application, often a web browser, renders the page content according to its HTML markup instructions onto a display terminal.

The pages of a website can usually be accessed from a simple Uniform Resource Locator (URL) called the homepage. The URLs of the pages organize them into a hierarchy, although hyperlinking between them conveys the reader's perceived site structure and guides the reader's navigation of the site. Some websites require a subscription to access some or all of their content. Examples of subscription websites include many business sites, parts of news websites, academic journal websites, gaming websites, file-sharing websites, message boards, web-based email, social networking websites, websites providing real-time stock market data, and websites providing various other services (e.g., websites offering storing and/or sharing of images, files and so forth).

The World Wide Web (WWW) was created in 1990 by CERN physicist Tim Berners-Lee. On 30 April 1993, CERN announced that the World Wide Web would be free to use for anyone. Before the introduction of HTML and HTTP, other protocols such as File Transfer Protocol and the gopher protocol were used to retrieve individual files from a server. These protocols offer a simple directory structure which the user navigates and chooses files to download. Documents were most often presented as plain text files without formatting, or were encoded in word processor formats.

Organized by function, a website may be

- A personal website
- A commercial website
- A government website
- A nonprofit organization website.

It could be the work of an individual, a business or other organization, and is typically dedicated to some particular topic or purpose. Any website can contain a hyperlink to any other website, so the distinction between individual sites, as perceived by the user, may sometimes be blurred.

Websites are written in, or dynamically converted to, HTML (Hyper Text Markup Language) and are accessed using a software interface classified as a user agent. Web pages can be viewed or otherwise accessed from a range of computer-based and Internet-enabled devices of various sizes, including desktop computers, laptops, PDAs and cell phones.

A website is hosted on a computer system known as a web server, also called an HTTP server, and these terms can also refer to the software that runs on these systems and that retrieves and delivers the web pages in response to requests from the website users. Apache is the most commonly used web server software (according to Netcraft statistics) and Microsoft's Internet Information Services (IIS) is also commonly used.

STATIC WEBSITE

A static website is one that has web pages stored on the server in the format that is sent to a client web browser. It is primarily coded in Hypertext Markup Language, HTML. Simple forms or marketing examples of websites, such as *classic website*, a *five-page website* or a *brochure website* are often static websites, because they present pre-defined, static information to the user. This may include information about a company and its products and services via text, photos, animations, audio/video and interactive menus and navigation.

This type of website usually displays the same information to all visitors. Similar to handing out a printed brochure to customers or clients, a static website will generally provide consistent, standard information for an extended period of time. Although the website owner may make updates periodically, it is a manual process to edit the text, photos and other content and may require basic website design skills and software.

In summary, visitors are not able to control what information they receive via a static website, and must instead settle for whatever content the website owner has decided to offer at that time.

They are edited using four broad categories of software:

- Text editors, such as Notepad or TextEdit, where content and HTML markup are manipulated directly within the editor program
- WYSIWYG offline editors, such as Microsoft FrontPage and Adobe Dreamweaver (previously Macromedia Dreamweaver), with which the site is edited using a GUI interface and the final HTML markup is generated automatically by the editor software
- WYSIWYG online editors which create media rich online presentation like web pages, widgets, intro, blogs, and other documents.
- Template-based editors, such as RapidWeaver and iWeb, which allow users to quickly create and upload web pages to a web server without detailed HTML knowledge, as they pick a suitable template from a palette and add pictures and text to it in a desktop publishing fashion without direct manipulation of HTML code.

DYNAMIC WEBSITE

A dynamic website is one that changes or customizes itself frequently and automatically, based on certain criteria.

Dynamic websites can have two types of dynamic activity: Code and Content. Dynamic code is invisible or behind the scenes and dynamic content is visible or fully displayed.

Dynamic code

The first type is a web page with dynamic code. The code is constructed dynamically on the fly using active programming language instead of plain, static HTML.

A website with dynamic code refers to its construction or how it is built, and more specifically refers to the code used to create a single web page. A dynamic web page is generated on the fly by piecing together certain blocks of code, procedures or routines. A dynamically-generated web page would recall various bits of information from a database and put them together in a pre-defined format to present the reader with a coherent page. It interacts with users in a variety of ways including by reading cookies recognizing users' previous history, session variables, server side variables etc., or by using direct interaction (form elements, mouse overs, etc.). A site can display the current state of a dialogue between users, monitor a changing situation, or provide information in some way personalized to the requirements of the individual user.

Dynamic content

The second type is a website with dynamic content displayed in plain view. Variable content is displayed dynamically on the fly based on certain criteria, usually by retrieving content stored in a database.

A website with dynamic content refers to how its messages, text, images and other information are displayed on the web page, and more specifically how its content changes at any given moment. The web page content varies based on certain criteria, either pre-defined rules or variable user input. For example, a website with a database of news articles can use a pre-defined rule which tells it to display all news articles for today's date. This type of dynamic website will automatically show the most current news articles on any given date. Another example of dynamic content is when a retail website with a database of media products allows a user to input a search request for the keyword Beatles. In response, the content of the web page will spontaneously change the way it looked before, and will then display a list of Beatles products like CDs, DVDs and books.

Purpose of dynamic websites

The main purpose of a dynamic website is automation. A dynamic website can operate more effectively, be built more efficiently and is easier to maintain, update and expand. It is much simpler to build a template and a database than to build hundreds or thousands of individual, static HTML web pages.

SOFTWARE SYSTEMS

There is a wide range of software systems, such as ANSI C servlets, JavaServer Pages (JSP), the PHP, Perl, Python, and Ruby programming languages, ASP.NET, Active Server Pages (ASP), YUMA and ColdFusion (CFML) that are available to generate dynamic web systems and dynamic sites. Sites may also include content that is retrieved from one or more databases or by using XML-based technologies such as RSS.

Static content may also be dynamically generated either periodically, or if certain conditions for regeneration occur (cached) in order to avoid the performance loss of initiating the dynamic engine on a per-user or per-connection basis. Plug ins are available to expand the features and abilities of web browsers to show *active content* or even create rich internet applications. Examples of such plug-ins are Microsoft Silverlight, Adobe Flash, Adobe Shockwave or applets written in Java. Dynamic HTML also provides for user interactivity and realtime element updating within web pages (i.e., pages don't have to be loaded or reloaded to effect any changes), mainly using the Document Object Model (DOM) and JavaScript, support which is built-in to most modern web browsers.

Turning a website into an income source is a common practice for web developers and website owners. There are several methods for creating a website business which fall into two broad categories, as defined below.

Content-based sites

Some websites derive revenue by selling advertising space on their site either through direct sales or through an advertising network. (see Contextual advertising).

Product- or service-based sites

Some websites derive revenue by offering products or services for sale. In the case of e-commerce websites, the products or services may be purchased at the website itself, by entering credit card or other payment information into a payment form on the site. While most business websites serve as a shop window for existing brick and mortar businesses, it is increasingly the case that some websites are businesses in their own right; that is, the products they offer are only available for purchase on the web. Websites occasionally derive income from a combination of these two practices. For example, a website such as an online auctions website may charge the users of its auction service to list an auction, but also display third-party advertisements on the site, from which it derives further income.

6

Resource Sharing and Webs Networking

INTRODUCTION

In the present era of Information technology, the information needs of the users have been increased so enormously that no single library on its own can meet their information needs. This has necessitated the need for effective linkages and cooperation between libraries and information centers for sharing of available resources and information through networking. The consortia for library can be considered as a major step towards library cooperation in sharing electronic resources. The consortium should take lead role in the development of a national strategy for information provision for research in higher education.

LIBRARY RESOURCE SHARING AND NETWORKING

The term resource applies to a thing, person or action to which one resorts to in times of need and sharing indicates allotting, apportioning or contributing something that is owned, to benefit others. Resource sharing, therefore, refers to reciprocity, implying a partnership where each member has something useful to contribute to others and which each is willing and able to make available when needed.

Resource sharing is an empty concept, but for the approach permitting resource sharing to work is that which

- Entails having resources to share
- Having a willingness to share them, and
- Having a plan for accomplishing resource sharing

Resource Sharing is an integral part of modern library services. In the developed countries, no library services can be thought without sharing of resources.

In the past, RS was limited to the interlibrary loan system. In the modern age, with the development of science and technology and innovations of techniques and devices, resource sharing has become easier and fruitful due to the availability of databases, information network, and online sharing facilities. Thus, the resource sharing system helps one library to access to resources of other libraries. When resource sharing is agreed upon by participating institutions, then the following aspects must be planned:

- Identify and locate major collections, sources and materials
- Assemble, publish and distribute collective information for all participating bodies
- Workout the basis for sharing, reference service, lending service, copying service, access to materials, delivery service, and lists of holdings
- Establish means of sharing ideas, development and problems in the form of a newsletter
- Plan for new developments in the knowledge of what others are doing
- Developing a National Information Policy

The following are the most important benefits of resource sharing to participating institutions:

- Easy access to materials
- Enables co-operating institutions to extend limited resources
- Allow greater staff specialization
- Improve services to users
- Avoids unnecessary duplication
- Reduces the number of places which will need to go for services
- Improves working relationships between cooperating libraries.

Resource sharing refers to a joint use of resources available on a system or a network by user or peripherals. In the language of information management, when we talk about resource sharing we simply mean collective use of information of all types by various end users from a control coordinating unit or from within a network component at a reduced cost with easy accessibility. Library cooperation and resource-sharing activity can take place in several forms and can happen at many levels, which include:

- Interlibrary loans/reciprocal borrowing privileges
- Exchange or sharing of expertise, resources, and facilities
- Exchange of publications and photocopies and other reprographic services
- Sharing of bibliographic information
- Cooperative acquisition, cooperative cataloguing, and cooperative collection development preparation of union list of holdings
- Cooperative relationship and network development

The implementation of resource sharing is largely depends on library networking. It gives an easy and wider access to information as members have an expanded information-base and service. A network is a form of arrangement or an administrative structure that links a group of individuals or organizations who have agreed to work together and/or share resources. Information networking entails the sharing of resources so that the information needs of both actual and potential users of information—from the local to national level—of all network participants are met. The network enables the participating bodies to facilitate and expand their users' access to literature and information without corresponding investment in purchase, and processing of information is exchanged through the network on a formal basis. The network may be responsible for coordinating, organizing and providing information and literature support at the national and international level. The main activities and functions of the network are as follows:

Acquisition of materials:

- Joint purchasing of materials
- Assignment of specialization in material acquisition
- Coordinated subscription
- Exchange of duplicate holdings

Technical services:

- Co-operative cataloguing
- Abstracting and indexing services
- Interlibrary loan
- Reciprocal borrowing privileges
- Reference and/or referral services

Publication program/repackaging information:

- Union catalogue/list of periodicals
- Mutual notification of purchase through lists of new arrivals or acquisition list
- Bibliography development
- Newsletters
- Joint directories of personnel, projects, consultants, resource persons, etc.
- Manuals

Coordination services:

- Clearing house functions
- Retrieval and storage function
- Referral center

Delivery/mailing service:

- Research, training and other special services
  - User interest surveys
  - Joint research projects
  - In-service personnel training
  - Workshops and meetings
  - Translation services

RESOURCE SHARING AND NETWORKS INITIATIVES IN BANGLADESH

In Bangladesh several Resource-sharing and networks initiatives was taken by different organizations in different sectors to launch Resource sharing and networking systems. Some of these are as follows:

- National Agricultural Information System (NAIS): The Agricultural Information Centre (AIC) was taken an initiative to develop a network of agricultural institution.
- Social Science Research Council (SSRC): Social Science Research Council, Dhaka was taken an initiative to develop a social science information network in Bangladesh.
- Health Literature, Library, and Information Service (HeLLIS) Network: The HeLLIS network was developed by SEARO (WHO), New Delhi, India and National Health Library and Documentation Centre (NHLDOC), Dhaka. All the health libraries of Bangladesh were brought under this network.
- Development Information Network on South Asia (DEVINSA): The DEVINSA network was organized by CSCD (Committee on Studies for Cooperation for Development in South Asia) through the Marga Institute, Colombo, Sri Lanka. All SAARC countries, except Bhutan, were the participants of this network.
- Information Network on Rural Development (INRD): Centre on Integrated Rural Development for Asia and the Pacific (CIRDAP), Dhaka was taken an initiative to develop a regional network on rural development.
- Women Information Network (WIN): Centre on Integrated Rural Development for Asia and the Pacific (CIRDAP), Dhaka was taken another initiative to develop a network on women information.
- Bangladesh Development Support Information and Communication (BDSIC) Network: Bangladesh Academy for Rural Development (BARD), Comilla was taken an initiative to launch a network of rural development institutions in Bangladesh
- National Science and Technology Information Policy (NASTIP): Under this policy, a four-tier science and technology information networking system has been recommended.
- The Association of Management Development Institutes in South Asia (AMDISA) Library Network: The Association of Management Development Institutes in South Asia was launched a library network on management development. The Headquarter of this network was located at the Administrative Staff College of India, Hyderabad. One institute in each SAARC country was selected as a focal point. The Institute of Business Administration Library, Dhaka University was selected as the National focal point for this network.
- University Libraries: Dhaka University Library took an initiative several years' back to develop a network of the university libraries,

initially by preparing a union catalogue of the holdings of the university libraries.

- The University Grants Commission of Bangladesh (UGC), in collaboration with the Asia Foundation, took an initiative to compile a union catalogue of the collections of different universities of Bangladesh and to establish an information network within the universities.
- Bangladesh National Scientific and Library Information Network (BANSLINK): Bangladesh National Scientific and Technical Documentation Centre (BANSDOC) was taken an initiative to build up a Network, known as BANSLINK, to develop a resource-sharing network having dial up connectivity with 15 libraries and information centres of the country.
- Sustainable Development Network Program (SDNP): SDNP is a UNDP funded program, which started a union catalog services in 2002 in their virtual library program. The SDNP virtual library prepared this union catalog of 13 libraries, all of which are using CDS/ISIS software for bibliographic record keeping. The SDNP virtual library union catalog is a webbased Online Public Access Catalog.

Bangladesh being a developing country cannot effort to waste its resources. To avoid this, an effective resource sharing and networking system is necessary. At present the following resource sharing and networking systems are working in the country:

- Population Information Network (POPIN): The National Institute of Population Research and Training (NIPORT) has taken an initiative to establish an information networking system in the field of health, population, family planning and maternal and child health in collaboration and cooperation with the government and non-government organizations, autonomous bodies, voluntary organizations, and international organizations.
- National Health Library and Documentation Centre (NHLDOC), (Ministry of Health, Government of Bangladesh) and International Centre for Diarrhoeal Disease Research, Bangladesh (ICDDR,B) signed in 1976 an agreement to facilitate library cooperation through an interlibrary loan system and agreed to cooperate with each other to avoid duplication of journal subscriptions. Subsequently, some other library named, BIDS, BIRDEM, USAID, Dhaka, Aga Khan Community Health Program, Dhaka, and the Bangladesh Rural Advancement Committee joined this programme by signing interlibrary loan agreements. The system has been working well.
- United Nations Library Network in Bangladesh (UN L-Net BD): In March 2002 United Nations Information Centre (UNIC) Library has

taken an initiative to establish the UN Library Network in Bangladesh (UN L-Net BD). Initially the Network consisted of twenty major libraries of different government, NGOs, including the UN agencies in Bangladesh. At present there are 26 members in this network. It was agreed that UNIC library would act as a focal point and secretariat of the network.

It is not possible for one libraries or information centers to hold the full stock of information resources or to procure all information, which may be in demand by its clientele. Even not a single library or information centers can meet the thrust of knowledge of all the readers from its holdings. To solve this problem, library cooperation started long ago, such as Inter-library loan, document delivery, library networks etc. At present the more accepted system of resource sharing is library consortia. Consortia approach is one of the many ways of maintaining cooperation and coordination among the libraries and in fact it has emerged as the 'state of the art' in library cooperation in recent years. The word 'consortia' was originated from the Latin in early 19th century in the sense of partnership. Oxford Advanced Learners Dictionary describes Consortia as 'a group of people, countries, companies, etc. who are working together on a particular project'. A library Consortia is an association of a group of libraries that agree to share their resources to satisfy the needs of users. Consortia may be formed on a local, regional, national, or international basis; on a functional or format basis; or on a subject basis.

BENEFITS OF CONSORTIA

The benefits of Consortia are many:

- A comprehensive collection is possible
- Building communication among different libraries
- Avoid duplication of core collection specially for core journals
- Scope of electronic archives
- Easy access to resource sharing on Internet by developing common resources databases
- Effective document delivery systems
- Better scope for developing a union catalogue
- Reduce cost of information
- Time saving
- Improved resource sharing
- More professional services to users
- Help to develop a competitive professionalism among LIS professionals

INTERNATIONAL EFFORTS FOR LIBRARY CONSORTIA

The development of library consortia is the outcome of the desire for resource sharing and consortia seem to be getting bigger. The global development of OCLC is prime example. Due to escalating cost of documents, decreasing budgets, inadequate storage area and competent staff, LIS professionals of the world are coming together to form consortia. There are several International efforts for library consortia are:

- Consortium of University Research Libraries (CURL)
- Consortium of Academic Libraries in Manchester (CALIM)
- Colorado Library Information Network,
- Washington Research Library Consortium (WRLC),
- BIBSYS (Shared University, Research and National Library of Norway)
- Queensland University Libraries Office of Cooperation (QUOLOC)
- China Academic Library & Information System (CALIS), China,
- Takatsu University Library Consortium (YULC), Japan
- Tokyo Western Regional Academic Library Consortium, Japan,
- Yamatesen Ensen Private University Libraries Consortium, Japan
- Korea Resource Sharing Alliance (KORSA), Korea,
- CONsortium on Core Eletronic Resources in Taiwan (CONCERT),
- Ministry of University Affairs (MUA). ThaiLIS.

INDIAN INITIATIVES FOR LIBRARY CONSORTIA

In India at present there are many consortia being run successfully by different organizations. Some of them are as:

- CSIR e-Journal Consortia,
- INDEST (Indian National Digital Library in Science and Technology) Consortia
- FORSA (Forum for Resource Sharing in Astronomy)
- UGC-INFONET
- IIM Library Consortia,
- ICICI Knowledge Park,
- DAE Library Consortium,
- ICMR Library Consortia,
- HELINET (Rajiv Gandhi University of Health Sciences, Karnataka).

BANGLADESH INITIATIVES

The information revolution has brought radical changes to the functions and services in all types of libraries. Many libraries in Bangladesh till today are not in a position to afford to procure all documents and subscribe to core journals in major discipline due to financial constraints. As a result, with the aim of ensuring rapid resource sharing among the major libraries and documentation centers in Bangladesh, many library networking and resources sharing efforts were started to help each other. The objectives of these consortia are for better resource sharing, to reduce information costs, for speedy delivery of documents, to keep abreast of new developments etc. Much emphasis should be given at the national level in Bangladesh for the development of documentary information resources, because it is considered as vital resources to promote the development of economy, science, technology and culture etc. University Grants Commission of Bangladesh (UGC) and Dr. Javed I. Khan of Kent State University have taken an initiative to develop a digital library system for Bangladesh. A 4-member committee was formed by the UGC to draft a concept paper on forming Consortia in Bangladesh, and the committee has already submitted the report to the UGC for their approval.

CONSIDERATION NEEDED TO FORM CONSORTIA

The following issues need to consider before building the consortia:

- Technology infrastructure
- Resources identification
- Budget and funding
- Pricing issues
- Subscription payment issues
- Access related issues
- Licensing and copyright issues
- Archival issues
- Usages and usability issues
- Coordination among partners
- Availability of efficient staff
- Overcoming political objections
- The egos of individuals and institutions
- Adequate professional training on ICT for the LIS professionals
- Sustainability issues

RECOMMENDATION

In this era of global communication, networks and consortia are highly important. A library consortium in the country is needed to achieve cost effectiveness and bridging of the digital divide. To develop library consortia in Bangladesh we have to overcome many hurdles such as inappropriate ICT infrastructure, inadequate funding, limited trained personnel, technological capability, lack of understanding of the concept of consortia. But anything new comes up with new challenges and opportunity, it is up to the individuals to take up the challenge and accept the opportunity. So, we can recommend the following suggestions for establishment of library consortia in Bangladesh.

- The Government and LIS Professionals bodies should take initiative to conduct some workshops on Consortia.
- The Government and LIS Professionals bodies should start a forum to bring the librarians/ Information professionals and the publishers/ vendors together for better communication and interactions.
- The Government should also make attempts to provide the necessary

ICT infrastructure such as high-speed links and a stable network to access the e-journals.

- Policy makers, both in national and international levels together with Internet Service Provider (ISP) should have a shared obligation to seek ways to achieve the wide spread use of the internet.
- Bangladesh should have a separate ministry to coordinate the overall development of the library and information system in the country.
- LIS professionals must market their services to the private sector for sponsorship and support.
- The government should encourage and must recognize the role of librarians and information professionals in building an information society for the development of the nation.
- Involvement of management of the parents organization for sustainability

CONCLUSION

Consortia in Bangladesh are still in table talk and there is a need to study the consortia models and guidelines and methodologies. It is recommended that the concept of Consortia can work well among similar organizations having similar situations such as sufficient additional funds available for the libraries of the consortia members and above all the committed mindsets of the library administrators. On the other side the subscription of e-journals are increasing day by day and the library budgets are shrinking, so it is needed for the library professionals to work together and formulate consortia for subscription to e-journals. Bangladeshi LIS professionals should seriously think and take initiative for consortium movement like western countries for maximum utilization of resources at the reduced cost, time and space.

7

Webs of Influence —Digital Libraries

INTRODUCTION

The Internet and the Web have been growing in leaps and bounds over the past few years, accelerating the problem of information explosion, a well-known phenomena to all of us. According to Nature, the publicly indexable Web contains an estimated 800 million pages as of February 1999, encompassing about 15 terabytes of information or about 6 terabytes of text after removing HTML tags, comments, and extra white-space. Indeed, the growing amount of Search Engines (SEs) that have popped up everywhere, reaching more than 2400 different SEs, enable us to access the cyberspace, but they also flood us with vast amounts of irrelevant information. Search engine coverage, relative to the estimated size of the publicly indexable Web, has recently decreased substantially, with no engine indexing more than about 16% of the estimated size of the publicly indexable Web.

It is interesting to note that 83% of the Web sites contain commercial content and only 6% contain scientific or educational content. The article is structured as follows. This section presents the resource repository hierarchy, defines the notion of the library and the development from paper to digital libraries. The next section classifies digital libraries, compares between the different types and introduces the logical harvesting model. The section following provides additional aspects regarding digital libraries. A concluding discussion ends the article.

RESOURCE REPOSITORIES HIERARCHY

Both Search Engines (SEs) and Digital Libraries (DLs) are Internet Resource Discovery (IRD) Tools. We introduce a resource repositories hierarchy with two major paradigms: search engines and digital libraries, where each branches to categories. SEs can be classified into three categories: Basic-SE, Directory, and Meta-SE. All the categories support search user interfaces, but with significant differences in their construction method:

- Basic-SE/Index - a tool that uses an automatic robot/crawler to gather metadata on items.

- Directory/Catalog/Guide - a tool that uses human judgement to collect and catalog items.
- Meta-SE - a tool that holds no database of its own, but rather queries Basic-SEs upon a user request.

LIBRARY

Before we delve into digital libraries, we define the notion of a library in general and of a digital library specifically.

Collection of data objects

A library holds a collection of data objects, also called holdings, items, resources, or just material. The items can be:

- Books and journals.
- Documents (e.g., HTML pages)
- Multimedia objects (such as pictures or images, tapes or video files, etc.).
- The library objects can be available locally in the library, or indirectly, by using a network to access them.

Collection of metadata structures

A library contains a collection of metadata structures, such as catalogs, guides, dictionaries, thesauri, indices, summaries, annotations, glossaries, etc.

Collection of services

A library provides a collection of services, such as:

- Various access methods (search, browse, etc.) for different users.
- Management of the library (purchase, shelf arranging, computerization, communication).
- Search (query formulation), browse, and consultation.
- Logging/statistics and Performance Measurement Evaluation (PME).
- Selective Dissemination of Information (SDI) or as it is called Push mode on the Internet.

Domain focus

A library has a domain focus and its collection has a purpose. For example: art, science, or literature. Also, it is usually created to serve a community of users, and therefore is finely grained. For example: academic, public, special, school, national, or state library.

Quality control

A library uses quality control in the sense that all its material is verified and consistent with the profile, or stereotype, of the library. The material is filtered before it is included in the library, and also its metadata is usually enriched (e.g., annotated), etc.

Preservation

Libraries and archives have served as the central institutional focus for preservation, and both types of institutions include preservation as one of their core functions. The purpose of preservation is to ensure protection of information of enduring value for access by present and future generations. Preservation includes regular allocation of resources for persistence, preventive measures to arrest deterioration of materials, and remedial measures to restore the usability of selected materia ls.

FROM PAPER TO DIGITAL LIBRARIES

In any case, the Web and the SEs do not substitute the classical, loved libraries. Looking backwards, libraries can be classified into 3 types:

- Paper/Analog Library (PL) - the classical paper library with its card catalog.
- Automated/Hybrid Library (AL) - a paper library with a computerized catalog.
- Digital Library (DL) - a computerized library in which most of the information is digital.

No one questions or disputes the long and lasting contribution of existing classical libraries. The concept of the paper library and the various services it provides are well established. The idea is that DLs should provide all these and more.

We use the term 'integrated services' in DLs to allude to that. These integrated services will add services that are made possible by use of the digital medium such as: varied search techniques resulting in focused results, faster provision of relevant resources, and access also to multimedia resources. The problems of our regular libraries are well known and need not be detailed here. On the other hand, it is less clear to us what a digital library is and how it works - this is the subject of this paper.

DIGITAL LIBRARIES

CLASSIFYING DLS

We classify the digital libraries into three categories:

- Stand-alone Digital Library (SDL),
- Federated Digital Library (FDL), and
- Harvested Digital Library (HDL).

We now detail:

- Stand-alone Digital Library (SDL): This is the regular classical library implemented in a fully computerized fashion. SDL is simply a library in which the holdings are digital. The SDL is selfcontained – the material is localized and centralized. In fact, it is a computerized instance of the classical library with the benefits of computerization.

Examples of SDLs are the Library of Congress (LC) and its National Digital Library (NDL), and the Israeli K12 Portal Snunit.

- Federated Digital Library (FDL): This is a federation of several independent SDLs in the network, organized around a common theme, and coupled together on the network. A FDL composes several autonomous SDLs that form a networked library with a transparent user interface. The different SDLs are heterogeneous and are connected via communication networks. The major challenge in the construction and maintenance of a FDL is interoperability. Examples of FDLs are the Networked Computer Science Technical Reference Library (NCSTRL) and Networked Digital Library of Theses and Dissertations (NDLTD).
- Harvested Digital Library (HDL): This is a virtual library providing summarized access to related material scattered over the network. A HDL holds only metadata with pointers to the holdings that are "one click away" in Cyberspace. The material held in the libraries is harvested (converted into summaries) according to the definition of an Information Specialist (IS). However, a HDL has regular DL characteristics, it is finely grained and subject focused. It has rich library services, and has high quality control preserved by the IS, who is also responsible for annotating the objects in the library. The HDL harvesting model is further detailed in section 3. Examples of HDLs are the Internet Public Library (IPL) and the WWW Virtual Library.

COMPARISON

To emphasize the different aspects of this DL categorization, let us get into the various DL types. In SDL and FDL, the items are electronically purchased or fully digitized/scanned. These items are stored in the local repository (in SDL), or in separate SDL repositories accessed using a network protocol (in FDL). Each SDL (and all together in a FDL) holds a huge repository containing both the items and some metadata structures to enable efficient retrieval. This material is updated every now and then, in a process similar to the one in classical library.

It is important to note that composing a FDL out of SDLs requires interoperability capabilities, and the use of a common protocol. In contrast to the SDL and FDL, the HDL's items are gathered from the network. These items are scattered on many servers, and accessed via direct retrieval using standard protocols such as HTTP, FTP, etc. The HDL holds only metadata on the items, and therefore its repository is small and compact. Because the items that belong to the HDL can be updated any time by their authors, their summaries have to be dynamically refreshed in the HDL using computerized procedures that are triggered automatically or initiated explicitly by the IS. An interesting point is that the profile of a HDL can be changed by the IS to enhance the library contents.

HARVESTING MODEL FOR HDLS

We will now describe our developed logical model for constructing HDLs. The model includes processes, data repositories (represented by rectangles) and auxiliary repositories (represented by parallelograms). The initiating IS invokes the Harvester with the DL harvesting request. The Harvester generates the initial DL profile and passes this as the harvesting query to the Locator component.

The Locator uses various network search techniques to enrich the initial collection of URLs to be harvested. The next component to be invoked is the Gatherer. It uses each top-level URL, in a recursive manner, to gather all referenced resources from the network providers, and passes them to the Filtering component. The Filtering component is responsible for blocking the non-relevant documents from reaching the focused DL. It uses various levels of filtering that all remaining documents have to pass to be considered relevant. A first level, for example, can use 'regular expressions' to match query keywords with the URL string tokens. A second level can use statistical techniques on the document itself, based on keyword counts and frequencies. A third level might use a Categorizer to classify the document and check if it belongs to the gathered DL categories. More levels or any geared combination of levels can ensure a cleaner DL devoid of 'noises'.

All relevant documents are passed now to the Summarizer. It extracts a summary of the document, and passes a stream of summaries to the Broker. The Broker indexes the summaries and organizes the DL. The IS builds for the DL a relevant topics-tree, possibly using advanced IR tools for categorization and clustering. The Retriever provides the DL user with a user-friendly interface.

IMPLEMENTATION OF HARVEST/KATSIR SYSTEM

To demonstrate HDLs, we focus on the Katsir HDL based on the Harvest system, an initial/partial implementation of the harvesting model for HDL. Katsir is currently being developed in Bar-Ilan University (BIU) as cooperation between the Mathematics and Computer Science department and the department of Information Studies.

The Harvest system, developed mainly at University of Colorado, USA, is an integrated set of tools to gather, extract, organize, search, cache, and replicate relevant information across the Internet. With modest effort users can tailor Harvest to digest information in many different formats, and offer custom search services on the Internet. Moreover, Harvest makes very efficient use of network traffic, remote servers, and disk space. The Katsir system is based on the Harvest system. Katsir can be directed to build a focused DL, based on both local and networked harvested materials. Katsir's enhancements over the original Harvest system are:

- Hebrew support: Full Hebrew support for both resources and interfaces was added to Harvest.
- Improved user interface: While Harvest's user interface supports keywords query, Katsir enable to user to retrieve information by keywords or conduct a guided tour by following a topics-tree that enables hypertext access to relevant materials.
- Improved Graphical User Interface for the IS: While the IS interface to Harvest is through Unix, using file editors to define harvesting options, Katsir implemented a GUI interface to define DL profile. The interface includes URLs for initialization, harvesting options, ports selection, etc. It also employs the standard browsers Bookmarks/Favorites utilities to define the initial DL Harvesting URLs.

The initial Katsir system was developed and implemented in an educational environment as a response to the unique requirements of the Israeli educational system. This project was part of a drive to enhance and assimilate information and telecommunication technologies in Israel, based on the public Internet. Both researchers and students of the departments of Information Studies and of Mathematics and Computer Science at BIU were involved in the development of Katsir.

Their cooperation in the framework of the demonstrative Gilo High-School project was complementary in knowledge and experience, and fruitful in its results. Moreover, the project itself was planned and executed with full cooperation of the Gilo user community. This begun in requirements analysis, in deciding the topics to be harves ted, in training the users in accessing the system, in conducting the control and evaluation process, and in reviewing and implementing the conclusions reached as part of the working methods of Katsir.

ADDITIONAL ASPECTS

PERSONAL DLS VS. PUBLIC DLS

All libraries can be personal or public, but this issue is mostly interesting in the implementation of HDL. HDL can support the harvesting of both personal and public DLs. A personal DL is one constructed for personal use by a seemingly only self-interested pers on. Here, the person is both the harvester and its user.

The personal and library profiles could be related or even be the same here. A public DL is geared to a wider range of audience. The harvester here is the IS, but the users are many. The library profile supports the library (users) stereotype and is maintained by the library IS. A public DL supports a large audience and has to have a higher level of integrated services, including support for pull and push modes.

TEXTUAL DLS VS. MULTIMEDIA DLS

Most DLs nowadays are mainly textually oriented libraries. However, a major advantage of being digital is the option of supporting libraries that contain Multi-Media (MM) resources. One major problem with MM DLs is how to summarize MM resources. The methods for summarizing MM resources are entirely different from textual ones; they include color, texture, shape, objects, etc. for visual information; pitch, rhythm, etc. for vocal information. Also, the repository generated is different, requiring special tools, such as multimedia and object oriented databases. Another hard problem is intelligent search and retrieval of MM resources. Usual IR tools are textually oriented. Some techniques for MM contents search and retrieval have been developed for use in MM-SEs. These techniques includes query by example, and the tools are sketching or giving an image as example to the query for images and video or based on singing a melody or humming a few notes for audio. There are several implementation of MM DL, few examples on the Web are:

- Webseek.
- Metaseek.
- Virage.
- Meldex.

However, most of these techniques are low-level using query by example or similarity measures, while DLs should also use higher-level methods based on object specification and recognition methods.

COMPOSING DLS

Another promising idea here is the composition of existing DLs to construct a coarser-grained DL. For example, we might have finely-grained DLs on the categories of Spaniels and Briards. These two can be composed to a coarser-grained DL on dogs. If we had additional DLs on cats, we could then combine them to a mammal DL. And similarly, further compose a DL on the category of animals and so on. The DLs participating in a composed DL can be physically distributed of course. The DL composition process uses techniques of open networking, shared file systems, replication servers, and resource caching.

DISCUSSION

Considering the vast amount of information, the Web is considered by many to be the world's ultimate virtual digital library - but is this solution the right one? We already confronted SEs with DLs to realize the differences between them. We can compare the different categories of SEs with the different categories of DLs. Basic -SE is similar to all DLs in the basic user interface, IR tools, and network access. Furthermore, Basic-SE is similar to HDL since they both hold metadata repositories rather than full items. A directory is even closer to a DL than a Basic-SE, since it is humanly compiled and therefore has quality control. But lets not forget it does not have domain focus and DL integrated services. Meta-SE is somewhat similar to FDL in the sense that both generate on-the-fly queries to other SEs/DLs to answer user queries. We elaborate more on the differences between SEs and DLs in the following section.

SEARCH ENGINES VS. DIGITAL LIBRARIES

The Search Engine (SE) paradigm and the DL one are really located at the extremes of a spectrum of data repositories and types of search. There are two sides to each of these coins: the data repository construction side and the user information search side. We will now discuss and contrast these aspects. As regards to the construction of SEs, this is a complex undertaking. It is clearly a long-term effort that is supported by commercial companies. The SE aims to build a quantitative global repository that represents as much information available on the Internet as possible or at least a large amount of it. The SE maintains various data structures, to represent its repository, like indices, directories, and catalogs. It also provides an elaborate user interface for search purposes.

The SE continuously employs various types of robots to search out and index pages on the Internet and to dynamically update its provided repository. Let's look now at the user side of SEs. Assume that a user needs some information on a certain topic that currently interests him. So he summons on a whim of a second his favorite SE to search for any relevant information. The SE is invoked with an ad-hoc query composed of a supposedly appropriate combination of keywords. The SE will certainly return a lot of information, which is bound to overload the user. He will then have to tediously sift through it all and manually filter the supplied references. The relevant information found will then be immediately used or temporarily kept in a cache for a short-term period of use.

Consider now the process of harvesting (i.e., constructing) a DL. A user, say an Information Specialist (IS), realizes a well-thought out need to build a qualitative data repository on an important focused topic. He decides to invest by harvesting and maintaining a long-term DL, described by a set of specific categories. So he interacts with an IS interface to carefully define his DL harvesting request. The DL is then harvested and made available to its users. It supports transparent user access methods using various data structures to enable efficient keywords search, touring a DL via a topics tree, and DB/SQL oriented views of the DL contents. The contents of the DL are continuously kept current and the DL can be annotated and enhanced with additional relevant material. Let's check now on the use of DLs. A serious user will tend to often need information on a topic included in his areas of interest. There is a good chance then that he already has access to a relevant DL, previously harvested. So he invokes the high-level DL interface and chooses an appropriate way to search this DL. The DL will return a reasonable amount of information (with high precision and recall) that the user can readily digest. The returned results will be made available at three levels of detail: first, a high-level summary (metadata); then, if requested, an additional abstract; and finally, if relevant, the referenced resource itself will be fetched and presented. Not much sifting will be necessary in any case. The relevant information can be further annotated by the user and later rediscovered whenever needed.

So, to summarize, SEs necessitate a huge organizational effort, provide the user with too much noisy information, but are useful for a one-time shot for quickly needed information. DLs, on the other hand, require a modest support effort, provide the user with focused information, but have to be made available beforehand while excelling in quality and ease of use. It is important to note that these two paradigms are neither conflicting nor exclusive, but are complementary in nature.

CONCLUSION

Digital libraries and search engines on the Internet are similar in many ways yet differ in others. The direction they are all going seems somewhat alike, yet, more research should be carried out to determine the real trends. Further research can also probe into the versatile types of SEs and DLs and their generations. More exploration into additional aspects discussed here, like multimedia, composition of libraries, and DL profiles should take place to promote these issues for the benefit of the millions of users surfing the net.

8

Internet

INTERNET TECHNOLOGIES

The use of the term Information and Communication Technology (ICT) rather than Information Technology (IT) emphasises this change. Computers now facilitate communication between people as well as between people and programmes or people and data.

Those who were involved in developing CAL packages in earlier decades usually point out that there is nothing new under the sun - which the lessons we are learning today about using the Internet for teaching were learnt before. Others would go further and point out that distance education with print has also covered a lot of the ground before and it is only because most lecturers are only accustomed to the face to face setting that they stumble into well mapped pitfalls when beginning to use internet technologies to teach. All of this is true but it is also true that using the Internet for teaching brings new challenges and necessitates the development of additional teaching skills.

The arrival of the Internet made communication between machines much easier and a number of open protocols and applications were developed to make use of this. Of these, E-mail was the forerunner and there can be few academics and students that do not have access to this now. E-mail has its limitations and it was the World Wide Web that really brought the world of networked computers to the general public.

The open standards of many of the technologies and the ease with which anyone could publish information encouraged participation by all and we need to remember what is about these technologies that makes them attractive when we try to deploy them for education. However, initially, a relatively small number of University lecturers adopted it for a range of teaching purposes but even fewer did more than post information about their courses or actual lecture notes - usually not modified in any way to take advantage of the strengths of the media such as hypertext.

One of the strengths and principle attractions of the Web is that it can provide authoring access to anybody and this is quite different from the one-way nature of education through CAL or any other media that predated it.

The fact that the technology facilitates this does not of course mean that it will take place but then this is true of any educational forum.

While far from needing programming skills, it still takes a certain amount of technophilia to publish a Web page. Creating them is trivial but actually publishing them can be tedious if the institution has not provided a simple means to do so. This is all about information rather than teaching and learning and it soon becomes obvious to any treading this path that you cannot take the people out of the learning equation entirely. Learning is about interaction and interaction with information alone is not enough.

HISTORY OF THE INTERNET

Many people mistakenly believe that Internet was developed in the 1990s. The history of the Internet actually goes much deeper than that. The Internet we use today has evolved over the past 40+ years from a simple communications network to one that spans the globe and includes participants in every country in the world. Many people are also surprised that the Internet started out as a Cold War military project.

The original concept for the Internet was developed in 1962 by Paul Baran of the RAND Corporation. RAND in the 1960s was a Cold War military think tank. RAND was commissioned by the US military to find a way to maintain military communication in the event of a nuclear attack. The idea was to create a network that has no central control that could be targeted in an attack. Baran laid out a plan using packet switching technology to maintain communications through a network of multiple communications paths. The idea for multiple paths allowed communications to continue in the even that any one or more sections of the network were neutralized due to a nuclear blast.

In 1968, a contract was awarded by ARPA (Advanced Research Projects Agency) to a company called BNN to build the first network model, which was then called ARPANET. The original ARPANET used a Honeywell computer to handle the network switching. The original network linked four nodes: the University of California in Santa Barbara, the University of California in Los Angeles, the University of Utah and SRI in Stanford.

A major event in the history of the Internet occurred in 1972 when Ray Tomlinson of BNN developed the first e-mail programme. Also in 1972, ARPA changed its name to DARPA (Defence Advanced Research Projects Agency). DARPA and Stanford were collaborating on the development of TCP/IP, which became the main communications protocol for the Internet. TCP/IP was a huge breakthrough because it allowed different types of computers on different networks to communicate with one another. Prior to this breakthrough, computers could only communicate with other computers on the same type of network. The name "Internet" was first used in the development of TCP

In 1976, Dr. Robert Metcalfe of Xerox's Palo Alto Research Facility developed Ethernet, which allowed data to be moved extremely fast. This breakthrough allowed local area networks (LANs) to become practical. Actually, in 1976, extremely fast meant a 56Kbps connection, which is the same speed that most narrowband dial-up connections still operate on due to the limitation of telephone wiring. In 1983, every computer connected to ARPANET was required to use TCP/IP, which became the core Internet communications protocol. Also in 1983, the University of Wisconsin developed the Domain Name System (DNS), which allowed TCP/IP packs to be delivered to a server representing a domain name. Because the Internet actually operates on IP addresses, domain names must be translated into IP addresses by Domain Name Servers. This made it much easier to remember addresses for different nodes on the Internet.

1984 saw the Internet split into two entities. MIL NET became focused on the needs of the military and military development projects. ARPANET became focused on advanced research. The US Department of Defence continued to fund and support both networks. Also in 1994, the first high-speed Internet backbones were installed by MCI. The new network was called NSFNET (National Science Foundation Network)

In 1985, the first.com domain name was registered by Symbolics, who still uses it today. In 1985, the Internet was strictly a text-based system. There were no images or web sites as we see today. Internet sites consisted of pages of text messages.

In 1990, the US Department of Defence replaced the old ARPANET infrastructure with the the new, high-speed NSFNET backbone. Also in 1990, Tim Berne's-Lee of CERN began working with a hypertext system that would eventually lead to the creation of the World Wide Web, for which he is best known. Tim Berners-Lee is frequently called the father of the world wide web due to his work in developing the concepts

In 1992, the World Wide Web was introduced by CERN. The World Wide Web incorporated hypertext linking capabilities, a standardized HTML scripting language, standardized resource identifiers (URIs/URLs) and utilized a client-server model for requesting web pages and objects using a hypertext transport protocol (HTTP) model.

In 1993, the National Science Foundation created interNIC, which leads to the implementation of several Internet services, including formalized domain registration services by Network Solutions. Marc Andersen and the University of Illinois introduced Mosaic, the first graphical user interface for the World Wide Web. Andreessen would go on to start Netscape in order to further develop and commercialize the use of browsers. Compuserve and other subscription information services began offering businesses and home users access to the Internet through their information networks. By 1995, large numbers of users were were joining the Internet community and business began thinking of ways to use the Internet to sell products and services. Since then, the evolution and growth of the Internet has been rapid. It is important to note that the Internet and the World Wide Web are not really one and the same. The Internet refers to the massive network of networks, which is basically the hardware infrastructure. The World Wide Web is a combination of methods and protocols for accessing the information over the Internet.

SIZE OF INTERNET

No one knows for certain because it is growing so rapidly. Estimates range from 12 billion web documents to over 20 billion. It could actually be much larger than that.

INTERNET FOR MILITARY

The original concept developed by RAND was for a military communications network. It evolved into more of an academic study involving better ways to communicate information. For many years the Internet was only available to universities and research facilities. There was military funding and research from DARPA, which kept the project alive, so there was a strong military interest as the project evolved through the 1960s, 1970s and early 1980s. There are people who played important roles in the history of the Internet project who say it was not a military project, but that is a bit of a denial regarding where the concept originated and where much of the funding came from. It is safe to say that by the time the concept of the World Wide Web started to emerge, the Internet was no longer a military project.

USING ADD-ON FOR FIREFOX

If you use the FireFox browser and are looking for a free FTP utility, try FireFTP. For a freebie browser add-on, FireFTP is a fairly full featured FTP tool. It will handle all of your common FTP needs. FireFTP is a FireFox-only add-on, which means that it will not work with Internet Explorer. Installation is simple. Just go to the FireFTP download page and click on the Download button. Make sure you are using FireFox when you visit the page. The browser add-on will automatically install in a few seconds.

After installation, you can find the FTP utility in the FireFox Tools menu. Click on it and it will open in a browser window. Just like FileZilla, FireFTP allows you to set up and save FTP connection accounts and allows quick connects for occasional FTP connections that you do not want to store. The only difference is that an Account is saved, while a QuickConnect is not. When you start up FireFTP, you will see multiple panes. The panes on the left side represent the local directories on your PC. The panes on the right display remote directories on your web site after you have connected to your server.

To set up an account, click on the Create an account... selection from the drop-down menu in the top left-hand corner. The Account Manager dialog box will display. From there you can enter the FTP information for your web site.

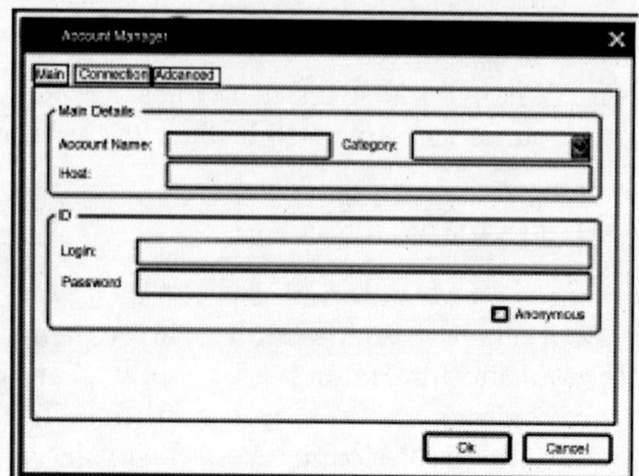

The Account Name will be displayed on the drop-down menu. The account information can be obtained from your hosting company. The Category is optional and can be used if you have a lot of FTP accounts that you want to set up in logical group sonthe menu.

The Host is typically your domain name, *i.e.*, tech-evangelist.com. If you are using a dedicated IP address, you can use the IP address.

Some hosting companies require the use of special Host addresses:

- The Login is your username for the FTP account.
- The Password is the password for the FTP account.

To set up an account, you only need to enter the Account Name. Any information that you enter will be stored when you same the account. If you are using a laptop that could be stolen, it is a good idea to leave the password blank. FireFTP will prompt you for missing information when you try to connect to your server. The Account Manager also has a Connection tab where you can set up any special connection information, such as a non-standard port number. You can also designate default directories for both the Local (your PC) and the Remote (the server) sides of the connection. This feature saves a lot of time because you do not have to search for files on your PC if you store them in a special location.

LOCAL FILES

Use the Browse button to the right of the path displayed just above the Local pane. You can select any location that you have access to on your network.

TRANSFERRING FILES

Make sure that the proper directories are selected in both the left-hand pane (Local) and the right-hand-pane (Remote). Highlight the files your wish to transfer in the left window and click the right arrow in the center bar. You can also transfer files from the server to your PC. It is important to make sure that you have the proper directories selected.

DISCONNECTING FROM A SERVER

To disconnect from your server, use the Disconnect button to the right of the drop-down menu. Once a connection is made, the Connect button turns into the Disconnect button.

VIEW HIDDEN FILES

This is easy to set up, although the location for the change is not very intuitive. On the top right-hand side of the FireFTP window there is a Tools selection. Select Tools > Options. Check the box named Show Hidden Files.

SETTING UP DEFAULT DIRECTORIES

This is found in the Connection tab in the Account Manager dialog box. The easiest way to set this up is to make the connection to your server, select the proper directories for both the left-hand and right-hand panes, then select the Edit button next to the drop-down menu. Select the Connection tab. You should see both the Local and Remote directory paths displayed. Click on the Use Current button next to each, and then click OK. The next time you connect to your server, the default directories will be used. If you need a real nice, lightweight and simple FTP utility, it is worthwhile to take a look at FireFTP. I was pleasantly surprised with this one.

WEB PROXY SERVER

A web proxy server, sometimes called a web proxy, can serve a variety of purposes. Many of the purposes for using a proxy server are legitimate, but others are suspicious and sometimes malicious.

Using a simple definition, a proxy is basically a server that sits between a user and the destination server that the user is accessing. It is an intermediary or go-between that requests resources from the destination server on the user's behalf.

On of the most common uses of a proxy server is for anonymous web surfing. When a user is connected through a proxy server, the IP address of the web proxy is used to communicate with the destination server and thus the IP address of the user is hidden. This can be used to allow a user access to systems where their access might normally be blocked, or because an IP address identifies a user's geographic location, it can be used to disguise the country where a user is located.

There are thousands of free proxy servers set up in countries around the world, and lists of these servers can easily be found on the web. When a user visits one of these sites, they enter the web address of the site they wish to visit. From that point on, the true IP address of the user is protected and the destination server only sees the IP address of the proxy server.

Students use web proxies to allow them to access web sites whose IP addresses are blocked by their school's server. For example, if a school has blocked all the known IP addresses for porn sites, students might still be able to access these sites through a proxy. Because of uses intended to circumvent normal security, lists of the IP addresses of known proxy servers are available, which can also be blocked by a company or school network.

If you are concerned about protecting your identity while on the web, a proxy server can help with anonymity. But be aware that these servers can have a malicious intent and can be used to cache information that passes through them, which means that you never want to use one of these intermediaries to log into your bank account or any web site where exposing user IDs and passwords can be detrimental. This can be a path to identity theft. There are other malicious uses for these servers. Many e-commerce sites capture the IP addresses of customers who purchase products. They are used to identify the geographic location of a customer to help prevent fraud. If a customer's street address is in Boston, but their IP address identifies their geographic location as Nigeria or China, the chances are more than good that a stolen credit card is being used. Many sophisticated online thieves use domestic drop points or freight forwarding companies where products are shipped and later forwarded to the thief. They have also learned to use web proxy servers to hide their location, or make it appear that they are located in a country not known for credit card fraud. There are many legitimate uses for proxy servers. AOL has traditionally cached commonly visited web pages and altered JPG images by compressing them to speed up web access for their users. They can also be used by schools and companies to filter content, and by ISPs that restrict access to family friendly content. If you are going to use a proxy server, try to identify those that are legitimate. Many are, but some are not. As a general rule, never access sensitive sites that require a user ID and password. This includes your e-mail accounts.

PHP SHOPPING CARTS

A shopping cart is an essential component of every e-commerce site. Although there are literally hundreds of shopping carts to choose from, only a few stand out. PHP is the preferred shopping cart language because it is the most popular web development language on the Internet. When combined with the MySQL database, PHP is unbeatable for cost effectiveness.

The selection of the best shopping cart for your web site is an issue that should not be taken lightly. The user-friendliness built into your shopping cart can be a major factor when it comes to retaining visitors and converting them into customers. Numerous studies have shown that the checkout process associated with a poorly designed cart can be a major factor affecting shopping cart abandonment during the checkout process. The following is brief list of the most popular shopping carts that utilize both PHP and MySQL. Both PHP and MySQL are free (no licensing issues) and are offered with almost all non-Microsoft web site hosting. This gives this combination a low-cost advantage, both for the cost of obtaining, modifying and maintaining your shopping cart system. Indeed, many of the most popular shopping carts using PHP and MySQL are free and most have a wide range of support available through numerous forums. All of these shopping cart options are complete e-commerce storefronts, complete with category pages, product pages, checkout processes and much more. All have a wide range of mods available that add functionality to the e-commerce sites.

OS COMMERCE

First and foremost is os Commerce, the biggest player in open source shopping carts. osCommerce has been around for more than six years and includes a large community of users and supporters. osCommerce is a complete e-commerce storefront. The basic osCommerce download is very functional and there is a wide selection of plugin mods that add functionality and features. More than 100 templates are available that change the look and feel of a storefront.

CRE LOADED

When considering shopping carts, CRE Loaded has been referred to as osCommerce on steroids. CRE Loaded is built on osCommerce. Different versions include large collections of already-installed mods so that you have a highly functional and heavily equipped version of of osCommerce as soon as it is installed. There are small one-time fees associated with purchasing a copy of CRE Loaded, but the costs are minimal.

ZEN CART

Zen Cart is a derivative of osCommerce. The group that focuses on this cart started with a version of osCommerce a few years ago and used it as a basis for building their own open source shopping cart. it is therefore similar to osCommerce in some ways, but has its own user and developer community. Support is provided through a very active forum where members help each other to solve issues related to e-commerce and the use of Zen Cart. The best part is that it is a very stable cart with loads of built-in functionality and it is free.

CUBE CART

This is another contender when it comes to popular and very functional shopping carts. Cube Cart has both a free and low-cost version available. They are both the same, but it will cost you $89.95 if you wish to remove the Cube

Cart copyright notice and link from the page footers. Sometimes this makes sense if you are in a competitive market and you do not want your competitors to know which shopping cart you are using.

OBSERVATIONS

Any of the choices listed above are good choices for an e-commerce web site. One thing to note is that most of the systems have all of the functionality turned on when you install the cart. This tends to degrade speed performance due to numerous unnecessary database lookups. After installing one of these shopping cart systems, you need to become familiar with the administration area and then should turn off every feature that you really do not need.

Most of these systems have manuals available, either in hardcopy or downloadable format. Your learning curve will likely be shortened if obtain the manual and go through it in great detail. Which one did we like best? We decided to go with Zen Cart due to the very active user forum and the superior support we see from the development staff. You should, of course, make your own decision. You cannot go wrong with any of these PHP shopping cart choices.

TROUBLESHOOTING

Outgoing e-mail problems can sometimes be more difficult to troubleshoot than incoming e-mail problems. Troublesh-ooting these types of problems in Mozilla's Thunderbird is fairly easy if you understand how outbound e-mail works. Outbound e-mail uses a process called SMTP (simple mail transport protocol). SMTP is the standard for e-mail transmissions across the Internet. SMTP is generally used to send messages from a mail client (Thunderbird) to a mail server.

The e-mail is stored on the server until retrieved by another e-mail client using a POP3 or IMAP retrieval protocol. Outbound e-mail problems can be frustrating to deal with because you rarely see an indicator as to what might be causing the problem. However, there are fewer factors involved when setting up the SMTP section in Thunderbird, so isolating the problem can be much simpler. Unlike setting up an e-mail retrieval for inbound e-mail, with SMTP, a single SMTP setup can be used to cover all of your e-mail addresses, regardless of how many different ISPs are involved. Most SMTP mail servers are set up to allow e-mail accounts from other ISPs to be run through them. Thunderbird identifies the first SMTP account that you set up as being the default account. That is because in most cases it can be shared by all of your e-mail accounts.

Most of the configuration issues with sending e-mail can be resolved in the Server Settings section in Thunderbird:

- Select Account Settings from the Tools menu.
- Scroll down to the bottom of the list if e-mail accounts.
- Select Outgoing Server (SMTP).

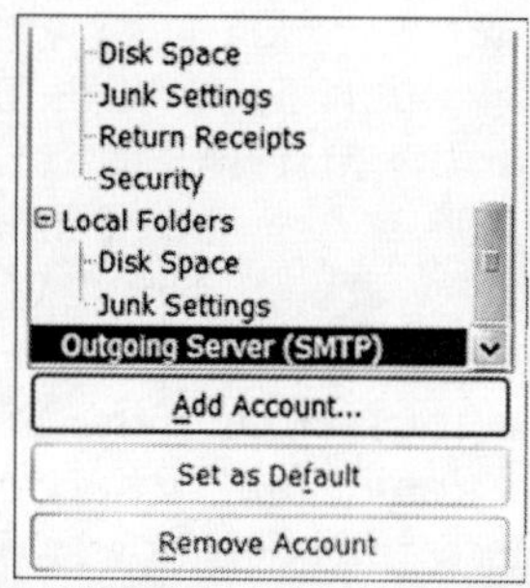

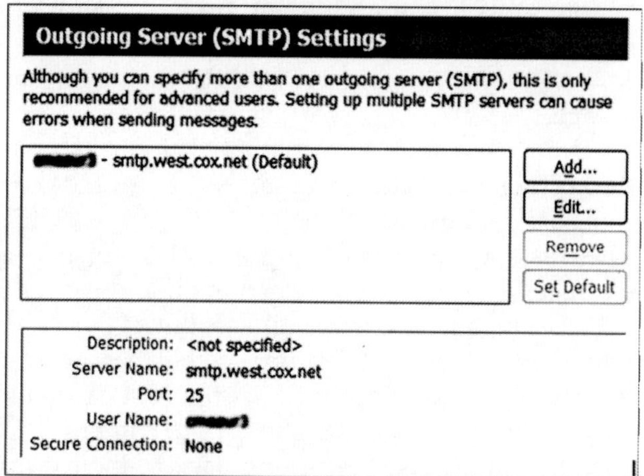

When you are sure that this information is correct, click the OK button, shut down Thunderbird and then start it up again to make sure that any new settings are loaded. If you have multiple e-mail accounts and you know that inbound e-mail is working, try sending a test message to another of your e-mail addresses. If it still does not work or you see an error, make sure that you Internet access is active. If you can access the Internet using your browser, you should be able to send e-mail messages once the SMTP information is correct. If you are still having trouble connecting to the SMTP server, Thunderbird will usually display a message, but depending on the type of error, sometimes it does not. Most of the time the User Name is just the account name, but some configurations may require a complete e-mail address. If one way does not work, try the other.

If your SMTP server requires a secure connection, you may have to check the SSL box. I sometimes use the SMTP server at my AT&T account. AT&T connections usually require that you check the SSL box.

If you are having connections problems, post your issues in the Comments below. Try to give us as much information as you can and we will see if we can help you to get connected.

IMPORTANT NOTE

- I have been receiving dozens of questions per week from people who are experiencing the same issues with SMTP server connections for outgoing e-mail with Thunderbird. The problems seem to start without warning. For the first time, I experienced the same issue.

- I have three SMTP server connections set up in Thunderbird. The only one that worked is my AT&T account, which uses a secure connection. I went into the SMTP server configuration described above and selected the SSL radio button for one of the two non-functioning SMTP server accounts and clicked OK. Guess what? The connection now works.
- Try doing this if you are having problems with outgoing e-mail with Thunderbird and let us know if it works. You may be asked to re-enter your password when you send your first message.
- Why did this work? At this point I don't have a clue because the SMTP server that I changed to use an SSL connection does not use SSL for e-mail.
- If this resolves your outgoing e-mail problems, you may also have to change the incoming e-mail setting to SSL under the Server Settings for each e-mail account.

- I have now experienced the problem that has been tormenting so many of you, but I still do not know the root cause of the problem. The morning after I made the changes to the SMTP configurations to enable SSL, I changed the setting back to their original state and everything is working fine.
  - So was Thunderbird the cause or did something else happen on my PC or the Internet? I find it hard to believe that two SMTP servers would experience the same problem, but nothing else on my PC or my internal network changed. The only thing that did change is that I upgraded to version 2.0.0.16 (20080708) after I experienced the problem. Thunderbird was working correctly after I booted the PC in the morning. You might want to try doing the update and then reboot your PC to make sure that everything refreshes. Just select "Check for updates" under the Help menu.
  - Let us know if it works for you.
- If you are using Symantec's Norton products and either incoming or outgoing e-mail mysteriously ceases to function with Thunderbird, try rebooting your PC to see if that resolves the issue. See Norton May Be Disabling E-Mail for more information.

THUNDERBIRD INCOMING E-MAIL PROBLEMS

Troubleshooting connection problems with an e-mail client, such as the freebie Mozilla Thunderbird e-mail programme can be frustrating and tricky.

If you are having problems retrieving your e-mail or getting it configured correctly, don't give up. Most solutions are pretty simple. In this article we cover some of the more common connection issues you might find when using Thunderbird. Most e-mail addresses today use the POP3 (Post Office Protocol 3) Internet protocol for receiving e-mail. With POP3 your e-mail is held on a mail server. You can download your mail to an e-mail client. Typically, the e-mail is deleted from the server when it is downloaded, but it can be set up to retain the e-mail messages.

An alternative Internet mail protocol is IMAP (Internet Message Access Protocol). IMAP provides some enhanced capabilities and is useful for dealing with large volumes of mail that may need to be organized. Most hosing companies today use POP3. If you are not sure about your situation, ask the ISP or hosting company. The e-mail documentation they provide will usually tell you which protocol you are working with. Most of the configuration issues with receiving e-mail can be resolved in the Server Settings section for each e-mail address in Thunderbird.

Each e-mail address is configured separately:

1. Select Account Settings from the Tools menu.
2. Select Server Settings under the e-mail address you wish to troubleshoot.

Server Settings

Server Type: POP Mail Server
Server Name: Port: 110 Default: 110
User Name:
Security Settings
Use secure connection:
Never TLS, if available TLS SSL
Use secure authentication

If anything in this section is incorrect, you will not be able to download your e-mail. After making each change, click the OK button on this screen, close Thunderbird, re-open Thunderbird, and try to download your e-mail messages once again. If you do not have detailed instructions from your ISP or hosting company, this is a trial-and-error process.

The first thing to check is the Server Name. This identifies your mail server. You will need to get this information from your hosting company or ISP. Most mail servers are identified by using a subdomain preceding the domain name, such as mail.tech-evangelist.com. Some use other subdomain names, such as ipostoffice.tech-evangelist.com. Once again, the only way to know is to find out how your mail server is configured.

Next, check the User Name. Sometimes this is the entire e-mail address and sometimes is is just the account name, which is the portion of the e-mail address to the left of the @ sign. The third item to test is the Security Settings.

Most mail servers do not use a secure connection, so Never would be checked. I've seen a few that use TLS (Transport Layer Security), which is a type of secure connection. If Never didn't work, try TLS, if available.

There are also a few e-mail servers that use SSL (Secure Sockets Layer) for secure connections. Secure connections encypt the messages as they are downloaded, which prevents others from intercepting your messages. I have an AT&T e-mail account that requires SSL. When you click the SSL radio button, the port number will change. You can also try checking the Use Secure Authentication box, but thus far I have never had to do that when setting up an e-mail account.

There is a very small possibility that your ISP or hosting company is using a non-standard port. Thunderbird does allow you to change the port, but you should never do that unless instructed to do so by your ISP or hosting company.

If the port is wrong, you will not make the proper server connection. If none of this works, make sure that you do indeed have an active Internet connection. If your browser can access the Internet, you should be able to retrieve your e-mail.

By now your problems receiving e-mail should have been resolved. Most of the time when I've run into issues setting up new e-mail accounts in Thunderbird, the issue was an incorrect User Name or Security Setting. Remember to save the settings each time you make a change by clicking the OK button. It is also best if you shut down and restart Thunderbird to make sure that your changes are reloaded. After that, test it again.

CREATING E-MAIL SIGNATURE

A signature in an e-mail is kind of like a footer on a web page. It is generally used to convey contact information, legal notices and other repetitive information. This is something that you may not want to re-type every time you send an e-mail message. Thunderbird allows you to create as many signatures as you wish. You can assign a different signature to each individual e-mail address. The first thing you need to know is that you must create the signature file in a pure text editor, such as Microsoft's Notepad. Do not use Word or any type of text editor that may embed codes in the text. You can save these files anywhere on your PC, but it makes sense to store them somewhere where they will not get separated from the rest of your Thunderbird files. In a previous tutorial, I changed the file location for the Thunderbird files in order to make it easier to back up these files. I simply created a new folder called "signatures" in the folder with the rest of the Thunderbird files. Like I said, you can store them anywhere, but when you do it this easy, the signatures stay with your Thunderbird files if you need to move them to another PC or if you have to restore a PC from your backup files.

Wherever you decide to store the files, keep them together and name each in a way that makes it easy for you to identify them. Next, you will need to assign a signature to each e-mail address. From the Tools menu, select Account Settings… Highlight an e-mail address on the left-hand column. On the right, check the box that says "Attach this signature:" and then click the Choose button to navigate to your signatures folder. Select the file that you want to attach. Click the OK button to save your settings. You will need to repeat this process for each e-mail address where you wish to add a signature.

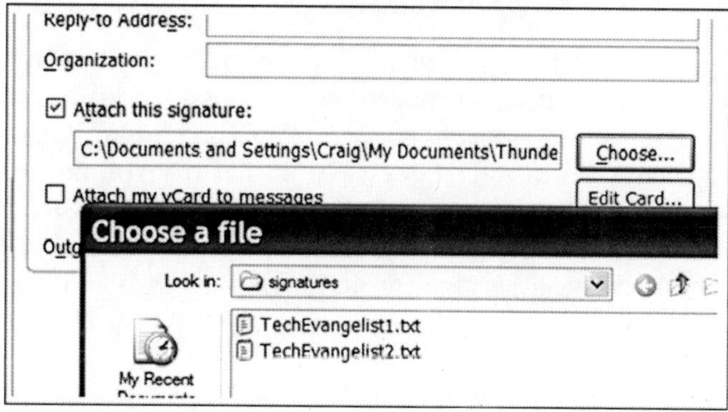

If you add a URL to the signature file, most e-mail clients will turn it into a hyperlink. But if you need to spruce it up of if you wish to use HTML in a signature instead of plain text, here is what you need to do. Create a text file in the same manner as described above. When you save the file, save it with a.html extension, rather than a.txt extension. Thunderbird will then recognize it as an HTML file. You can then use coloured fonts, hyperlinks or just about any type of CSS, as long as you use inline CSS styles.

When you are using CSS in e-mail messages, make sure that you fully specify the URLs to images and store the images on your server. Don't try to embed images or send them with the message. It won't work well with many browsers.

One more thing that has to be mentioned about HTML in signatures is that the message must be sent in HTML mode for the HTML and CSS to work. When you send any message that contains HTML, Thunderbird will ask you if you want to send it in in Plain Text. You do have to click on the Send in

HTML Only or Send in Plain Text and HTML for the HTML and CSS to render properly.

SPAM AND JUNK MAIL FILTERS

No one want to receive spam, but today it is almost inevitable that most e-mail addresses will eventually end up on spam lists. I have always protected my e-mail addresses, but recently ended up receiving more than 100 spam messages per day on my most important e-mail address used only by my business clients. It turns out that a client thought she was doing me a favour when she posted it on a forum, along with a recommendation. As part of my battle to eliminate spam, I found that Thunderbird contains some amazingly powerful spam and junk mail controls that are very effective at filtering unwanted e-mail. This tutorial shows you how to turn these filters on and configure them to meet your needs. There are actually several methods for filtering out spam using Thunderbird's tools. I used all of them in conjunction and found that Thunderbird effectively filtered out almost every undesirable message. It is also amazingly accurate and only very rarely grabs a legitimate message and identifies it as spam.

PRE-FILTERING SPAM MESSAGES

The first level for setting up spam filtering is to do it at the server level or on your personal computer. If you have a web site, your hosting company might already offer spam filtering software, such as Spam Assassin or Spam Pal. This step is not absolutely necessary, but it does make the process of identifying and filtering spam more effective. SpamAssassin is commonly found on Linux or Unix Apache servers. SpamAssassin checks messages coming through a hosting service's e-mail system. It does not actually filter the spam out, but rather uses heuristic algorithms that analyse a message. It then assigns a spam score. Thunderbird can use this score to determine if a message is likely to be spam. If your web site runs on Unix or Linux and uses a control panel such as Pleske or cPanel, check to see if SpamAssassin is included. You will find it under Mail, SpamAssassin. If the message near the top indicates that SpamAssassin is disabled, click the box labeled Enable SpamAssassin. Do not click the box labeled Enable Spam Box. SpamPal is a different type of filtering system that installs on your PC. SpamPal uses spam block lists (lists of IP addresses used by spammers) to identify spam messages. I have not tried it, but if your hosting company does not use SpamAssassin, or if you do not have a web site (and therefore do not use a hosting company), you might want to try installing it. You will find it atspampal.org.

CONFIGURING JUNK MAIL

The first step is to configure Junk Settings:

- Select Account Settings from the Tools menu. Thunderbird allows you to configure each e-mail address separately.

- Select Junk Settings under one of your e-mail addresses.
- Check all of the boxes in the Junk Settings display. If you don't use SpamAssassin or SpamPal, skip that checkbox. If you do use one of these tools, make sure the box is checked and the proper filter selected.
- Checking "Move new junk messages to Junk folder" will create a Junk folder under the selected e-mail address. You can set the nuber of days before spam is deleted from the junk folder. It is a good idea to move the messages to this folder so that you can periodically review it for messages that may not be spam.

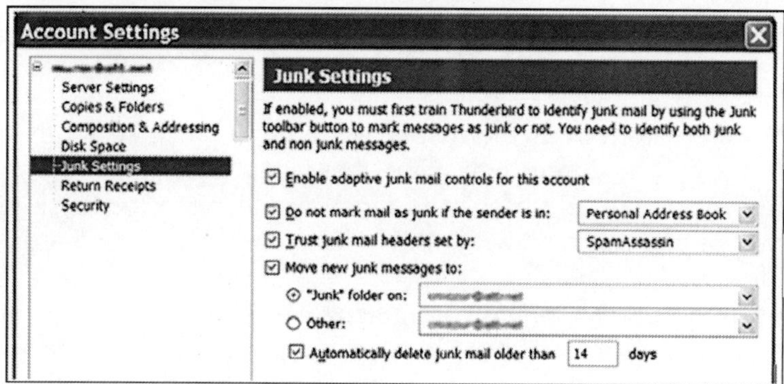

CONFIGURING PRIVACY SETTINGS

- Select Tools, Options.
- Select the Privacy button.
- Select the Junk tab.
- Choose how you want spam to be handled when you manually select it when reviewing your e-mails. When you are viewing messages and you identify a spam message, you can click on the column to the left of the date to send the message to the Junk folder. This also helps the system identify spam messages.

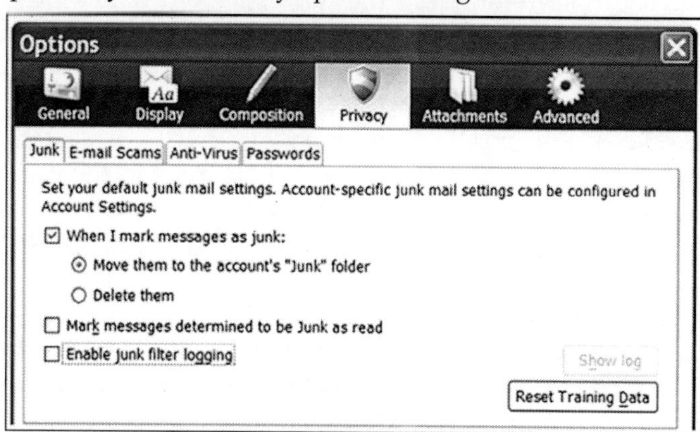

CONFIGURING MESSAGE FILTERS

When all else fails to identify spam, this is the way to do it. Message filters will search new messages for any keywords you designate. This section is pretty easy to figure out.

Once again, you have to set up individual message filters for each e-mail address:

- Highlight an e-mail address in the main screen.
- Select Tools, Message Filters from the top menu.
- Click on the New button.
- Name your message filter at the top.
- Select the e-mail element that you wish to filter. Most spam keywords are going to be found in the Subject or Body.
- Select Contains.
- Enter the keyword or phrase you wish to use as a filter.
- Near the bottom of the displayed dialogue box, select the location to move any identified spam messages. The Junk folder for the current e-mail address is the most logical place for these messages so that you can review them.
- Click OK.

That's about all there is to configuring Thunderbird to filter out spam messages. Although the configuration sections are a bit scattered throughout Thunderbird, once you know where to find them they are easy to use.

VIEW SOURCE

If you are an avid Internet user and use Internet Explorer as your browser, you have probably noticed that there are times when the View Source function in Internet Explorer occasionally stops working. For a Web developer or designer who likes to view the HTML code for a Web site, this can be frustrating. Fortunately, both the explanation to the problem and the solution are usually simple. The root of the problem is that the browser cache has filled because of all the Web page code and images stored by the browser. The solution is to clear these temporary files and start out with a fresh cache.

To do this:

- Select Tools on the top menu in Internet Explorer
- Select Internet Options...
- Click Delete Files in the Temporary Internet Files section

It may take several minutes to delete all the files in the cache, so don't panic if it appears like your PC has locked up. As soon as the hour glass once again turns into a mouse pointer, you can shut down Internet Explorer and start it up again. The View Source feature should now work once again.

If this does not fix the problem, you may have a more serious issue, such as a corrupted or deleted Notepad.exe programme file or problems related to the temporary files directory in Windows. Those problems are beyond the scope of this article. Other issues that have been reported that sometimes disable View Source include having a shortcut to Notepad on your desktop or having a shortcut named Notepad on your desktop. Renaming the shortcut should resolve those issues. Most of the time, the problem tends to be related to the cache, so if you spend a lot of time on the Internet, it might be a good idea to clear the cache once a week.

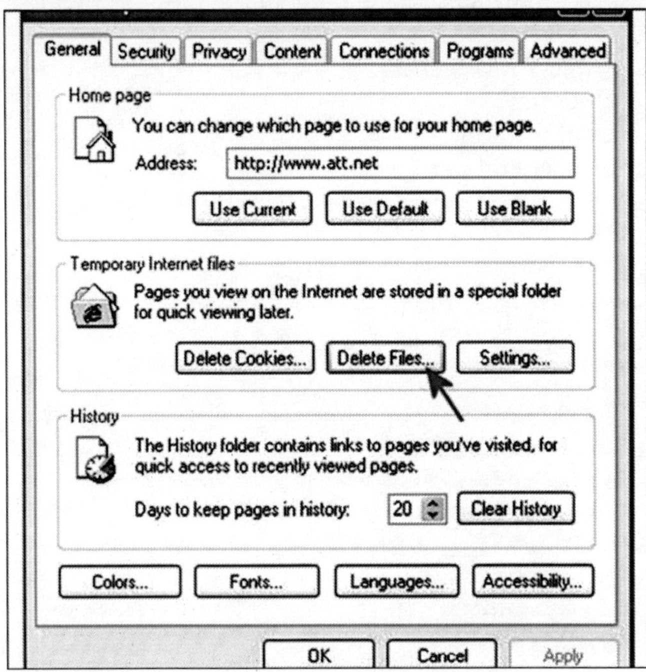

MOZILLA THUNDERBIRD TIPS AND FAQS

Mozilla Thunderbird is, in my opinion, the absolute best free e-mail programme available. It doesn't have the vulnerabilities found with Outlook, primarily due to the fact that it is not an "attack target" like Microsoft products. Even when vulnerabilities are found, they are quickly patched by the community of developers that support Thunderbird.

We've put together a list of tips to make your use of the Thunderbird e-mail application more enjoyable. If you have a specific question regarding how to do something with Thunderbird, post a comment below and if we have a solution we will include the answer on either this tips page or in a separate tutorial.

Where do I Find the Download for Thunderbird

You can find the most current version at the Mozilla Thunderbird download page. Installation is pretty simple. If you are using Outlook, Eudora or another e-mail client, you can easily import your address book and messages during the installation.

Including Previous Message Text

We found this to be one of the annoying default features with Thunderbird. Unless you change the settings, when you forward a message with Thunderbird it will include the forwarded message as an attachment. I personally prefer that the forwarded text be included in the body of the message that I send.

This is easy to change:

- Click on the Tools menu
- Select Options
- Select Composition
- Select the General tab
- *At the top change Forward messages*: "As Attachment" to "Inline"
- Click OK

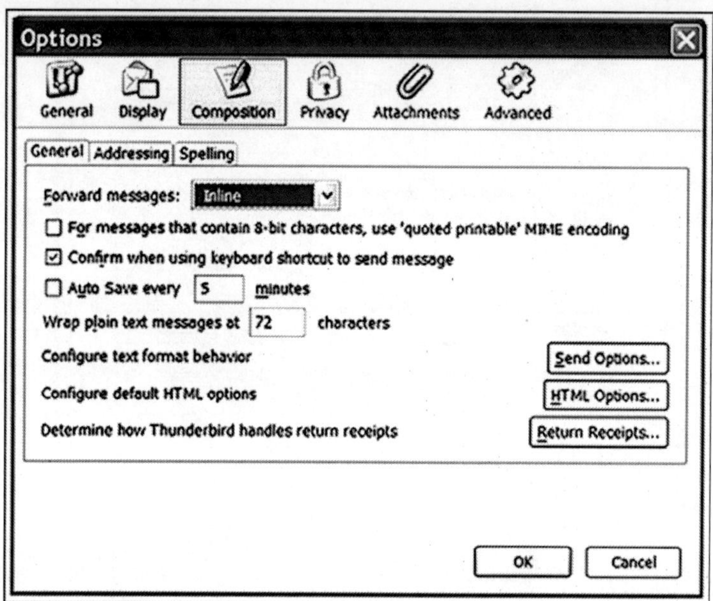

Your forwarded messages should now include the text of the forwarded message in the body of the e-mail just below any message text that you add.

How Do I Upgrade Thunderbird

If you selected the default settings during the installation, Thunderbird will automatically download updates and let you know when they are ready for installation. You will find the settings for this under Tools, Options, Advanced and then select the Update tab.

How Do I Set up Mailing Lists

Check out our tutorial about setting up Thunderbird mailing lists. This is really simple to do, but like many things with open source software, the solution is not always intuitive.

How do I Eliminate Spam

This is an area where Thunderbird excels. We did a separate post on that called Thunderbird spam and junk mail filters. We tried several different methods to eliminate spam and this was the only system that eliminated it almost completely and at zero cost. We were very impressed.

String E-mail Messages

They are hidden, but you can find them using the tips we offer in Thunderbird file location. This is very useful information if you wish to move the location to a Windows folder that can be easily backed up.

Changing Passwords

Ah-h-h, grasshopper. Passwords used to access your e-mail accounts are easy to change if you follow the instructions we offer in Changing Thunderbird Passwords

Adding Signature to my Messages

That is also very easy to do if you just follow the steps in our creating an e-mail signaturetutorial.

Making Mozilla Thunderbird

When you set up Thunderbird as the default e-mail client, it will automatically open whenever you click on an e-mail address on a web page that uses the HTML mailto: protocol. To configure Thunderbird as the default e-mail client, simply Open the Tools menu, select Options and click on the General icon. Under system Defaults, check the box that says, "Always check to see if Thunderbird is the default e-mail client on startup."

Click OK to save the setting. From now on, whenever the PC is booted it will check to see if Thunderbird is the default e-mail client. If one of the Windows programmes tries to change the setting to Outlook or if another programme changes it to something else, a message will be displayed that will allow you to change it back.

How do I Permanently Delete E-mail Messages in Thunderbird

Most people are not aware of this, but when you delete an e-mail message with most e-mail clients, you do not actually delete the message. The message is simple flagged so that it does not appear in the e-mail list. Thunderbird never actually deletes a message unless you take some extra steps. First, select File, Empty Trash. Second, select File, Compact Folders. This deletes all of the flagged messages in the data files.

Using Thunderbird with Yahoo E-mail Account

Yes and no. This issue keeps coming up. It looks like you can use

Thunderbird with a Yahoo account if you subscribe to Yahoo Mail Plus. The standard freebie Yahoo account does not offer POP3 access. See the following articles.

You will find all of the proper configuration information posted there:

- Can I use Thunderbird to read and send my Yahoo! Mail?
- Can I POP my mail into a different e-mail client (like Thunderbird)?
- Yahoo outgoing e-mail problems with Thunderbird.

Preventing Thunderbird

This was a feature that was turned on by default in older versions of Mozilla Thunderbird. I think the default is turned off in newer versions. It is something that is not only annoying, but also presents security issues.

Turning the embedding feature off is easy. Just select the View menu. Make sure that Display Attachments Inline is unchecked.

Preventing Thunderbird from Embedding

Changing Thunderbird's behaviour with outgoing e-mail attachments is easy to do, but is buried in the Config Editor. Make sure that you are using a current version of Thunderbird. The location of the Config Editor has changed several times with different versions.

Select the Tools menu, then Options, select the Advanced button, then the General tab and click on the Config Editor button. Scroll down until you find mail. content_ disposition_type. If the value is not set to 1, double-click on that line and an Enter Integer Value dialog box will pop up. Change the value to 1 and click OK. Shut down Thunderbird and restart it for the change to take effect.

PROGRAMMER JARGON

When a non-technically inclined web site owner speaks with an experienced programmer, technical jargon frequently enters the conversation. Some programmers do that intentionally, just to show off their expertise. For others, it is just the way they talk because they are immersed in a technical working environment. If you get confused talking with IT people, you may find this jargon guide to be handy.

The technical language of programmers can sometimes be very difficult to understand. It is loaded with shortcuts, euphemisms and analogies. Frequently, the full name or technical term for the many special symbols or characters used in programming is just too cumbersome or boring to use in everyday technical conversations.

Unique names or monikers for programming symbols has evolved. Most are intended to be humorous and help to liven up the communications between programmers. The following are a few of the most common jargon and techno-terms used by professional programmers in everyday conversations amongst themselves. Step outside of your box for a few moments and compare the special characters to the jargon terms and you can easily envision the evolution of the terms.

- . *(dot)*: A dot is just a period in a file name or domain name, as in google-dot-com.
- * *(star, splat or spider)*: An asterisk is a wild card symbol used with servers and computer programmes.
- # (hash, pound, crunch, sharp) – Most commonly referred to as a hash, this symbol is commonly used to designate comments in many programming languages.
- *! (bang, pling, shriek, not)*: The exclamation point serves different purposes in different programming languages, but it is most commonly used to reverse a Boolean evaluation. In other words, if a statement is true, it reverses it to false.
- *#! (hash-bang or sh-bang)*: When used as the first two characters on the first line of a programming script, a hash-bang causes Unix and Linux operating systems to execute that script using the interpreter specified by the rest of that line.
- *' (tick):* This is a single quote commonly used to surround a string of characters.
- *" (snakebite, rabbit ears)*: A standard double quote. This jargon goes way back to the 1980s, so if you hear this, you are talking to an old-timer.
- *$ (buck, bling, cash)*: Used to designate a string variable in many programming languages.
- *() (left paren, right paren, open, close)*: Commonly used to group portions of algorithms or comparison statements. Algorithms and evaluations of statements always start with the inner-most set of parens in all programming languages.
- */ (wack, slash, stroke)*: A common slash character, most commonly used in directory paths on servers or to define a mathematical division.
- \ *(backslash, backwack, hack)*: A common blackslash used in some networking paths and also as a common designation for a escape character, which means that the next character in line should be taken literally and not executed.
- *{ } (left curly, right curly, hitchcocks*: Think Alfred Hitchcock silhouette, left banana, right banana) – Curly braces commonly used to group multiple programming statements.
- *~ (squiggle)*: A tilde character.
- | *(bar, pipe)*: A vertical bar character.
- ^ *(hat)*: A caret character.
- *% (mod, grapes)*: Commonly used as a mathematical modulo character in programming languages.
- *& (amp, amper)*: An ampersand symbol.

W3C HTML/SXHTML VALIDATOR

The World Wide Web Consortium, also known as the W3C, is the organization tasked with setting and maintaining the international standards for common Web scripting languages, such as HTML, XHTML and cascading style sheets (CSS). Their web site offers several valuable tools that assure that a Web site is compliant with international coding standards. First and foremost is the W3C HTML and XHTML code validator.

You may find it interesting to learn how to eliminate every error message the W3C validator produces. It can be an educational process even if you are a very experienced developer. Although you may think you know a lot about HTML or XHTML, you will likely find that you do not know as much as you thought you knew about the W3C's coding standards.

There are some very good reasons for validating Web page code:

- Browsers are designed to interpret standards. Compliance with standards helps assure consistent rendering among different browsers. In other words, it helps a site to look the same in Internet Explorer, and Netscape, and FireFox, and Opera, etc.
- Browsers are very forgiving and automatically fix many coding errors, but this frequently requires re-rendering which slows down the final display of the page. Did you ever watch a Web page flash as the browser displays a page, or watch a page rearrange itself several times while attempting to display the page? This is frequently caused by poor coding methods. Each flash of the page is another attempt at rendering.
- Browsers are very forgiving, but search engine spiders may not be. Spiders are designed to read and dissect clean code that meets established standards. If a search engine spider cannot read the code properly, it may not be able to dissect the page and find the content. This results in either abandonment of the page by the spider or a missed opportunity that might have resulted in a high ranking page.

Before you use the validator, a page needs to have a Doctype declaration. The Doctype declaration, or DTD, needs to be the very first line of code on a Web page. The DTD sets the standard to be used in the validation. It also serves another purpose. Many modern browsers contain multiple rendering engines. If you do not set a standard to be used for rendering, the page may not look consistent across different browsers.

Note that all valid DTDs from HTML 4.01 on contain a link to a standards document. If your web page editor already adds a DTD with every Web page, it may not be valid if it does not contain a URL to the actual standards document.

Using the W3C validator is very easy. Just cut-and-paste or enter a complete URL to the Web page you wish to test. You may find some of the validation messages to be a bit cryptic, but the W3C provides links with most error messages that lead to additional information. There are some common page elements that always produce errors or warnings, even though they do not negatively affect either browsers or search engine spiders. Microsoft-specific entity codes, such as copyright and other symbols may not be code compliant. The validator handles these errors well and typically offers the code compliant equivalent.

Body tag attributes such as leftmargin, right margin (Internet Explorer), marginheight, marginwidth (Netscape) are browser extensions that are not part of the official coding standards. These types of issues will not typically produce negative effects with either browsers or spiders, but do show up as errors because they do not comply with the standard.

One type of nuisance error is a missing alt attribute in image tags. Current standards do require the use of the alt attribute in order to push designers and developers to use this attribute because it is beneficial for Internet users with vision impairments who utilize special browsers that describe images though the use of alt attributes. It may not make sense, however, to include text with every alt attribute. The code compliant workaround is to simply include an empty string value (alt="") for lines and other page elements that need no explanation.

It can sometimes be very beneficial to eliminate every error message displayed, and to assure complete and 100% compliance with the DTD standard you chose. Once a page has been validated as compliant, the W3C offers a cut-and-paste snippet of code that can be added to your Web pages as both a "gold star" certification of compliance and as a link to re-validate the code when you make changes.

AVOIDING SPAM

Despite anti-spam laws, the amount of spam e-mail messages I receive has grown enormously. You probably feel the same way. The problem with spam laws is that someone has to enforce them, but the e-mail spam problem is so enormous that only the largest and most aggressive USA spammers get prosecuted.

Foreign spammers are not subject to USA laws and are much harder to identify. There are, however, some fundamental things that you can do to lessen the amount of spam that you receive, particularly if you have a business. First and foremost, the best way to prevent your e-mail address from finding its way to a spam list is to never, under any circumstances, publish the e-mail address on a web page. Why? Because most e-mail ends up on spam lists because one of the hundreds of spam bots–also called e-mail harvesters–found it on a web site and automatically added it to a spam list.

If you need to publish an e-mail address, create an image file for the e-mail address and display that. Spambots cannot read text in images, so they will not find the e-mail address if you display it in an image.

Second, never, ever click on a spam message or any links in a spam message. This includes links that assure that the message will be removed from the spammer's database. While this may work for legitimate sources of e-mail, I am willing to bet that few spammers really care about the laws, especially if they are in a foreign country. When you click on any link, you are very likely just verifying that your e-mail address is valid, which pretty much guarantees that it will be added to hundreds of spam lists.

Third, much of the spam that we receive comes from spammer programmes that randomly generate e-mail account names using the domain names of popular ISPs and then send an e-mail to that address. If it bounces back, they know the e-mail address is not valid. If it does not bounce back, it may be a valid e-mail address.

Many spammers use a library of account names that are attached to other libraries of domain names. The account name if the portion of the e-mail address found to the left of the @ symbol. The domain is the part to the right.

Due to the fact that we run several web-based businesses, we have noticed a pattern of account names that many spammers use to see if an e-mail address is valid. The account names are attached to lists of domain names that can easily be found on the web and are used to generate spam for commonly used e-mail addresses. The following is a list of account names that are frequently used with spam messages. If you wish to cut down on the amount of spam that you receive, it may be wise to avoid using these names.

- Customerservice
- E-mail
- Info
- Information
- News
- Orderstatus
- Postmaster
- Sales
- Support
- Techsupport
- Test
- Webmaster
- www

If you run a business and you need to use a sales-related e-mail address, try using simple variations, such as salesrequest@yourdomain.com or salesinfo@yourdomain.com. If you avoid using some of the most commonly used account names, you can avoid wasting a lot of time trying to separate legitimate e-mail from spam.

FUTURE INTERNET TECHNOLOGY

The Internet has become critical to everyday life in domains as diverse as education, health, defence, commerce, travel and entertainment. The Internet was not designed for its current level of usage, and there is a need for simple constructs to allow the network to do better in terms of security, mobility and quality of service, among other things.

A number of global and local programmes of research (in the US, EU and further afield, eg Asia) are looking at future network architectures and building testbeds to evaluate new protocols and systems based on these new ideas. The most notable, in the US are the NSF Find programme and the GENI project to build infrastructure. In Europe we find a number of projects, with some interesting high-level thinking (eg the Eiffel project) and a set of testbed initiatives under the FIRE Programme. While some researchers think there is a need for a 'clean slate' design of the network of the future, much successful work is evolutionary rather than revolutionary, and this can be seen in the articles in this issue. For this special theme on Future Internet Technology, we issued a call for papers and invited four well known researchers in addition, to cover the following topics as well as possible.

ARCHITECTURES AND INFRASTRUCTURES

Future core networks will leverage IP over simple, super-fast optical core networks. A major trend is that of virtualization, featuring the construction of optimized virtual networks that answer the needs of a collection of users or applications. A wide variety of wired and wireless access networks are available or being developed: FTTH/FTTO in the wired domain, and 3G/ CDMA, LTE, WiFi, WiMax and Satellite in the wireless setting.

INTERNET MODELLING, SIMULATION AND MEASUREMENTS

It is quite important to comprehend how the complex systems that we build actually operate. This requires basic research on network modelling and simulation, eg, in order to derive the fundamental laws on network dynamics and control or to evaluate the ultimate capacity of self-organized wireless networks. It also requires advances in network measurements: traffic statistics, Internet probing and measurement, network inference and detection of anomalies and attacks.

INTERNET ALGORITHMS AND SOFTWARE

The future of the Internet will require a wide range of computer science tools: verification; distributed algorithms (eg for consensus, and election and epidemic diffusion); resource management algorithms: resource allocation and scheduling; database algorithms: content storage, update and retrieval, content replication and consistency; search engines and the semantic Web.

SELF-MANAGING NETWORKS

A key cost in networking is the operations and management overheads.

The scalability of the Internet is well known, but as distributed applications proliferate, a more autonomic approach is increasingly required. Spontaneous and self-organized networks emerge both in the wireless setting (eg with Wifi meshes or infrastructure-less wireless networks [MANETS]) and in the wired network setting (eg in peer to peer).

EMBEDDED INTERNET, INTERNET OF THINGS

The Internet started by connecting computers and users to information, and then went on to connect users to each other with audio, video, games and social networking tools. Now the rapid evolution of pervasive, embedded networked devices means that we connect various types of devices to each other. There are far more computers in the world embedded in everyday objects (cars, domestic appliances etc) than there are on desktops.

The interconnection of the Internet with the physical world through sensors and agents and the tagging of industrial production by RFIDs will lead to new traffic and architecture challenges, with possibly hundreds of billions of new devices that will collect information and will have to be upgraded and managed remotely and conveniently. This will require new paradigms for routing, search, naming, maintenance, data survival etc.

VEHICULAR INTERNET

The Internet of things extends to cars and other vehicles. Here the key potential is in safety: ABS in cars could communicate road surface conditions to following vehicles, setting speed and braking reactions sooner rather than too late. Traffic management and pollution sensing on cars can also make use of networking between cars, and from cars to roadside infrastructure. Tracking goods in transit on the road would allow logistics companies to optimize their freight operations, saving time and energy and perishable goods.

MEDIA INTERNET/MEDIA-DRIVEN NETWORKS

There is an important diversification of the nature of the content transported across the Internet: initially it was files, then real-time games, video, telephony and whiteboards, and now TV, video on demand etc. There has also been diversification of the localization of contents: with each user potentially a content producer (peer-to-peer applications). New interactions with data are appearing, as in Web 2.0 or the semantic Web, and applications continue to evolve and require new systems, measurements and management tools.

IDENTITY MANAGEMENT/SECURITY

Since its beginnings in 1992, the World-Wide Web has offered remote transactions for goods and services. Recently we have seen a rapid growth in the number of attacks on identity, since acquiring such information allows miscreants to commit fraud that is hard to detect.

ENERGY SAVING AND THE INTERNET

Estimates vary, but the Internet and all its services consume something on the order of 4% of the energy in the developed world. Only simple measures are required to improve this by a factor of two. Furthermore, the Internet, as we have discussed above, can be used to monitor and control external devices (things, vehicles, services) and significantly reduce their unnecessary power consumption.

Figures as high as 30% have been quoted for possible national savings of energy, if unused devices in all homes could be remotely turned off. The investment necessary to achieve this is relatively low, with what seems like a very big potential return.

THE INTERNET SERVICES

We are moving from a Web of documents to a Web of services and Web of knowledge. This has triggered an explosion of new applications such as SecondLife, FaceBook and LinkedIn. And there is more to come, with augmented reality, virtual worlds, real-time games and telepresence. New concepts such as service orchestrations are also emerging, and with them, new business models.

Setting the Context

- The invited article 'Starting the Debate: Agreeing on Disagreements' by Dirk Trossen, B.T., U.K., is a meta-discussion note, on how to trigger debate. As such, it is quite interesting as a methodology for encouraging architectural thinking in the long term.
- 'The Internet Engineering Task Force and The Future of Internet' by Emmanuel Baccelli, Thomas H. Clausen and Philippe Jacquet, INRIA Saclay, France, provides a useful reminder of the processes by which standards are created, and an analysis of how future research might be delivered in the short to medium term.

Architecture

- 'Network Virtualization, a Perspective' by Anja Feldman, Mario Kind, Olaf Maennel, Georg Shaffrath and Christoph Werle: Virtualization, briefly defined above, can be seen as a way to overcome the ossification of the Internet, namely the general idea that one should not change a system or architecture that works well. The technical challenges and the business models associated with overlay networks and more generally with virtualization are thoroughly discussed in this invited paper.
- 'Y-COMM: A New Architecture for Mobile Heterogeneous Communications' by Glenford Mapp suggests that the symmetric architecture we are used to in the Internet is perhaps not well

adapted to wireless, and proposes an alternative, useful for promoting discussion (cf the EU ANA Project).

Modelling, Measurement and Management

- 'Epidemic Information Dissemination' by Laurent Massoulie (Invited paper): Epidemic algorithms became popular at the turn of the century with Peer-to-Peer applications. They are now being investigated by major companies designing efficient distributed live streaming mechanisms over the Internet. This beautiful line of research combines the design of innovative algorithms and the modelling of their execution over a large network, which allows one to prove their quasi-optimality.
- Understanding traffic entails delivering information efficiently to humans so that they can decide on actions to take. The article 'iMyNetScope- a Platform for Network Traffic Visualization and Analysis' by Pavel Minarik discusses one approach to this, and presents one particularly interesting topic for today - the element of Cyber Defence.
- 'Unified Access to Internet Measurement Data' by Felix Strohmeier, Martin Nilsson and Demetres Antoniades: like the previous article, this touches on a timely topic - making sure we can all (as researchers or operations) access data easily (see also www.crawdad.org for an example of traffic archives in a standard form). Since the Internet is a federation of a vast number of networks (300 ISPs in the UK alone), we need clear and standard methods for exchanging data about operations. This applies equally to research networks such as those in FIRE.
- 'Privacy Aware Network Monitoring' by Peter Dorfinger, Carsten Schmoll and Felix Strohmeier describes a problem relevant to the research and operations community. Much work on the future Internet requires monitoring of research, but at the same time, real users require privacy. This article reminds us how important and difficult it is to reconcile these two aspects. Indeed, in gathering data about network use there are legal requirements relating to intercept laws and user privacy that must be met.
- '*Breaking the Weakest Link*: Becoming a Trusted Authority on the Internet' by Marc Stevens is a reminder of the danger of security failures. The fact that even the basic technology of security is sometimes flawed is interesting. Systems are never perfect, and this is never more true than for security: we can never prove a system is secure, but only discover (eventually) when it no longer is!

Correctness and Robustness (And Self-Managed to Some Extent)

- '*ResiliNets*: Resilient and Survivable Networks' by David Hutchison and James P.G. Sterbenz: As discussed above, we need secure networks that are efficient and well managed. We also depend on these networks, and since individual components are never 100% immune from faults and failures, we need techniques to make the overall system more resilient than its components.

- 'Standardized Testware for Internet-Based Telecommunication Services' by Bostjan Pintar, Axel Rennoch, Peter Schmitting and Stephan Schulz: As Internet protocols grow in number and complexity each year, we need assurance that systems will behave correctly. This article outlines industrial solutions on the correct operation of the software systems (protocols) that make the Internet and its telecommunication infrastructure work.
- 'Network Description Tools and Standards' by Freek Dijkstra, Jeroen van der Ham and Ronald van der Pol: Setting up high-speed network connections - light paths - is still a manual effort taking two to three weeks. The network engineers need a clear picture of the network topology in order to plan and configure light paths. The Network Markup Language (NML) standardizes network topology and state information. The University of Amsterdam and SARA Computing and Networking Services in the Netherlands are contributing to this effort, with the ultimate goal being to automatically set up and manage light paths.

Novel Applications, Especially Multimedia

- 'Delay-Tolerant Bulk Internet Transfers' by Nikolaos Laoutaris and Pablo Rodriguez (invited paper): Using disruption-tolerant networking (DTN) techniques, but on the Internet rather than on challenged networks, produces very interesting results in terms of capacity. Throughput can be significantly increased for some applications, and there are some very well-motivated examples, such as backing up information between large data centres, using spare capacity in a smart and autonomic way.
- 'Resource Management for IPTV Distribution' by Henrik Abrahamsson and Per Kreuger: IPTV on AT&T and Telefonica's networks now has in excess of 12 million users, each with hundreds of channels of broadcast quality content. This makes for non-trivial deployments,– and the importance of resource management for the various different technologies is unquestionable.
- 'VISTO: Visual Storyboard for Web Video Browsing, Searching, and Indexing' by Marco Pellegrini describes exciting work on future Internet killer applications.
- 'The New Role of Humans in the Future Internet' by Daniel Schall and Schahram Dustdar: Current service-oriented architectures

typically orchestrate Web services. This article addresses architectures that combine Web and human services, where the latter are not limited to service consumption but may also undertake service production. The main emphasis is on the interfaces required in such architectures.

In the Home (Internet of Things, and Energy!)

- 'Orchestrating your Surroundings' by Pau Giner, Carlos Cetina, Joan Fons and Vicente Pelechano, UP Valencia, Spain, is an example of the 'Internet of Things' being at the centre of future Internet visions.
- 'An Autonomic Home Networking Infrastructure' by Thomas Luckenbach, Mario Schuster and Marc-Oliver Pahl: in line with the previous article but articulated with a vision of autonomic computing, this is on the important topic of home net automation. Home users are non-technical: they really do not want to become network managers, operators or system administrators. It is thus essential to make home networks 'plug and play'.
- 'Load-Balancing Energy-Usage of Household Appliances' by Lennart E. Fahlen: Energy is a highly relevant topic, as described above, and using the Internet to control consumer electronics in the household is a promising way to reduce unnecessary consumption.

On the Road, Vehicular

- 'The Internet of Vehicles or The Second Generation of Telematic Services' by Markus Miche and Thomas Michael Bohnert: Like the Internet of Things, vehicular networking is just taking off. There are car-to-car and car-to-infrastructure communications standards as well as integration of satellite navigation, traffic monitoring, tracking, and cellular map systems.
- 'Web-Enabled Tracking Operations in Distributed Supply-Chains' by Zsolt Kemény and Elisabeth Ilie-Zudor: Using the Web to track logistical information about goods in the real world is already a huge business. This is a very useful article on the topic, which also relates to the previous article.

Awareness, Identity and Society

- 'Knowledge-Based Collaboration Patterns in Future Internet Enterprise Systems' by Gregoris Mentzas and Keith Popplewell is supporting virtual community patterns, a bit like eScience community work.
- 'Experiences from the Public Safety Arena for the Future Internet' by Socrates Varakliotis, Peter Kirstein and Steve Hailes: Since the Boxing Day tsunami and Hurricane Katrina, it has become clear that

the Internet might be better used in support of communications during disasters. This is a useful note on work in the area.

- 'With Joint Forces - Establishing Situation Awareness for the Future Internet' by Tanja Zseby and Thomas Hirsch: Like Mentzas' article, we can build systems to track patterns of use. This can be used to support collaboration or to detect misbehaviour. Increasingly, though, agencies are beginning to monitor social networks for this purpose.
- 'Social Networking for a Pervasive Future Internet: the SOCIALNETS Project' by Stuart M. Allen, Marco Conti, Andrea Passarella and Roger M. Whitaker: A timely article on an increasingly important topic. This outlines several new aspects of social networking that our readership should know about.
- 'Owner-Centric Networking: A New Architecture for a Pollution-Free Internet' by Claude Castelluccia and Mohamed Ali Kaafar proposes a new Owner-Centric Networking architecture that provides individuals control over their contents. This architecture would considerably improve privacy on the Internet by limiting data pollution.
- 'Semantic Web for e-Commerce' by Bernd Gruber: The Web is the basis for most new applications (Web mail, photo sharing, social nets, maps) and is the basis for commerce, which drives real economies.

Wireless, Embedded

- 'Management of Future Mesh-Based Radio Access Networks' by Vangelis Angelakis, Vasilios Siris and Apostolos Traganitis: Community mesh wireless nets are becoming pretty widespread in some areas as an alternative to expensive cellular data services. Automating management is important; related work at Intel and Microsoft in the last couple of years has covered some aspects (AP selection) but the topic continues to be relevant.
- 'Testing Mobile Data Applications on Smartphoes with SymPA' by Almudena Díaz and Pedro Merino discusses further the shortcomings of operating system platforms for data networking on cell phones and related devices. This is important, since the largest growth in Internet-capable devices is currently in this area.

9

Web Technologies

BACKGROUND

This section provides information about web technologies that relate to the interface between web servers and their clients. This information includes markup languages, programming interfaces and languages, and standards for document identification and display.

SECTION ORGANIZATION

Markup Languages Section

Includes all markup languages including HTML, XML, and SGML. Documentation in this section currently includes an HTML Guide, XML Guide, and a Document Type Definition (DTD) reading reference.

CGI Section

Includes four documents describing implementation of the client to server web interface. It includes information about the common gateway interface (CGI), server side includes (SSI), JavaScript, and writing perl script programmes

HTTP Section

Thic section currently includes an HTTP Reference which is based on RFC 2616. It has brief descriptions of the HTTP request and response headers and also lists the possible response headers such as 404 (not found). PHP - PHP is a scripting language that runs on the web server and the script code is embedded in the HTML document. It is easy to use with syntax similar to C which is why it is so popular. This section includes a

PHP INTRODUCTION MANUAL

JAVA Section

Documentation is being generated for this section. It currently contains some web links.

MIME Section

This section describes Multipurpose Internet Mail Extension along with its purpose and it also includes a few MIME related web links.

Graphics

Gif files used to add graphics to web pages.

TECHNOLOGIES TO BE INCLUDED IN THIS SECTION

- Streaming audio and video

WORLD WIDE WEB COORDINATING GROUPS

There are many types of technologies which are used to support the world wide web and more are being developed all the time. There are several groups involved in the development and coordination of these technologies.

IAB

Internet Architecture Board. Web site: IAB. The IAB websites states that "The IAB does not aim to produce polished technical proposals on such topics. Rather, the intention is to stimulate action by the IESG or within the IETF community that will lead to proposals that meet general consensus."

IANA

Internet Assigned Numbers Authority. Web site: IANA. They control the assignment of internet addresses and domain names.

IESG

The Internet Engineering Steering Group. Web site: IESG. According to RFC 2418, the IESG "has responsibility for developing and reviewing specifications intended as Internet Standards."

IETF

The Internet Engineering Task Force. Web site: IETF. Their web site says "The Internet Engineering Task Force (IETF) is a large open international community of network designers, operators, vendors, and researchers concerned with the evolution of the Internet architecture and the smooth operation of the Internet."

InterNIC

Internet Network Information Center, the authority for allocating internet addresses. Web site: InterNIC.

IRTF

Internet Research Task Force. Web site: IRTF. Their web site states their mission is "To promote research of importance to the evolution of the future Internet by creating focused, long-term and small Research Groups working on topics related to Internet protocols, applications, architecture and technology."

- *Isoc*: Internet Society, promotes internet policies. Web site:ISOC.
- *Istf*: Internet Societal Task Force. Web site: ISTF. Their mission is "To assure the open development, evolution and use of the Internet for the benefit of all people throughout the world".
- *W3c*: World Wide Web Consortium, sets standards for the web working with the IETF. W3C
- *Oasis*: Organization for the Advancement of Structured Information Standards. OASIS
- Internet2 Internet2 An Organization that supports internet related technologies including XML, DHTML, JAVA and more.
- *Irt*: Internet Related Technologies. Internet Related TechnologiesTheir website states "Internet2, led by over 180 U.S. universities working in partnership with industry and government, is developing and deploying advanced network applications and technologies, accelerating the creation of tomorrow's Internet."
- Graphic Communications Association A trade association that provides standards for the printing and publishing industries.

Intnernetn Technology

- *TCP/IP*: Understand basic networking and how TCP/IP provides a standards based network to interconnect computers.
- *Perl*: A quick introduction to the Perl programming language. We will just use the basic parts of the language. There will be a one-time section to introduce Perl.
- *HTML/HTTP*: Understand how HTML and HTTP work to build the Web. 1 CS193i Handout #1 Summer 2004 Kelly A. Shaw Java A quick introduction to the Java programming language. As with Perl, we will introduce the minimum necessary to write the programs we want.
- *HTTP Server programming*: Understand how HTML forms and the CGI work together to build web applications.
- *HTTP Servlet programming*: Understand Java servlets and JSPs - a more sophisticated structure for building web applications. Miscellaneous Advanced Depending on how things go, we'll look at some combination of: security, XML, Javascript, Java Thick Clients.

Web Technology

- *UNIT* I: Introduction and Web Development Strategies History of Web, Protocols governing Web, Creating Websites for individual and Corporate World, Cyber Laws Web Applications, Writing Web Projects, Identification of Objects, Target Users, Web Team, Planning and Process Development.

- *UNIT II*: HTML, XML and Scripting List, Tables, Images, Forms, Frames, CSS Document type definition, XML schemes, Object Models, Presenting XML, Using XML Processors: DOM and SAX Introduction to Java Script, Object in Java Script, Dynamic HTML with Java Script.
- *UNIT III*: Java Beans and Web Servers Introduction to Java Beans, Advantage, Properties, BDK, Introduction to EJB, Java Beans API (10) Introduction to Servelets, Lifecycle, JSDK, Servlet API, Servlet Packages: HTTP package, Working with Http request and response, Security Issues.
- *UNIT IV*: JSP Introduction to JSP, JSP processing, JSP Application Design, Tomcat Server, Implicit JSP objects, Conditional Processing, Declaring variables and methods, Error Handling and Debugging, Sharing data between JSP pages- Sharing Session and Application Data.
- *UNIT V*: Database Connectivity Database
Programming using JDBC, Studying Javax.sql.* package, accessing a database from a JSP page, Application-specific Database Action, Developing Java Beans in a JSP page, introduction to Struts framework.

WEB TECHNOLOGY RESOURCES

SUB CATEGORIES

HTML

This section provides HTML documentation and HTML information. It describes HTML and XHTML which is very basically HTML with some simple additional rules such as all tags are in lower case and all attribute values are in quotes. XHTML is the curent World Wide Web Consortium standard for web content. This section also covers information and documentation about cascading style sheets (CSS) which is covered in this section's HTML Guide.

HTML stands for Hypertext Markup Language and is the main language used to display information to web browsers across the web. This language is based on asc text and relies on tags which are surrounded by the asc characters < and >.

The tags allow for what is called the markup which defines how the text between the tabs is displayed. Read the HTML guide for information about the various tags and how they are used.

Current Documentation

Documentation in this section currently includes:

- *HTML Guide*: Describes how to build a web page with information about most HTML elements and attributes. It provides many examples of how to use the HTML elements. Included elements are ABBREV, A (anchor), APPLET, AREA, AU, B (bold), BASE, BASEFONT, BGSOUND, BIG, BLOCKQUOTE, BR, BODY, CODE, DIR, DD, DEL, DFN, DL (definition list), DOCTYPE, DT, EM, FONT, FORM, FRAME, FRAMESET, headers (H1, H2, H3, H4, H5, H6), HEAD, HR, HTML, IMG, INS, I, KBD, LI, MAP, MENU, META, NOFRAMES, OL (ordered list), P (paragraph), PRE, Q (quotation), SAMP, SMALL, SPAN, STRIKE, STRONG STYLE, SUPER, TABLE, TD, TH, TR, TITLE, TT, U (underline), and UL (unnumbered list).

XML

This section contains XML information and XML documentation. It describes XML on a practical level. This section also provides XSL documentation and will be expanded to include information about other subcategories of XML. XML stands for extensible markup language. It is a language for the world wide web, and is defined by SGML. XML differs slightly from SGML since it requires both a beginning and ending tag on all elements. Also It does not require a DTD if the XML document is "well-formed".

Current Documentation

- *XML Guide*: This guide briefly describes the structure and uses of XML documents giving some examples along the way. It outlines the use of XSL for applying style to XML documents.

This section currently includes some XML web links.

XML Categories

XML has several different categories that have slightly different purposes. *A few are listed below with descriptions:*

- *XML*: The all encompassing category which includes the categories listed below. Specifically it refers to XML as used with a "well-formed" or valid document.
- *XSL*: Extensible Stylesheet Language is used to include additional style on XML pages. HTML code may even be embedded in the.xsl stylesheet file. This form of style sheet control is much more powerful and complicated than extensible style sheets.
- *DSO*: The data source object programming model is a technology provided by Microsoft which is used with small database support. It is a set of controls which can be used to allow a user to page

through a table of information displayed on an HTML page which is linked to XML. This technology is not cross platform compatible.

- *DOM*: Document Object Model is a programming model that represents parts of an XML document as objects. Each object is thereby accessible by referring to the object and subobjects with periods between them. Each object supports specific attributes and methods which allows dynamic content using XML. The DOM is cross platform compatible.
- XLink
- *RDF*: Resource Description Framework
- *SOAP*: Simple Object Access Protocol

CGI SCRIPTING SECTION INTRODUCTION

This section includes basic technologies that are used on both sides of the client/server CGI interface.

Therefore it includes:

- Client side JavaScript
- Server side Perl Script
- *CGI*: Basic information about the CGI interface itself
- *SSI*: Information about server side includes which enhances ability to use server side script programmes.

This section will not include other technologies that may also perform the same function such as PHP which have their own sections. This section is intended only as an introduction to CGI and the various tools involved.

CGI Definition

CGI stands for common gateway interface. CGI is required in order for information passed from the client to the server using HTTP to be processed by a programme which is running on the server. CGI is a defined standard that provides for the passing of data between a web server and a CGI application. The CGI defines a set of environment variables that are used to pass the data. A CGI application may be written in C, C++, Perl, Unix shells, TCL, JAVA, visual basic or other languages. The CGI variables may be set on the client side using client side embedded script code such as JAVA script or VB script.

The Defined method for getting data from an HTML page which may include a script form, is to use the GET or POST method.

Scope of this Section

Because there are many ways and tools that may be used to communicate between the client and the server, this section includes information about the following technologies:

- The CGI Interface and CGI environment variables.

- Perl server side script writing.
- JavaScript client side script writing.
- Server Side Includes (SSI) can enhance your page and make calling server side script programmes easier, but it is not without penalties.

The reader should read the CGI section first to understand how data is passed from client to server and how to get the information. Then client or server script writing may be studied. I believe it is best to learn client script writing first, but it is a matter of preference.

This section assumes the reader has familiarity with HTML and how to set up forms using the FORM tag in HTML. If not, the reader should refer to the HTML section. The information passed between the client and server is passed using the HTTP protocol, and the reader is referred to that section for information about that protocol.

Current Documentation in this Section

- *CGI Manual*: Describes the CGI interface and how to use it. Describes data access methods such as GET and POST. Also describes the required headers for document description between the client and server. An example of a form posting is shown so the reader can see the format of the data transfer. A list of CGI variables is shown with examples for many and general CGI operation is documented. CGI environment variables are listed and described.
- *JavaScript Manual*: This manual includes descriptions of variables, operators, programme flow control, and available javascript objects. It describes the javascript object heirarchy.
- *Perl Script Manual*: This is a brief Perl script manual with some examples to enable the reader to understand the server side script process.
- *SSI Manual*: This manual lists and describes SSI variables and commands. Examples are given for each command.

HTTP

This section provides HTTP information and HTTP documentation. HTTP stands for Hypertext Transfer Protocol and is the means by which your internet browser and web server communicate. HTTP provides the capability not only for your web browser to request pages and files from the webserver, but also HTTP provides the ability for your browser to send information back to the server.

Usually this information is in the form of text box information, check boxes, and radio buttons you click on or fill out when you register on a particular website, respond to a poll, or submit any form.

This section will describe how HTTP works and is applied. Therefore this section will also include some information about client and server side scripting. Any information about these areas may be found in this section.

Lets say, you are browsing the web and you see a web page that provides a poll that may be filled out.

From the time you click on the link to open the web page containing the poll, here's roughly what happens:

- Your web browser sends a request for the page to the server using the HTTP protocol as a communications media. The universal resource locator (URL) or address of the page is included with the request not only so the correct server is located, but the server will know where to get the page. This step excludes the description of how the server is found.
- The server finds the page and sends it over the web lines to your computer which your browser receives and displays.
- In this case, the web page you have received, includes some client side script language. Your browser understands this language and can run the script programme. The script programme causes a form to be displayed with the other content of the web page. This form may contain text boxes, radio buttons, check boxes and more.
- You put some text in the text box, select a radio button, and possibly check one or more check boxes. Then you click on the submit button.
- The information you entered is sent to the server using HTTP in the form of commands with information you entered.
- The server is running a programme which may be a script programme (server side script) receives the commands and data, and stores the information. The programme running on the server side can be any programme such as a binary programme, but must read the HTTP commands. It could be written in the C language.
- The server updates its database, then may send to you, the client, an updated copy of the web page, such as the current status of the poll.
- Your web browser will receive this new updated web page and display it.

Current Documentation

Documentation in this section currently includes:

- *HTTP Reference*: Based on RFC 2616, it contains brief descriptions of the HTTP request, entity headers, and response headers and also lists the possible response headers such as 404 (not found).

PHP

This section contains PHP documentation and PHP information. PHP stands for Hypertext Preprocessor and is used as a scripting language that is embedded in HTML and runs on the web server. The PHP code is run on the server when the page is requested.

Anyone who knows HTML and the C or C++ language can easily programme PHP. PHP uses much of the same syntax of C, but is much easier to use and provides access to variables and their values as submitted using HTML forms without the need to parse information. Also PHP is designed to work easily with most SQL servers including the open source SQL server, MySQL. The above example will output the quoted text on the HTML page where the PHP code is embedded.

Many webservers support PHP out of the box although depending on the version, they may not support the latest version of PHP (Currently 4). If using PHP on the web, it is wise to run the latest version since it has some security enhancements.

If you're just using PHP to learn on a local network using the latest PHP version is not as imperative. For example the Apache webserver that comes with Redhat Linux version 6.1 supports PHP3.

Depending on how the webserver is setup, it may be required to name the HTML files that contain PHP code with an extension like ".php4".

MIME

This section contains information and documentation about MIME. MIME stands for Multipurpose Internet Mail Extensions. The purpose of MIME is to allow the use of a wide variety of media types through internet mail. The Internet Engineering Task Force (IETF) Working Group defined the standard for MIME in 1992.

Current MIME RFC's include:

- 2045: MIME Part One: Format of Internet Message Bodies
- 2046: MIME Part Two: Media Types
- 2047: MIME Part Three: Message Header Extensions for Non-ASCII Text
- 2048: MIME Part Four: Registration Procedures
- 2049: MIME Part Five: Conformance Criteria and Examples

Terms

- *Rendering*: The act of presenting the information in a document to the user.
- *Parsing*: The scanning and filtering of the information in a document into the context of the elements the information is structured for.

WEB DEVELOPMENT STRATEGIES

SIMPLE WEB DEVELOPMENT STRATEGIES

At the time of developing a website you must be sure that you should the website in a way to put your website and web development Delhi company in the best and above all. Today customers have many option, so make sure that your website should not take more than 5-6 seconds to open otherwise visitors will swap on other website as visitors have a click away from the others websites. You should develop in such a way that the customers should find the product and web development Delhi services with detailed information easily so that customers should not thing himself that you product is not more web development Delhi beneficial for him.

So make the web development Delhi Navigation of each button or link very easy accessing and don't loads lot things in single pages otherwise it will take long time open a page. The last thing you want is your customers to become frustrated with your website because they can't find what they're looking for. Visitor usability and the overall web development Delhi loading speed are two vital elements of web development.

Your website should be visually gratifying. Comprise graphics and proper images which match the overall theme of your website easily understood what you want to gratify the customers from these images. At the time putting graphics on your websites, be careful. Don't exaggerate it with too many showy graphics, it will hamper your loading speed and take attention away from the main web development Delhi principle of your website. Having an efficient website doesn't take a ton of plan, go for uncomplicated and friendly.

You should also web development Delhi ask what you have offered to visitors so that they would visit your website again and again. And help to bring your website at the first. Offer your visitors with the best content with best and effective to the web development Delhi visitors as possible as. Search engines will also help to achieve the rank of your website with lots of targeted traffic if your web development Delhi website has good fresh quality content. If you have the time and writing skill abut any thing then, write the content yourself. If you require help, it's web development Delhi comparatively easy to find someone that's willing to ghostwrite for you online. Your website pages should all have proper titles and Meta tags. Both are considered important for the search engine optimization of your website, and properly set tags will help bring more people to your sites from the engine search results.

- CSS Instead of Tables
- Choosing Good Icons
- Look and Feel of your site
- Google Guidelines Web Development
- The Importance of W3C Web Development Delhi
- Guidelines for Web Development India
- Technology of Web Development
- Attracts Visitors
- Importance Of Web Builders
- Flout Of Accessibility Web Development India
- 5Website Builder Tool
- Software Development Tools
- Classified Ad Web Development

- Meaning Of Googleism
- Staying Software Project
- Capture Process
- Domain Development Corp
- more Info on web development...
- Web Development India Articles
- Webservices
- Process Centric Organization
- Google Quality Web Development Delhi
- E-mail Tips And Tricks Development
- Building Trust
- How To Successfully Delegate
- Recruiting Programming
- Cut Your Using Simple Web Development India
- Creating Request Web Proposal
- Website Or Blog Development
- Bridge The Web Development India
- What Is A Website Development ?
- The Changing Face Of Web Development
- Indian Service Provider
- Maintenance Web Development India
- Methodology Web Development Delhi
- Core Organizational Values
- Improve Profitability For Web Development
- Development Methodology
- User Centered Development
- Simple Tips For Web Development
- Risk Model For Software Development
- Methodology Of Web Development India
- Effective Time Difference Of Web Development Delhi
- Some Basic Of Web Development Delhi
- The Reasons To Web Development India
- Guide To Successful Ecommerce Development
- How Web Development Of Website Designing India
- The Single Page Website
- Important Google Of Web Development Delhi
- India Is Software Web Development Delhi
- Typically Closed Search Engines Development
- Competition For Web Development Delhi

HISTORY OF WEB

HISTORY OF THE WORLD WIDE WEB

Before the World Wide Web the Internet really only provided screens full of text (and usually only in one font and font size). So although it was pretty good for exchanging information, and indeed for accessing information such as the Catalogue of the US Library of Congress, it was visually very boring. In an attempt to make this more aesthetic, companies like Compuserve and AOL began developing what used to be called GUIs (or graphical user interfaces). GUIs added a bit of colour and a bit of layout, but were still pretty boring.

Indeed IBM personal computers were only beginning to adopt Windows interfaces - before that with MSDOS interfaces they were pretty primitive. So the Internet might have been useful, but it wasn't good looking. Probably the World Wide Web saved the net. Not only did it change its appearance, it made it possible for pictures and sound to be displayed and exchanged. The web had some important predecessors, perhaps the most significant of these being Ted Nelson's Xanadu project, which worked on the concept of Hypertext - where you could click on a word and it would take you somewhere else.

Ted Nelson envisaged with Xanadu a huge library of all the worlds' information. In order to click on hyperlinks, as they were called, Douglas Engelbart invented the mouse, which was to later become a very important part of personal computers. So the idea of clicking on a word or a picture to take you somewhere else was a basic foundation of the web. Another important building block was the URL or Uniform Resource Locator. This allowed you a further option to find your way around by naming a site. Every site on the worldwide web has a unique URL (such as www.nethistory.info). The other feature was Hypertext Markup Language (html), the language that allowed pages to display different fonts and sizes, pictures, colours etc. Before HTML, there was no such standard, and the "GUIs we talked about before only belonged to different computers or different computer software. They could not be networked.

It was Tim Berners Lee who brought this all together and created the World Wide Web. The first trials of the World Wide Web were at the CERN laboratories (one of Europe's largest research laboratories) in Switzerland in December 1990. By 1991 browser and web server software was available, and by 1992 a few preliminary sites existed in places like University of Illinois, where Mark Andreesen became involved. By the end of 1992, there were about 26 sites.

The first browser which became popularly available to take advantage of this was Mosaic, in 1993. Mosaic was as slow as a wet week, and really didn't handle downloading pictures well at all - so the early world wide web experience with Mosaic, and with domestic modems that operated at one sixths of current modem speeds at best, were pretty lousy and really didn't give much indication of the potential of this medium. On April 30, 1993 CERN's directors made a statement that was a true milestone in Internet history.

On this day, they declared that WWW technology would be freely usable by anyone, with no fees being payable to CERN. This decision - much in line with the decisions of the earlier Internet pioneers to make their products freely available - was a visionary and important one. The browser really did begin to change everything. By the end of 1994 there were a million browser copies in use - rapid growth indeed!!

In the same year Marc Andreesen founded Netscape Corporation, and the World Wide Web Consortium, which administers development of Word Wide Web standards, was formed by Tim Berners Lee. Then we really started to see growth. Every year from 1994 to 2000, the Internet saw massive growth, the like of which had not been seen with any preceding technology. The Internet era had begun.

The first search engines began to appear in the mid 1990s, and it didn't take long for Google to come on the scene, and establish a dominant market position. In the early days, the web was mainly used for displaying information. On line shopping, and on line purchase of goods, came a little bit later. The first large commercial site was Amazon, a company which in its initial days concentrated solely on book markets. The Amazon concept was developed in 1994, a year in which some people claim the world wide web grew by an astonishing 2300 per cent! Amazon saw that on line shopping was the way of the future, and chose the book market as a field where much could be achieved.

By 1998 there were 750,000 commercial sites on the world wide web, and we were beginning to see how the Internet would bring about significant changes to existing industries. In travel for instance, we were able to compare different airlines and hotels and get the cheapest fares and accommodation - something pretty difficult for individuals to do before the world wide web. Hotels began offering last minute rates through specially constructed websites, thus furthering the power of the web as a sales medium. And things went even further - in some fields of travel, individuals would outline where they wanted to travel to and from, and travel companies would then bid for the business. All these developments rapidly changed the way traditional markets worked. In some industries, the world would never be the same again.

HISTORY OF THE INTERNET PROTOCOLS

In this section we are talking about the central systems and protocols that make the Internet run - and I'm going to try and do this without sounding too technical! So wish me luck! The Internet base protocols and systems were mainly devised in the 1970s and 1980s. Many were established initially as a means to connect mainframe computer systems for timesharing purposes.

The system introduced for this fairly trivial purpose has expanded to become a global multimedia information and communications system, connecting PCs, phones, and tens of millions rather than the few devices foreseen by the original inventors. Parts of the system are now over 20 years old, and the Internet is required to perform a number of important functions not included in the original design. Various patches have been applied to base protocols and systems, not always evenly. How well does it perform these tasks? Well that's a matter of some debate, and we may need another series of tapes to examine those issues.

But for now lets look at the core systems and how theyevolved. And we should start with the mother of all systems, the world's largest database, the Domain Name System or DNS. Each host on the Internet has a range of IP (or Internet protocol) numbers. The Domain name system (DNS) maps the numbers to names of hosts or websites (eg www.google.com, www.hotmail.com). Thus, when a user enters a name, the Internet knows which number to send the query to by looking up the DNS database. The DNS was introduced in 1984, several years before commercial traffic was able to be part of the Internet.

Associated with the DNS is the WHOIS database, which stores details of the names and addresses of domain owners and technical contacts. It was named after a UNIX operating system command (whois) which gave basic details about system users. Whois was established essentially to allow technical managers of hosts to contact their peer. In those days, there were no privacy issues or privacy laws to think about.

However that's changed, and some problems associated with the current system include the ease with which contact details could be used for spam mailing lists, and the nuisance domain name renewal business which exploits the openness of the database. These factors in particular are leading to calls for changes to WHOIS so that certain personal details are kept private. But on another level, DNS in its current state is proving unsuitable for multilingual domain names. Now as the Internet spreads, the 80% of people on Planet Earth who don't use English as their primary language want to use the Internet to communicate.

It currently works well for some similar European languages, but when we start to use Japanese and Arabic character sets, for instance, a whole lot of problems emerge. This is because the DNS uses a system called ASCII, or the American Standard Code for Information Interchange. ASCII doesn't accommodate these other languages well, thus one of today's current internet problems emerges. It will be interesting to see how it is resolved.

The protocol which they say determines what the Internet is, is TCP/IP, or Transmission Control Protocol-Internet Protocol. Essentially, TCP/IP describes a protocol which will work on any sort of computer and operating system for transportation of data across the internet between different systems. Invented in the 1970's, largely adopted in the late 1980s, TCP/IP hit its first big problem in the early 1990s when it became apparent that the numbering system was going to run out of numbers in the foreseeable future. Therefore in 1995, after several years of work, TCP/IP Vs 6 was released to solve this problem. Adoption has been very slow. TCP/IP has proven to be remarkably robust, but is very basic. SMTP, or the Simple Message Transfer Protocol, is the basic standard for e-mail, and again exists since the 1980s when the Internet was small and honest. Perhaps more than any other system on the Internet, e-mail has seen a number of improvements and different protocols, each of which has been adopted by only part of the Internet e-mail community. This capacity not to adopt standards is a feature of the Internet, making dealing with change more difficult than it otherwise might be.

There is another thing about SMTP that stands out. SMTP comes from an innocent age, and no-one thought it would be necessary to prove that the person sending a message was who they said they were. The basic flaws in SMTP authentication are now causing significant problems, particularly the ease with which e-mail sender details can be forged. This helps the transfer of some viruses and a lot of the worst spam, and makes Internet fraud a lot easier than it might otherwise be. Now not all viruses and spam can be attributed to problems with protocols, but better protocols sure would help.

Another important protocol which dates from pre 1972 is FTP, or the file transfer protocol. This simply is the way to upload or download a file from an Internet computer. Just about everyone who owns a website uses this one. With the coming of the World Wide Web, we see another powerful protocol - http, or hypertext transfer protocol. HTTP allows us to click on the name of a site and visit it. Simple, but very powerful.

So there you have it - some of the base set of protocols that make todays Internet work. In fact there are thousands of standards, each carefully worked out by engineers from all over the world to make various functions on the Internet work. Some of them are over 20 years old now - given their origins, it's remarkable they have lasted this long. Will they last long into the future? In our next and last segment, the future history of the internet, we will start to examine this.

HISTORY OF WEB APPLICATION

Earlier in client- server computing, each application had its own client programme and it worked as a user interface and need to be installed on each user's personal computer. Most web applications use HTML/XHTML that are mostly supported by all the browsers and web pages are displayed to the client as static documents. A web page can merely displays static content and it also lets the user navigate through the content, but a web application provides a more interactive experience.

Any computer running Servlets or JSP needs to have a container. A container is nothing but a piece of software responsible for loading, executing and unloading the Servlets and JSP. While servlets can be used to extend the functionality of any Java- enabled server. They are mostly used to extend web servers, and are efficient replacement for CGI scripts. CGI was one of the earliest and most prominent server side dynamic content solutions, so before going forward it is very important to know the difference between CGI and the Servlets.

Common Gateway Interface (CGI)

The Common Gateway Interface, which is normally referred as CGI, was one of the practical technique developed for creating dynamic content. By using the CGI, a web server passes requests to an external programme and after executing the programme the content is sent to the client as the output. In CGI when a server receives a request it creates a new process to run the CGI programme, so creating a process for each request requires significant server resources and time, which limits the number of requests that can be processed concurrently. CGI applications are platform dependent. There is no doubt that CGI played a major role in the explosion of the Internet but its performance, scalability issues make it less than optimal solutions.

Java Servlets

Java Servlet is a generic server extension that means a java class can be loaded dynamically to expand the functionality of a server. Servlets are used with web servers and run inside a Java Virtual Machine (JVM) on the server so these are safe and portable. Unlike applets they do not require support for java in the web browser. Unlike CGI, servlets don't use multiple processes to handle separate request. Servets can be handled by separate threads within the same process. Servlets are also portable and platform independent.

CREATING WEBSITES FOR INDIVIDUAL AND CORPORATE WORLD

CREATING PERSONAL WEB SITES

This is a two-part article about creating a web site on the web and the tools that you need to do that. During the last decade we have truly entered the information age. More and more people are becoming a part of the ever growing and wondrous community called the Internet. It was just over a decade ago that 'Internet' was just another new concept that a lot of people were skeptical about.

Today however, it would be difficult to imagine living in the world without this amazing phenomenon. It really has enabled humans to reach new heights. Some basic terminology that you should take a look at before proceeding further: Web Page: A document that contains information created with the help of HTML. Web Site: A collection of web pages on a particular subject. HTML: Also known as Hyper Text Markup Language, this is used for the creation of web pages.

Information is written in between HTML tags (<>) to instruct the web page as to how information will be displayed. You can also put images into the web page by using this language. Some other languages like JavaScript, VB script, ASP, ASP.NET etc. are also used to display dynamic content on web pages and for performing user driver events. There are basically two main categories of web sites:

Personal web site: These include websites that are about individual human beings/people. Business web site: Includes web sites that advertise and inform users about the products and services that a company is selling. This article will deal with creating personal web sites and putting them on the web. You too can make your presence felt on the web (if you have not already done so) by creating a web site. The demand and popularity of personal web sites have increased at a great rate since the start of the web. People have found web sites a great way to express themselves.

A personal web site is your message center where you can upload information about friends and family and share them with the rest of the world. They can even act as a personal Blog (on-line journal).

Having a personal web site on the Internet has a lot of advantages:

- Gives you the freedom of self-expression. You can tell the world about your favourite hobbies, special interests, post your resume etc. for the whole world to see.
- Ability to keep in touch share your life) with friend and family who are far away.
- Great opportunity for making new friends and forming online communities.

Now comes the question of actually creating a web site. Surprisingly it is not a difficult task at all. In fact there are a lot of web sites that will provide you with all the tools you need to create your own web site and put it on the web, and you do not even have to know HTML to make them! You do not even have to worry about buying up web space; almost all these sites will provide you with free hosting services.

The only disadvantage is that they will probably put in banners (advertisements) of their sponsors on the site. For example: http://geocities.yahoo.com/ members.lycos.com These are two of the most popular web sites where you can create your own web pages. Yahoo gives you multiple options for creating web pages. It has yahoo page wizard and yahoo page builder, which are two very powerful yet simple editors for creating pages and have a point and click interface. http://www.webspawner.com/http://maxpages.com/ www.expage.com/ These are some other sites where you can create your own web pages. You can also search on the Internet for more sites like these as well. All you need to do is register and then you can create your own web pages. However, there is one little drawback when creating a site on these sites: you do not get your own personal domain name, so the address of your website will be something like http:www.site_where_you_registered.com/ yourname Where 'yourname' is the name under which you registered. However, taking everything into consideration, this is the simplest way to get on the web and start expressing yourself. This is the second part of a two-part article about creating a web site on the Internet and the tools that you will need to do it.

Some basic terminology that you should take a look at before proceeding further:

- *Web Page:* A document that contains information created with the help of HTML.
- *Web Site:* A collection of web pages on a particular subject. *HTML:* Also known as Hyper Text Markup Language it is used for the creation of web pages. Information is written in between HTML tags (<>) to instruct the web page as to how the information will be displayed. You can also put images into the web page by using this language. Some other languages like JavaScript, VB script, ASP, ASP.NET etc. are also used to display dynamic content on web pages and for performing user driver events. There are basically two main categories of web sites: Personal web site: These include websites that are about individual human beings. Business web site: Includes web sites that advertise and inform users about the products and services that a company is selling. This article will deal with creating web sites for small businesses and putting them on the web. Web Page: A document that contains information created.

The Internet is one of the best ways to reach out to people and advertise your services. If you are a small business you will think twice before advertising your services in traditional forms of media like radio, TV and newspapers.

However, advertising on the Internet is very cheap, for a fraction of the price that you might pay for advertising on TV you can reach out to millions of people. Your site acts as a virtual storefront through which you can sell almost any type of good or service. Having a presence on the web gives you a competitive edge and puts you on equal ground with others to compete while enabling you to reach millions of customers who browse the Internet on a daily basis. You can create your own site and you do not even need to have knowledge of programming. All you need is creativity and an eye for design. It must be mentioned that you can create your site by going to web sites that provide free hosting services. On the other hand, you will notice that these kinds of sites do not give you your own domain name. You will always get something like:

`http://www.somesite.com/yoursitename`

This simply doesn't look very professional if you want to project an image of a serious business. Think about it yourself, would you buy from a site that does not even have its own domain name? There is lots of software out there that can help you make a web site. These types of software are basically

WYSWYG editors *i.e.* 'What You See Is What You Get'. They have a point and click interface and are suited for both beginners and advanced users.

`1st Page 2000 -http://www.evrsoft.com/1stpage2.shtml NVU - http://www.nvu.com/`

These are two of the best sites that I would recommend and have a very easy learning curve.

ROLE OF A WEBSITE IN BUILDING CORPORATE

A website is an online identity of an individual or an organization on World Wide Web that helps to serve lot of purposes -personal, professional, organizational or public. Technically speaking, a website is a bunch of web pages, graphics, images, animation, and videos that is accessible to one and all in this world through the medium of internet. Hence, a website is not a local or regional identity but a global image of an individual or organization.

Of late, websites are widely being used to meet corporate needs and ambitions. As business and other commercial activities in 21st century are mostly being executed through worldwide online connectivity, it is essential for a company to have a user friendly website to accomplish its project in a smooth way. Globally, websites of different kinds like static website, dynamic website, CMS website, e-commerce website and others are designed and developed by professional designers or web design companies according to specific needs of individuals or companies.

A website nicely designed and technically (through programming) integrated with good functionality helps customers/clients to take the services offered by any company in smooth and effective way. Smooth navigation or browsing, information of services or products offered by the company better presented (web content), quick online payment modes and other facilities integrated with the website help clients do online business transactions effectively. Hence, it (website) creates a positive image for the company in the mind of customer. And a customer fully satisfied with the services provided by a company is a good source of advertisement in favour of the company. His links and interactions with people in day to day activities give back support to the company and help in creating good corporate and public image for the company.

Maximum number of people in developed countries and well educated people in developing countries like India and china are tech-savvy and generally use internet and do online shopping. If a company from any part of the world offers online service to millions of these tech-savvy people must have a good website. eBay and Amazon.com furnish ideal examples in this online shopping category. These two have their websites integrated with very good functionality and linkage. They provide online shopping services successfully to their customers globally through their outstanding websites. The market grip of these two companies help us easily understand how a good website can build corporate image and boost business irrespective of the sector any company deals in.

CREATE A WEBSITE

Welcome! My name is Ian. I've been creating websites since 1996. If you need to create a website, but don't know where to start, you've come to the right place! Here, I explain how to create a website. I also explain how to get your own domain name (eg,www.yourname.com), and how to host your website (make it available to the world). Creating a website is much easier than you might think. By following these steps, you will be able to create your own website in no time at all!

No Experience Needed

Did you know that anyone can create a website? Not only that, but did you know that you could make your own website within the next 30 minutes? Well, I'm about to show you the quickest and easiest way to create a website.

Website Tonight

Check out this video to see how easy it is to use Website Tonight. Website Tonight is a website builder that makes it easy to create a website. It is especially useful if you just want to make a website quickly without having to learn the technical stuff like HTML, CSS, etc. One of the great things about Website Tonight is that it is an online website builder. This means that you don't need to download anything. Everything is done online. To give you an example of how easy it is to create a website using this website builder, here's a sample website that I created in about 5 minutes. I could have added a lot more to it, but I wanted to show you what can be done within 5 minutes. As you can see, it looks like a finished website.

Create Your Website Now

The above link takes you to Website Tonight, a professional online website builder by our partner site, ZappyHost. Website Tonight includes free hosting, and you can get a domain name for $1.99. Domains for this price are almost unheard of, but this is part of the special package, so make sure you register your domain and Website Tonight at the same time.

A Warning about Free Websites

You might occasionally encounter someone offering you a free website. Basically these enable you to sign up, and start building your website for free.

But... a word of caution! There are things they might not tell you when they're trying to sell you a free website. While a few companies will be completely upfront about these extra costs, others will fail to mention them...until you've signed up: Your "free" website does not have it's own domain name (*i.e.* www.yourname.com). If you want your own domain name, you'll have to pay for it. And you will probably pay more than you should. Your "free" website may have ads displayed all over it. This enables the company (not you), to earn money from your website. To remove the ads, you will usually have to pay money for a premium package.

Most of the really good features are actually part of a "premium" package - which you have to pay for. Of course, it's entirely up to you which way you go. But there is one thing I will always recommend: Get your own domain name - now! Registering your own domain name is the best piece of advice I can give. Without this, your website does not have it's own "web address". This might not sound like much now, but later, once you've built up a fantastic website with loads of content, you will see what I mean. Without your own domain name, your "web address" is not actually yours, it's the company who provides your "free" website. If they decide to change something, you could lose all your hard work. Imagine losing months, or even years, of hard work, just because you chose not to register a domain name! So, if you're shopping around, check for those three things before you sign up with anyone.

The Website Creation Process

Now if you choose not to use a website builder, you are probably curious to know what is involved in making a website. Here I explain the three main steps of creating a website.

Creating a website basically involves the following 3 steps:

TEP 1 >>	STEP 2 >>	STEP 3 >>
Register a Domain Name A domain name is the thing that looks likemysite.com. You register these on an annual basis. Domain names can cost anywhere between $10 and $50 per year. I'll show you how to get one for $1.99 (below).	Get a Web Host A web host is a company that enables your website to be viewed by the rest of the world, 24/7. A good hosting plan can be anywhere between $10 per month and many thousands per month. Below, I'll show you excellent hosting plans starting from $5.35 per month.	Build your Website You can either build it yourself or use a website builder. Below, I'll show you an online website builder that includes template-sand hosting. And the great thing is, it's cheaper than most hosting plans!

CYBER LAWS WEB APPLICATIONS

REGULATORY NORMS IN INDIAN CYBERSPACE

The arrival of the Internet and the World Wide Web made it possible for people to communicate and transact over cyber space. It was a revolutionary step for humanity, but it also created a significant need for the regulation and governance of these activities, a requirement that lead to the creation and implementation of cyber laws across the globe. India became the 12th nation in the world to adopt a cyber law regime during 2000.

The country's cyber laws are contained in the Information Technology, Act 2000. The Act came into effect following the clearance of the Information Technology Bill 2000 in May 2000 by both the houses of the Parliament. The Bill received the assent of the President Of India in August 2000 (IT Act 2000). The IT Act 2000 aims to provide the legal infrastructure for e-commerce in India. At this juncture, it is relevant to understand what the IT Act 2000 offers and its various perspective.

Chapter-II of the Act specifically stipulates that any subscriber may authenticate an electronic record by affixing his digital signature. It further states that any person can verify an electronic record by use of a public key of the subscriber.

Chapter-III of the Act details about Electronic Governance and provides inter alia amongst others that where any law provides that information or any other matter shall be in writing or in the typewritten or printed form, then, notwithstanding anything contained in such law, such requirement shall be deemed to have been satisfied if such information or matter is – rendered or made available in an electronic form; and accessible so as to be usable for a subsequent reference The said chapter also details the legal recognition of Digital Signatures.

ADVANTAGES OF CYBER LAWS

The IT Act 2000 attempts to change outdated laws and provides ways to deal with cyber crimes. We need such laws so that people can perform purchase transactions over the Net through credit cards without fear of misuse. The Act offers the much-needed legal framework so that information is not denied legal effect, validity or enforceability, solely on the ground that it is in the form of electronic records.

In view of the growth in transactions and communications carried out through electronic records, the Act seeks to empower government departments to accept filing, creating and retention of official documents in the digital format.

The Act has also proposed a legal framework for the authentication and origin of electronic records/ communications through digital signature:

- From the perspective of e-commerce in India, the IT Act 2000 and its provisions contain many positive aspects. Firstly, the implications of these provisions for the e-businesses would be that e-mail would now be a valid and legal form of communication in our country that can be duly produced and approved in a court of law.

- Companies shall now be able to carry out electronic commerce using the legal infrastructure provided by the Act.
- Digital signatures have been given legal validity and sanction in the Act.
- The Act throws open the doors for the entry of corporate companies in the business of being Certifying Authorities for issuing Digital Signatures Certificates.
- The Act now allows Government to issue notification on the web thus heralding e-governance.
- The Act enables the companies to file any form, application or any other document with any office, authority, body or agency owned or controlled by the appropriate Government in electronic form by means of such electronic form as may be prescribed by the appropriate Government.
- The IT Act also addresses the important issues of security, which are so critical to the success of electronic transactions. The Act has given a legal definition to the concept of secure digital signatures that would be required to have been passed through a system of a security procedure, as stipulated by the Government at a later date.
- Under the IT Act, 2000, it shall now be possible for corporates to have a statutory remedy in case if anyone breaks into their computer systems or network and causes damages or copies data. The remedy provided by the Act is in the form of monetary damages, not exceeding ₹ 1 crore.

WEB APPLICATIONS

In software engineering, a web application is an application that is accessed via a web browser over a network such as the Internet or an intranet. The term may also mean a computer software application that is hosted in a browser-controlled environment (*e.g.* a Java applet) or coded in a browser-supported language (such as JavaScript, combined with a browser-rendered markup language like HTML) and reliant on a common web browser to render the application executable. Web applications are popular due to the ubiquity of web browsers, and the convenience of using a web browser as a client, sometimes called a thin client.

The ability to update and maintain web applications without distributing and installing software on potentially thousands of client computers is a key reason for their popularity, as is the inherent support for cross-platform compatibility. Common web applications include webmail, online retail sales, online auctions and many other functions.

Writing Web Applications

There are many web application frameworks which facilitate rapid application development by allowing the programmer to define a high-level description of the programme. In addition, there is potential for the development of applications on Internet operating systems, although currently there are not many viable platforms that fit this model. The use of web application frameworks can often reduce the number of errors in a programme, both by making the code simpler, and by allowing one team to concentrate just on the framework. In applications which are exposed to constant hacking attempts on the Internet, security-related problems can be caused by errors in the programme. Frameworks can also promote the use of best practices such as GET after POST method.

Applications such as Content Management Systems (CMS), Wikis, Portals, Bulletin Boards, and discussion forums are being used by small and large organizations. Every week hundreds of vulnerabilities are being reported in these web applications, and are being actively exploited. The number of attempted attacks every day for some of the large web hosting farms range from hundreds of thousands to even millions.

All web frameworks (PHP.NET, J2EE, Ruby on Rails, ColdFusion, Perl, etc) and all types of web applications are at risk from web application security defects, ranging from insufficient validation through to application logic errors. The most exploited vulnerabilities are:

PHP Remote File Include

PHP is the most common web application language and framework in use today. By default, PHP allows file functions to access resources on the Internet using a feature called "allow_url_fopen". When PHP scripts allow user input to influence file names, remote file inclusion can be the result.

This attack allows (but is not limited to):

- Remote code execution
- Remote root kit installation

On Windows, internal system compromise may be possible through the use of PHP's SMB file wrappers.

SQL Injection: Injections, particularly SQL injections, are common in web applications. Injections are possible due to intermingling of user supplied data within dynamic queries or within poorly constructed stored procedures.

SQL injections allow attackers:

- To create, read, update, or delete any arbitrary data available to the application
- In the worst case scenario, to completely compromise the database system and systems around it

Cross-Site Scripting (XSS)

Cross site scripting, better known as XSS, is the most pernicious and easily found web application security issue. XSS allows attackers to deface web sites, insert hostile content, conduct phishing attacks, take over the user's browser using JavaScript malware, and force users to conduct commands not of their own choosing – an attack known as cross-site request forgeries, better known as CSRF.

Cross-site Request Forgeries (CSRF)

CSRF forces legitimate users to execute commands without their consent. This type of attack is extremely hard to prevent unless the application is free of cross-site scripting vectors, including DOM injections. With the rise of Ajax techniques, and better knowledge of how to properly exploit XSS attacks, CSRF attacks are becoming extremely sophisticated, both as an active individual attack and as automated worms, such as the Samy MySpace Worm. Directory Traversal: Directory traversal (file access via ".." or many encoded variants) allows attackers access to controlled resources, such as password files, configuration files, database credentials or other files of the attacker's choosing.

C1.2 How to Determine If You Are at Risk Web scanning tools can help find these vulnerabilities, particularly if they are known bugs. However, to find all potential vulnerabilities requires a source code review. This should be done by the developers prior to release. Inspect your web application framework's configuration and harden appropriately. System administrators should consider scanning web servers periodically with vulnerability scanners, particularly if they run a large diverse range of user supplied scripts, such as a hosting farm. It is impractical for system administrators to perform detailed penetration tests.

How to Protect Against Web Application Vulnerabilities

From the PHP system administration and hosting perspective:

- Upgrade to PHP 5.2 as it eliminates many latent PHP security issues and allows for safer API, such as PDO
- Always test and deploy patches and new versions of PHP as they are released
- Frequent web scanning is recommended in environments where a large number of PHP applications are in use
- Consider using the following PHP configuration:
- Register_globals (should be off, will break insecure apps)
- Allow_url_fopen (should be off, will break apps that rely on this feature, but protect against a very active exploit vector)
- Magic_quotes_gpc (should be off, will break older insecure apps)
- Open_basedir (should be enabled and correctly configured)
- Consider using least privilege execution features like PHPsuexec or suPHP
- Consider using Suhosin to control the execution environment of PHP scripts
- Use Intrusion Prevention/Detection Systems to block/alert on malicious HTTP requests. Consider using Apache's mod_security to block known PHP attacks

- As a last resort, consider banning applications which have a track record of active exploitation, and slow response times to fix known security issues.

From the Developer Perspective

- If you use PHP, migrate your application to PHP 5.2 as a matter of urgency.
- To avoid the coding issues above:
- Develop with the latest PHP release and a hardened configuration (see above)
- Validate all input appropriately
- Encode all output using htmlentities() or a similar mechanism to avoid XSS attacks
- Migrate your data layer to PDO - do not use the old style mysql_*() functions as they are known faulty
- Do not use user-supplied input with file functions to avoid remote file inclusion attacks
- Join secure coding organizations, such as OWASP (see references) to boost skills, and learn about secure coding
- Test your apps using the OWASP Testing Guide with tools like WebScarab, Firefox's Web Developer Toolbar, Greasemonkey and the XSS Assistant

WRITING A WEB APPLICATION

As you probably know only too well, writing a web application can be a daunting task. A web application programmer must understand concepts related to distributed applications and services, the HTTP protocol, Common Gateway Interface (CGI) programming, HTML/JavaScript programming, user authentication and authorization, session management, data exchange from disparate sources, and so on. If you are writing web applications or if you have ever been tempted to write web applications, you can use Java technologies and tools provided by Novell and IBM to write an application for IBM WebSphere Application Server for NetWare. (For more information about WebSphere Application Server, visit www.novell.com/products/websphere.) This article explains the concepts you need to know to write a web application and outlines the steps for writing a simple web application that runs on WebSphere Application Server for NetWare.

Specifically, this article explains the following:

- Understanding how web application concepts relate to Java-based web application servers
- Applying the Model/View/Controller (MVC) pattern to the web application domain
- Using command beans to handle business logic tasks

- Using format beans to simplify complex presentation code
- Understanding technologies that provide a framework for Novell's Directory-Enabled Network Infrastructure Model (DENIM)
- Finding the right edition of WebSphere Application Server for your company
- Using IBM development tools to create a web application
- Applications Available Today

Web Application Concepts

A typical web application starts when a user clicks a link in an HTML page and causes the browser to instigate an HTTP request/response transaction with a web server, CGI programme, and web application server. For the purposes of this article, I will refer to the web server, CGI programme, and web application server as the targeted server.

The targeted server receives the HTTP request and dispatches the request and its associated data (such as headers and query parameters) to the desired resource residing on the targeted server. In the simplest case, the targeted server responds with a static HTML page, which the browser interprets and presents to the user.

In more complex web applications, the targeted server must perform other functions such as the following:

- Execute business logic
- Retrieve data according to query parameters
- Authenticate and authorize users
- Reestablish a session from a former request
- Exchange data with legacy systems
- Build the HTML response page dynamically to be passed back to the browser

The Java 2 Platform, Enterprise Edition defines a set of architectures, technologies, and frameworks that simplify and standardize distributed web application programming using the Java programming language. Java-based web application servers incorporate some of these architectures, technologies, and frameworks such as servlets, Java Server Pages (JSP), and Enterprise JavaBeans (EJB) to provide a common programming platform for web application programmers. WebSphere Application Server for NetWare is a Java-based web application server, thus enabling you to use these technologies to build web applications.

THE MVC PATTERN

Servlets are server-side Java programmes that extend a web server to handle HTTP requests and responses. A servlet's request-handling methods are expected to extract information from request parameters, perform business logic, and then send back HTML responses to a client.

JSP extend HTML with a set of custom HTML tags that allow developers to embed Java code in an HTML page. A JSP is converted into a Java servlet and compiled the first time it is requested. Subsequent requests are simply routed through the cached instance. This process allows content to be added to a page dynamically and sent to the client.

You can use the MVC pattern to implement an architecture that uses servlets to handle HTTP requests and perform business logic and uses JSP to handle the HTML presentation. The components of this pattern are explained below:

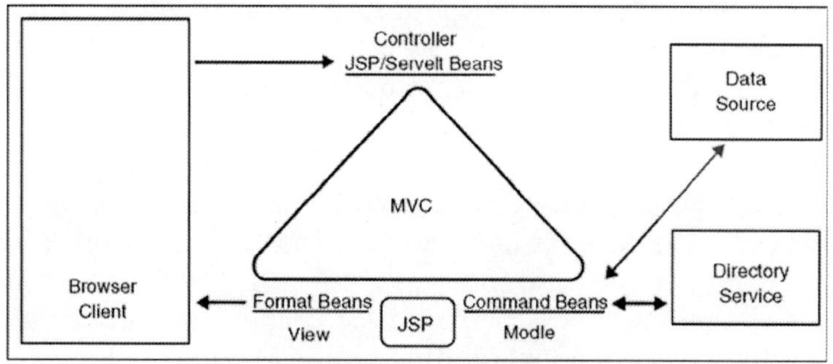

Fig The Interaction between the Elements Involved in A Java-based Web Application

- *Model*: The model components expose the business logic for a particular web application or service.
- *View*: The view components build HTML pages that a web application returns to a user in response to HTTP requests.
- *Controller*: The controller components or services drive the model and view components.

Using an MVC pattern to build web applications decouples the development process, thereby allowing HTML authors to build web pages and Java programmers to work on business logic. Novell's MVC Beans for eBusiness takes this development process one step further by separating business logic into Java components called command beans and separating the complex user interface into Java components called format beans.

An HTTP transaction that uses command and format beans is processed in the following way:

- The HTTP request is handled by a target servlet.
- The servlet instantiates and calls methods belonging to one or more command beans to perform the business logic of the request.
- The command beans that are implementing the business logic access relational databases, connectors, directory services, file systems, and so on while performing their specific actions.
- The servlet invokes a JSP after storing command bean instances in the applicable context object for use by the JSP.

- The content is dynamically generated by the JSP using a combination of HTML and the output properties of the command beans that are retrieved from the context object. The HTML page is then sent to the client. This process may leverage formatting beans, other JSP, and static resources such as HTML files and image files.

Command Beans

A command bean is a JavaBean that encapsulates a single business logic task.

To use a command bean, you complete the following steps:

- Create the command bean.
- Initialize the state of the command bean by setting specific input properties of the bean.
- Instigate the command bean to execute its specific business logic task by calling its perform method and then getting the values of the bean's output properties. (The perform method is explained below.)

This programming model helps isolate changes in the web application by factoring the business logic into fine-grained components that are easily managed and less reliant on other components. This model also allows easier distribution of processing using serialization to send the command bean over protocols, such as Internet Inter-ORB Protocol (IIOP) or HTTP, to a remote server. The remote server then executes the command bean and sends back the results. The primary interface for the command bean is the Command interface, which consists of four methods: isReadyToCallPerform, perform, executeCommand (used if executing remotely), and reset.

A command bean can be in one of the following states during its life cycle:

- *New*: The command bean is in the new state immediately after it is created. In this state, the isReadyToCallPerform method will return false, and the output properties should not be retrieved.
- *Initialized*: The command bean is in the initialized state after all required input properties have been set. In this state, the isReadyToCallPerform method will return true, but the output properties should not be retrieved.
- *Executed*: The command bean is in this state after the perform method has been called. In this state, the isReadyToCallPerform method will return true, and the output properties can be retrieved.

Command beans that execute locally (on the same Java Virtual Machine [JVM] as the web application) implement the Command interface. If a command bean is to be executed remotely on another server, the command bean implements the TargetableCommand interface. An extension of the Command interface, the TargetableCommand interface allows for remote execution.

Regardless of whether the command bean executes locally or remotely, the JSP or servlet executes the command bean in the following way:

1. The servlet instantiates the command bean and then sets the command bean's input properties. Next, the servlet calls the perform method on the command bean. If the command bean executes locally, step 2 begins. Otherwise, these additional steps occur: A. The perform method determines the target environment for the command bean. B. The perform method calls the executeCommand method on the CommandTarget object passing itself (the command bean) as an input argument. This step may entail serializing the command bean and sending it via some protocol (such as IIOP) to the target server for execution. C. After potentially de-serializing the command bean, the command target calls the command bean's executeCommand method, which encapsulates the business logic.
2. The perform method, if successful, returns with its output properties set to the results of the underlying business logic task.
3. Control flows to the JSP, which is now free to query the output properties of the command bean.

FORMAT BEANS

Format beans support JSP and help format various types of dynamic content. In fact, you can use one or more format beans to handle complex data formatting.

Formatting is usually specific to the characteristics of the user, such as the locale of the user. For this reason, each format bean class method comes in at least two forms: one that takes the servlet request object as a parameter and one that does not. When the request object is provided, the method will extract information from the request object to customise the formatting operation. When the request object is not provided, the method will use default values or server-wide values such as the default locale.

Most of the format beans produce locale-specific results. By convention, the format beans determine the locale from the request context value "JSPLocale" which must be a java.util.Locale value. If "JSPLocale" is not set in the request context or the request context is not available, the system's default locale will be used.

Each of the format classes also allows the locale to be configured into a format bean. In this case, the configured locale takes precedent over the JSPLocale value, if this value is specified.

A Framework For Denim

The Novell Web Application Servers team has designed an architecture consisting of JavaBeans, EJBs, JSP, servlets, and auxiliary Java classes to form a complete web application framework for Novell's DENIM platform. Part of this framework consists of the MVC Beans for eBusiness, a suite of command and format beans that uses the MVC pattern to expose NetWare services to web applications. By abstracting functionality required by many applications, software frameworks provide a common design and a partial implementation for a set of similar problems. Developers then provide application-specific functionality. This approach to software development provides a number of benefits including unbeatable design-to-market time frames, centralized bug fixes and feature enhancements, and compatible application infrastructures.

Domain frameworks capture expertise for particular problems such as network management, inventory control, and point-of-sale. Novell plans to provide a number of domain frameworks built around the MVC Beans for eBusiness and other components, using common data interchange interfaces such as XML and WML. Novell plans to begin distributing these domain frameworks (such as a web portal framework, a storefront framework, an NDS eDirectory management framework, and a server-health management framework) at the end of this year.

Websphere Editions

WebSphere Application Server for NetWare provides the infrastructure you need to deliver powerful web applications on the NetWare platform.

Novell offers two editions of WebSphere Application Server for NetWare:

1. Standard Edition, which allows you to create dynamic web sites based on JSP and Java servlets. This edition ships with NetWare 5.1 and 5.
2. Advanced Edition, which allows you to use EJBs and middleware connectors. (For more information about this edition,

WebSphere Application Server for NetWare includes an administrative console that allows you to manage the web application life cycle. The administrative console allows you to perform tasks such as creating web applications, setting options for loading local and remote servlets and initialization parameters, specifying servlet aliases, creating servlet chains and filters, and monitoring resources used by WebSphere Application Server.

You can also configure resources such as HTML pages, servlets, file system directories, and JSP into single units that WebSphere Application Server manages as web applications. These web applications can have their own relative URL (called a web path), their own classpaths for servlet execution, and their own document directories for HTML and JSP documents. After you create a web application in the administrative console, you can group this application with other web applications or other resources and secure it using WebSphere's extensible security model. WebSphere's security model uses NDS eDirectory via Lightweight Directory Access Protocol (LDAP).

TOOLS

IBM's WebSphere Studio, which ships with NetWare 5.1, provides a comprehensive set of tools that reduces the time and effort required to build dynamic web applications. Using a visual layout tool for dynamic web pages created through JSP, HTML, and JavaScript, WebSphere Studio allows you to quickly and easily develop and maintain web applications.

IBM's VisualAge for Java is one of the industry's favourite visual, integrated development environments (IDE) for Java. VisualAge for Java provides support for building, testing, and deploying 100 per cent pure Java applications, JavaBean components, servlets, and applets. Applications developed with WebSphere Studio and VisualAge for Java can be debugged either from within the IDE or remotely on the web application server.

To demonstrate how easy creating your own web applications is, the following sections explain how to create a simple web application that can access NDS eDirectory to retrieve a list of NDS trees on the network. To create this application, you will use WebSphere Studio, VisualAge for Java, WebSphere Application Server for NetWare, and Novell's MVC Beans for eBusiness.

WebSphere Administrative Console

- In the WebSphere Administrative Console, select the Tasks tab, and expand the Configuration node.
- Select the Configure a Web Application node, and click the green button on the button bar.
- Name the web application, and select the Enable File Servlet: checkbox and the Serve Servlets by Classname: checkbox. Also, click the Enable JSP 1.0 radio button. Click Next.
- From the Select a Servlet Engine page, expand the Nodes tree until the servletEngine node appears. Select the servletEngine node, and click Next. When the next page appears, click Next, and when the next page appears, click Finished.
- When the Command "Web Application.create" Completed Successfully dialog box appears, click OK.
- Select the Topology tab, and expand the node that matches your host name until you see your new web application node, which should be a child node of the servletEngine node.
- Right-click your web application node, and select Restart Web App.
- When theCommand" webappname.setRefresh Config" Completed Successfully dialog box appears, click OK.

WebSphere Studio

- Create a new project using the File->New Project... menu item.
- In the Publishing View, make sure the Test publishing stage is active,

right-click the Test node, and insert a server. Name the server the full Domain Naming System (DNS) name of your host server (such as >myserver.mydomain.com).

- Right-click the new server, and select the File System Publish radio button. Define the publishing targets as follows:A. Modify the HTML publishing target to match the web directory of your web application. B. Modify the servlet publishing target to match the servlets directory of your web application.
- Right-click the servlet node in the file view, and select insert file. Select the Use Existing tab. Browse for the EDirCMD.jar file found on your server in the<vol>:\java\beans directory.
- Expand the servlet node in the file view, right-click the EDirCMD.jar node, and select Properties. Select the Publishing tab, and uncheck the Set Publishable check box.
- Select the top node in the file view, and then select the Tools->Wizards->JavaBean Wizard menu item. From the JavaBean: list, select the com.novell. web.command.beans.edir.ListEDirTrees JavaBean, and click Next.
- Select the Create an Input Page and Create a Results Page checkboxes, and click Next. When the next page appears, click Next because you will not be setting any input properties from your input page.
- The Results page appears. Select the treeNames check box, and click Next.
- From the Methods page, check the perform() check box, and then click Next. When the Session page appears, click Next, and then click Finish.
- At this point, the output page (Bean1Results.jsp) contains code to display the treeNames output property as a Java string. The treeNames output property is an array of strings, so you must modify this line of code to display the names in the manner that best suits your needs. To do this, right-click the Bean1Results.jsp node, select the Edit with->ScriptBuilder menu item, and edit the file as needed. Save the file, right-click the Bean1Results.jsp node, and select the Check In menu item.
- Right-click the top node in the file view, and select the Publish Whole Project menu item. Select the OK and/or Yes buttons until the publishing phase finishes.
- Start VisualAge for Java. Create a new project that matches the name of your WebSphere Studio project.
- In VisualAge for Java, select the Window->Options menu item. Select the Remote Access to Tool API node. Click the Start Remote Access to Tool API button, and then click OK.

- In Websphere Studio, expand the servlet node, and select Project->VisualAge for Java->Send to VisualAge menu item. The VisualAge dialog box appears; select the project that matches the WebSphere Studio project.

Visual Age for Java

- After exporting your servlet from WebSphere Studio to VisualAge for Java, right-click the project that matches the name of your WebSphere Studio project, and select the Import... menu item. Click the Jar file radio button, and then click Next. Browse for the njcl.jar file on your server in the<vol>:\java\lib directory. Click Finish. If you encounter any problems relating to other packages that have not been imported (particularly Swing classes), import the jar files containing these classes as well.
- Select the Import... menu item. Click the Jar file radio button, and then click Next. Browse for the EdirCmd.jar file on your server in the<vol>:\java\beans directory. Click Finish. When the Modify Palette dialog box appears, create a new category, name it, select the ListEDirTrees bean and any other beans that you would like to use from the Available Beans list.
- Expand the project until you find the servlet that was created in WebSphere Studio. Select the method of the servlet that you want to edit. Edit as needed, and save the project.
- In WebSphere Studio, expand the servlet node, select the Project->VisualAge for Java->Update from VisualAge menu item. Right-click the Bean1class node and select the Check In menu item. Right-click the Bean1.java node, and select the Compile menu item. Right-click the Bean1.java node, and select the Publish Selected Files menu item.

EXISTING APPLICATIONS

MVC Beans for eBusiness are distributed with WebSphere Application Server for NetWare and NetWare 5.1 and are also available on Novell's developer web site (>developer. novell.com). You will also find documentation, sample code, and usable applications, such as the following: an application that uses JSP and format beans to manage NDS objects in a tree-view from a web browser, an application that uses JSP and command beans to authenticate a user and to perform operations on an NDS tree in proxy for the user, and an application that uses JSP and format beans to view and direct a server console.

Many other applications are available within the MVC Beans for eBusiness. You can customise and extend these applications as needed.

TARGET USERS

This variety of stakeholders is absolutely necessary in order to obtain a

Pan-European base cartography, uniform and shared with a great number of states. The cartography sample based on data provided by partners will ensure a significant coverage of the European territory. Nevertheless, a wide vision of users' requirements and needs will be provided by the direct involvement of GISIG (European association including around 100 GIS stakeholders: public authorities, data providers, researchers, services providers, software producers).

As far as definition of community standards and guidelines defined by governmental and standardisation bodies at EU level is concerned, European bodies need the support of each European Member State, above all for the enforcement and validation of standards.

The most important aspects for each level of Public Administrations are the re-use policies, aiming at saving time and money. In this way national, regional and local public entities will be able to re-use a shared base cartography and its tool, without spending much money and wasting time. Other kinds of users are data providers: national data providers link European standardisation bodies and other levels of data providers. For example regional data suppliers, which arrange for the identification of comparable experience, learning from "good practice" case study, and local data providers, and which need shared specifications for geographical data modelling and re-modelling.

Also the European and National/Regional Environmental Agencies are interested in having a shared base cartography, in order to georeference each environmental event and to prevent remarkable accidents and ecological damages, also at local level.

Each kind of European GI Agencies (*e.g.* mapping, cadastre, infrastructure, hydrography) will greatly benefit from this uniform normative context, while National GI Agencies need a European base cartography above all in order to compile national GI shared rules. Technological Enterprises will play a role as providers of tools and GI services, and their aim is to increase their knowledge, taking from other European experiences, and to enlarge their business in the greater part of the European countries.

The Research community (Research Institutes and Universities) is also very active in the GI field and it will play a relevant role in defining specifications and guidelines for the realisation of this shared base cartography. At the same time, Research Centres and Universities will carry out their research and training projects thanks to the definition of GIS4EU specifications. All GI users of GIS4EU will benefit from the interoperable and accessible base cartography, solving their usual cross-border, cross-scale and cross-languages problems.

The Critical Mass of the GIS4EU project is developed by the different types of organisation and user involvement, but also by the different types of data provider from the local to the national level, and by the different types of database included in the project. This document specifies requirements that, if satisfied by user agent developers, will lower barriers to accessibility.

This document includes the following:

- This introduction provides context for understanding the requirements listed in section 2.
- Section 2 explains 12 general principles of accessible design, called "guidelines." Each guideline consists of a list of requirements, called "checkpoints," which must be satisfied in order to conform to this document. Note: Section 2 is numbered differently than the other sections; it consists of a list of guidelines. In section 2, "checkpoint 1.2" refers to the second checkpoint of the first guideline. "Section 1.2" refers to a subsection of the Introduction.
- Section 3 explains how to make claims that software components satisfy the requirements of section 2. An appendix offers a summary of this document's principal goals and structure [UAAG10-SUMMARY].
- A second appendix lists all the checkpoints for convenient reference (*e.g.*, as a tool for developers to evaluate software for conformance) [UAAG10-CHECKLIST].

A separate document, entitled "Techniques for User Agent Accessibility Guidelines 1.0" (the "Techniques document" from here on) [UAAG10-TECHS], provides suggestions and examples of how each checkpoint might be satisfied. It also includes references to other accessibility resources (such as platform-specific software accessibility guidelines) that provide additional information on how a user agent may satisfy each checkpoint.

The techniques in the Techniques document are informative examples only, and other strategies may be used or required to satisfy the checkpoints. The UAWG expects to update the Techniques document more frequently than the current guidelines. Developers, W3C Working Groups, users, and others are encouraged to contribute techniques.

RELATION TO WAI ACCESSIBILITY GUIDELINES

"User Agent Accessibility Guidelines 1.0" (UAAG 1.0) is part of a series of accessibility guidelines published by the Web Accessibility Initiative (WAI). The documents in this series reflect an accessibility model in which Web content authors, format designers, and software developers have roles in ensuring that users with disabilities have access to the Web. The accessibility-related interests of these stakeholders intersect and complement each other as follows:

Designers of formats (*e.g.*, HTML, XHTML, XML, SVG, SMIL, MathML, and XForms) and protocols (*e.g.*, HTTP) create specifications that allow communication on the Web. Format designers include features in these specifications that authors should use to create accessible content and that user agents should support through an accessible user interface. The "XML Accessibility Guidelines (XAG)" [XAG10] explains the responsibilities of XML format designers; many XAG requirements make sense for non-XML formats as well.

Authors make use of the accessibility features of different format specifications, use markup appropriately, write in clear and simple language, and organize a Web site consistently. The "Web Content Accessibility Guidelines 1.0" [WCAG10] explains the responsibilities of authors in meeting the needs of users with disabilities.

The "Web Content Accessibility Guidelines (WCAG) 1.0" is considered within UAAG 1.0 to be the reference set of requirements to make Web content accessible. The "Authoring Tool Accessibility Guidelines 1.0" [ATAG10] explains the responsibilities of authoring tool developers. An accessible authoring tool facilitates the creation of accessible Web content and may be operated by users with disabilities. User agent developers design software that meets the needs of users with disabilities through conformance to other specifications, an accessible user interface, accessible documentation, and communication with other software (notably assistive technologies).

The requirements of this document interact with those of the "Web Content Accessibility Guidelines 1.0" [WCAG10] in a number of ways:

- UAAG 1.0 checkpoint 8.1 requires implementation of the accessibility features of specifications. Features are those identified as such and those that satisfy all of the requirements of WCAG 1.0 [WCAG10].
- UAAG 1.0 checkpoint 12.1 requires conformance to WCAG 1.0 for user agent documentation.
- UAAG 1.0 also incorporates some terms and concepts from WCAG 1.0, a consequence of fact that the documents were designed to complement one another.

Some requirements of this document take into account limitations of formats, authors, and designers. For example, formats generally do not enable authors to encode all of their knowledge in a way that a user agent can fully recognize. A format may lack features required for accessibility. An author may not make use of the accessibility features of a format or may misuse a format (which can cause problems for user agents). A user agent designer may not implement a format specification correctly or completely.

Some of these limitations are taken into account as follows:

- UAAG 1.0 includes requirements to satisfy the expectations set by WCAG 1.0 "until user agent" clauses. These clauses make additional requirements of authors in order to compensate for some limitations of deployed user agents.
- UAAG 1.0 includes several repair requirements (*e.g.*, checkpoints checkpoint 2.7 and checkpoint 2.10) for cases where content does not conform to WCAG 1.0. Furthermore, this document includes

some requirements to address certain widespread authoring practices that are discouraged because they may cause accessibility or usability problems (*e.g.*, some uses of HTML frames).

- Except for the indicated repair checkpoints, UAAG 1.0 only requires user agents to handle what may be recognized through protocols and formats. For example, user agents are not expected to recognize that the author has used "clear and simple" language to express ideas (WCAG 1.0, checkpoint 14.1). See the section on checkpoint applicability for more information about what the user agent is expected to recognize.

The Web Accessibility Initiative provides other resources and educational materials to promote Web accessibility. Resources include information about accessibility policies, links to translations of WAI materials into languages other than English, information about specialized user agents and other tools, accessibility training resources, and more.

Note: The Web Accessibility Initiative is developing new versions of both the Web Content Accessibility Guidelines and the Authoring Tool Accessibility Guidelines. The User Agent Accessibility Guidelines Working Group expects to follow the progress of those documents. UAAG 1.0 refers only to the WCAG 1.0 and ATAG 1.0 Recommendations, which will remain available and unchanged.

TARGET USER AGENTS

This document was designed specifically to improve the accessibility of user agents with multimedia capabilities running in the following type of environment (typically that of a desktop computer):

- The operating environment includes a keyboard (or keyboard equivalent)
- Assistive technologies may be used in the operating environment and may communicate with the conforming user agent
- The target user agent is one designed for the general public to handle general-purpose content in ordinary operating conditions.
- This document does not forbid conformance by other types of user agents, but some requirements (*e.g.*, implementation of certain application programming interfaces, or APIs) are not likely to be satisfied in environments (*e.g.*, handheld devices or kiosks) other than the target environment. Future work by the UAWG may address the accessibility of user agents running on handheld devices, for example.

Technologies not addressed directly by this document (*e.g.*, those for braille rendering) will be essential to ensuring Web access for some users with disabilities. Note that the ability of conforming user agents to communicate well with assistive technologies will depend in part on the willingness of assistive technology developers to follow the same standards and conventions for communication.

COMPOSITION OF CONFORMING USER AGENTS

In general, a conforming user agent will consist of several coordinated components, such as a Web browser, a multimedia player, several plug-ins, features or applications provided by the operating environment, and documentation distributed with the software or available on the Web. These components may run on the user's computer or on a server. A conforming user agent may also include assistive technologies and applications provided by the operating environment. The current document places no restrictions on the type or number of components used for conformance.

This does not mean that every component that one has chosen as part of the user agent has to satisfy every single requirement; some requirements may not be relevant for a particular component.

For instance, if a component does not have a user interface, the user interface requirements would not be relevant. On the other hand, if a component has a user interface, the user interface requirements are relevant. Conformance addresses the composite user agent as a whole.

USE OF OPERATING ENVIRONMENT FEATURES

The UAWG encourages developers to satisfy the requirements of this document by adopting operating environment conventions and features that benefit accessibility. When an operating environment feature (*e.g.*, the operating system's audio control panel, including its user interface) is adopted to satisfy the requirements of this document, it is part of the user agent.

See additional information on conformance of user agents running in multiple operating environments.

KNOWN LIMITATIONS OF THIS DOCUMENT

People with (or without) disabilities access the Web with widely varying sets of capabilities, software, and hardware.

Some users with disabilities:

- May not be able to see, hear, move, or speak.
- May not be able to perceive, read, or process some types of information easily or at all.
- May not have or be able to use a keyboard or pointing device.

This document does not include requirements to meet all known accessibility needs. Some known limitations of this document include the following:

INPUT MODALITIES

This document only includes requirements for keyboard, pointing device, and voice input modalities. This document includes several checkpoints related to voice input as part of general input requirements (*e.g.*, the checkpoints of guideline 7 and guideline 11) but does not otherwise address voice-based navigation or control.

Note: The UAWG intends to coordinate further work on the topics of voice input and synthesized speech rendering with groups in W3C's Voice Browser Activity and Multimodal Interaction Activity.

OUTPUT MODALITIES

This document does not include requirements for braille rendering. Some requirements are specific to graphical rendering and others specific to audio output or synthesized speech output. Speech rendering requirements are made by checkpoint 4.9 to checkpoint 4.13. Many of the requirements of this document are generic enough to apply to a variety of output modalities, including braille. User agents conform to this document by supporting some combination of graphical and audio/speech rendering output; see the section on Content type labels for more information.

- Size and colour of non-text content
- This document includes some checkpoints to ensure that the user is able to control the size and colour of visually rendered text content (checkpoints 4.1 and 4.3). This document does not in general address control of the size and colour of visually rendered non-text content (*e.g.*, images).

Note: A user agent may implement resizing functionalities as part of conformance to other specifications (*e.g.*, Scalable Vector Graphics [SVG]).

BACKGROUND IMAGE INTERFERENCE

The requirement of checkpoint 3.1 to allow the user to turn off rendering of background images does not extend to multi-layered rendering.

User control of every user interface component. This document distinguishes user interface features that are part of the user agent user interface and those that are part of content. Some checkpoints (*e.g.*, those in guideline 5) require user control over rendering and behaviour that is driven by content only. This document does not always explicitly require the same control over features of the user agent user interface. Nevertheless, this document (see checkpoint 7.3) does require user agents to follow software usability guidelines. The UAWG expects such usability guidelines to include requirements for user control over user interface behaviour.

Note: It is more difficult for users to distinguish content from user interface when both are rendered as sound in one temporal dimension, than it is when both are rendered visually in two spatial dimensions. Thus, the UAWG encourages developers of user agents that include audio output or synthesized speech output to apply the requirements of this document to both content and user agent components.

TIME PARAMETERS

This document includes requirements (see checkpoints 2.4, 4.4, 4.5, and 4.9) for control of some time parameters. The requirements are for time parameters that the user agent recognizes and controls. This document does not include requirements for control of time parameters managed on the server.

DIGITAL RIGHTS MANAGEMENT

The User Agent Accessibility Guidelines Working Group recognizes that further work is necessary in the area of digital rights management as it relates to accessibility. Digital rights management refers to methods of describing and perhaps enforcing intellectual property associated with Web resources.

Note: The User Agent Accessibility Guidelines Working Group may address these and other topics in a future version of the User Agent Accessibility Guidelines. Even though UAAG 1.0 does not address these topics, the UAWG encourages user agent developers to consider them in their designs.

RELATION TO GENERAL SOFTWARE DESIGN GUIDELINES AND OTHER SPECIFICATIONS

One the goals of the authors of this document is to ensure that the requirements are compatible with other good software design practices. However, this document does not purport to be a complete guide to good software design. For instance, the general topic of user interface design for computer software exceeds the scope of this document, though some user interface requirements have been included because of their importance to accessibility. The Techniques document [UAAG10-TECHS] includes some references to general software design guidelines and platform-specific accessibility guidelines (in particular, see checkpoint 7.3). Involving people with disabilities in the design and testing of software will generally improve the accessibility of the software.

This document promotes conformance to other specifications as part of accessible design. Conformance to specifications makes it easier to design assistive technologies, and helps ensure the implementation of built-in accessibility functions. This document also includes some requirements to implement an accessibility feature that may only be optional in another specification. In rare cases, a requirement in UAAG 1.0 may conflict with a requirement in another specification. UAAG 1.0 does not define a process for resolving such conflicts. The authors of this document anticipate that developers will consider accessibility implications in determining how to resolve them.

INSTALLATION

Installation is an important aspect of both accessibility and general software usability. On platforms where a user can install a user agent, the installation (and update) procedures need to be accessible. Furthermore, the installation procedure should provide and install all components necessary to satisfy the requirements of this document, since the risk of installation failure increases with the number of components (*e.g.*, plug-ins) to be installed.

This document does not include a checkpoint requiring that installation procedures be accessible. Since this document considers installation to be part of software usage, the different aspects of installation (*e.g.*, user interface, documentation, and operating environment conventions) are already covered by the complete set of checkpoints.

SECURITY CONSIDERATIONS

Some of the requirements of this document may have security implications, such as communication through APIs, and allowing programmatic read and write access to content and user interface control. This document assumes that features required by this document will be built on top of an underlying security architecture. Consequently, unless permitted explicitly in a checkpoint (as in checkpoint 6.5), this document grants no conformance exemptions based on security issues.

Developers should design user agents that enable communication with trusted assistive technologies. Sensitive information that the user agent can access through the user agent's user interface should also be available to assistive technologies through secure means. For instance, if the user types a password in the user agent user interface, do not communicate substitute characters (such as asterisks) through an API, but rather the real password, properly encrypted. Note also that appropriate user agent behaviour with respect to security may depend on the user's context. For instance, hiding typed passwords with asterisks is much less important for someone alone in a room than for someone in a crowded room. Similarly, while unencrypted passwords rendered as synthesized speech should not be broadcast in a crowded room, they may pose no security risk if the user is wearing an earphone. For information related to security, refer to "XML-Signature Syntax and Processing" [XMLDSIG] and "XML Encryption Syntax and Processing" [XMLENC].

USER CONTROL

This document emphasizes the goal of ensuring that users, including users with disabilities, have control over their environment for accessing the Web. Key methods for achieving that goal include: optional self-pacing, configurability, device-independence, interoperability, direct support for both graphical and auditory output, and adherence to published conventions. Chapter addresses these issues in detail.

This document also acknowledges the importance of author preferences and the proper implementation of specifications. However, this document includes requirements to override certain author preferences when the user would not otherwise be able to access that content.

CONTROL OF AUTOMATIC BEHAVIOUR

Many of the requirements in this document give the user additional control over behaviour that would otherwise occur automatically. For instance, there is a requirement to allow configuration to not open a viewport automatically (checkpoint 5.3) and one that requires user confirmation before submitting a form (checkpoint 5.5). This type of manual configuration option may be essential for some users with disabilities, since automatic behaviour may be disorienting or interfere with navigation.

CONFIGURABILITY

This document includes requirements for users with a variety of disabilities, in part because some users may have more than one disability. In some cases, it may appear that two requirements contradict each other. For instance, a user with a physical disability may prefer that the user agent offer more automatic behaviour (to reduce demand for physical effort) than a user with a cognitive disability (for whom automatic behaviour may cause confusion). Thus, many of the requirements in this document involve configuration as one way to ensure that a functionality designed to improve accessibility for one user does not interfere with accessibility for another.

Also, since a default user agent setting may be useful for one user but interfere with accessibility for another, this document prefers configuration requirements to requirements for default settings.

Finally, there may be some cases where, for some content, a feature required by this document is ineffective or causes content to be less accessible, making it imperative that the user be able to turn off the feature.

- To avoid overwhelming users with an abundance of configuration options, this document includes requirements that promote ease of configuration and documentation of accessibility features.
- Device independence, spatial independence, and temporal independence
- Many requirements in this document promote different kinds of independence:
- Input and output device independence. This document includes some requirements to promote device-independence natively, as well as requirements for interoperability with assistive technologies that provide complementary input and output functionalities.
- Spatial independence. Some users may not navigate effectively in two-dimensional visual space (*e.g.*, users who do not use a pointing device) or may be constrained to one temporal dimension (*e.g.*, users of audio-only output).
- Temporal independence. Some users (*e.g.*, users with a physical or cognitive disability) may not be able to interact with content that changes over time, or interaction with content that is time-sensitive.

Additional Benefits of Accessible User Agent Design

In meeting the goals of users with disabilities, user agent developers will also improve access to the Web for users in general.

For example, users without disabilities:

- May have a text-only screen, a small screen, or a slow Internet connection (*e.g.*, via a mobile phone browser). These users are likely to benefit from the same features that provide access to people with low vision or blindness.
- May be in a situation where their eyes, ears, or hands are busy or interfered with (*e.g.*, driving to work or working in a noisy environment). These users are likely to benefit from the same features that provide access to people who cannot use a mouse or keyboard due to a visual, hearing, or physical disability.
- May not understand fluently the natural language of spoken content. These users are likely to benefit from the same visual rendering of text equivalents that make spoken language accessible to people with a hearing disability.
- The UAWG expects that software which satisfies the requirements of this document will be more flexible, manageable, extensible, and beneficial to all users. For example, a user agent architecture that allows programmatic access to content and the user interface will encourage software modularity and reuse, and will enable operation by scripting tools and automated test engines in addition to assistive technologies.

10

Global Network

USE OF COMPUTER

The Internet is a global network of computers. Every computer that is connected to the Internet is considered a part of that network. This means even your home computer. It's all a matter of degrees, you connect to your ISP's network, then your ISP connects to a larger network and so on. At the top of the tree is the high-capacity backbones, all of these interconnect at'Network Access Points''NAPs' at important regions around the world. The entire Internet is based on agreements between these backbone providers who set in place all the fibre optics lines and other technical aspects of the Internet. The first high speed backbone was created by the'National Science Foundation' in 1987.

The Internet was first created by the Advanced Research Projects Agency (ARPA) of the U.S. government in 1960's, and was first known as the ARPANet. At this stage the Internet's first computers were at academic and government institutions. They were mainly used for accessing files and to send e-mail. From 1983 onwards the Internet as we know it today started to form with the introduction of the communication protocol TCP/IP to ARPANet.

Since 1983 the Internet has accommodated alot of changes and continues to keep developing. The last two decades has seen the Internet accommodate such things as network LANs and ATM and frame switched services. The Internet continues to evolve with it becoming available on mobile phones and pagers and possibly on televisions in the future.

The actual term"Internet" was finally defined in 1995 by FNC (The Federal Networking Council). The resolution created by the The Federal Networking Council (FNC) agrees that the following language reflects our definition of the term"Internet"."Internet" refers to the global information system that,

EVOLUTION

The underpinnings of the Internet are formed by the global interconnection of hundreds of thousands of otherwise independent computers, communications entities and information systems. What makes this interconnection possible is the use of a set of communication standards, procedures and formats in common among the networks and the various devices and computational facilities connected to them. The procedures by which computers communicate with each other are called"protocols." While this infrastructure is steadily evolving to include new capabilities, the protocols initially used by the Internet are called the"TCP/IP" protocols, named after the two protocols that formed the principal basis for Internet operation.

On top of this infrastructure is an emerging set of architectural concepts and data structures for heterogeneous information systems that renders the Internet a truly global information system. In essence, the Internet is an architecture, although many people confuse it with its implementation. When the Internet is looked at as an architecture, it manifests two different abstractions. One abstraction deals with communications connectivity, packet delivery and a variety of end-end communication services. The other abstraction deals with the Internet as an information system, independent of its underlying communications infrastructure, which allows creation, storage and access to a wide range of information resources, including digital objects and related services at various levels of abstraction.

Interconnecting computers is an inherently digital problem. Computers process and exchange digital information, meaning that they use a discrete mathematical "binary" or"two-valued" language of 1s and 0s. For communication purposes, such information is mapped into continuous electrical or optical waveforms. The use of digital signaling allows accurate regeneration and reliable recovery of the underlying bits. We use the terms"computer,""computer resources" and"computation" to mean not only traditional computers, but also devices that can be controlled digitally over a network, information resources such as mobile programmes and other computational capabilities.

The telephone network started out with operators who manually connected telephones to each other through"patch panels" that accepted patch cords from each telephone line and electrically connected them to one another through the panel, which operated, in effect, like a switch. The result was called circuit switching, since at its conclusion, an electrical circuit was made between the calling telephone and the called telephone.

Conventional circuit switching, which was developed to handle telephone calls, is inappropriate for connecting computers because it makes limited use of the telecommunication facilities and takes too long to set up connections. Although reliable enough for voice communication, the circuit-switched voice network had difficulty delivering digital information without errors.

For digital communications, packet switching is a better choice, because it is far better suited to the typically"burst" communication style of computers. Computers that communicate typically send out brief but intense bursts of data, then remain silent for a while before sending out the next burst. These bursts are communicated as packets, which are very much like electronic postcards. The postcards, in reality packets, are relayed from computer to computer until they reach their destination.

The special computers that perform this forwarding function are called variously"packet switches" or"routers" and form the equivalent of many bucket brigades spanning continents and oceans, moving buckets of electronic postcards from one computer to another. Together these routers and the communication links between them form the underpinnings of the Internet.

Without packet switching, the Internet would not exist, as we now know it. Going back to the postcard analogy, postcards can get lost. They can be delivered out of order, and they can be delayed by varying amounts. The same is true of Internet packets, which, on the Internet, can even be duplicated. The Internet Protocol is the postcard layer of the Internet. The next higher layer of protocol, TCP, takes care of re-sending the"postcards" to recover packets that might have been lost, and putting packets back in order if they have become disordered in transit.

Of course, packet switching is about a billion times faster than the postal service or a bucket brigade would be. It also has to operate over many different communications systems, or substrata. The authors designed the basic architecture to be so simple and undemanding that it could work with most communication services. Many organizations, including commercial ones, carried out research using the TCP/IP protocols in the 1970s. E-mail was steadily used over the nascent Internet during that time and to the present. It was not until 1994 that the general public began to be aware of the Internet by way of the World Wide Web application, particularly after Netscape Communications was formed and released its browser and associated server software.

Thus, the evolution of the Internet was based on two technologies and a research dream. The technologies were packet switching and computer technology, which, in turn, drew upon the underlying technologies of digital communications and semiconductors. The research dream was to share information and computational resources. But that is simply the technical side of the story.

Equally important in many ways were the other dimensions that enabled the Internet to come into existence and flourish. This aspect of the story starts with cooperation and far-sightedness in the U.S. Government, which is often derided for lack of foresight but is a real hero in this story. It leads on to the enthusiasm of private sector interests to build upon the government funded developments to expand the Internet and make it available to the general public. Perhaps most important, it is fueled by the development of the personal computer industry and significant changes in the telecommunications industry in the 1980s, not the least of which was the decision to open the long distance market to competition. The role of workstations, the Unix operating system and local area networking (especially the Ethernet) are themes contributing to the spread of Internet technology in the 1980s into the research and academic community from which the Internet industry eventually emerged.

Many individuals have been involved in the development and evolution of the Internet covering a span of almost four decades if one goes back to the early writings on the subject of computer networking by Kleinrock, Licklider, Baran, Roberts, and Davies. The ARPANET, described below, was the first wide-area computer network. The NSFNET, which followed more than a decade later under the leadership of Erich Bloch, Gordon Bell, Bill Wulf and Steve Wolff, brought computer networking into the mainstream of the research and education communities. It is not our intent here to attempt to attribute credit to all those whose contributions were central to this story, although we mention a few of the key players

ROLE OF DARPA

Modern computer networking technologies emerged in the early 1970s. In 1969, The U.S. Defence Advanced Research Projects Agency (variously called ARPA and DARPA), an agency within the Department of Defence, commissioned a wide-area computer network called the ARPANET. This network made use of the new packet switching concepts for interconnecting computers and initially linked computers at universities and other research institutions in the United States and in selected NATO countries.

At that time, the ARPANET was essentially the only realistic wide-area computer network in existence, with a base of several dozen organizations, perhaps twice that number of computers and numerous researchers at those sites. The programme was led at DARPA by Larry Roberts. The packet switches were built by Bolt Beranek and Newman (BBN), a DARPA contractor. Others directly involved in the ARPANET activity included the authors, Len Kleinrock, Frank Heart, Howard Frank, Steve Crocker, Jon Postel and many many others in the ARPA research community.

Back then, the methods of internetworking (that is interconnecting computer networks) were primitive or non-existent. Two organizations could interwork technically by agreeing to use common equipment, but not every organization was interested in this approach. Absent that, there was jury-rigging, special case development and not much else. Each of these networks stood on its own with essentially no interaction between them - a far cry from today's Internet.

In the early 1970s, ARPA began to explore two alternative applications of packet switching technology based on the use of synchronous satellites (SATNET) and ground-based packet radio (PRNET). The decision by Kahn to link these two networks and the ARPANET as separate and independent networks resulted in the creation of the Internet programme and the subsequent collaboration with Cerf. These two systems differed in significant ways from the ARPANET so as to take advantage of the broadcast and wireless aspects of radio communications.

The strategy that had been adopted for SATNET originally was to embed the SATNET software into an ARPANET packet switch, and interwork the two networks through memory-to-memory transfers within the packet switch. This approach, in place at the time, was to make SATNET an"embedded" network within the ARPANET; users of the network would not even need to know of its existence. The technical team at Bolt Beranek and Newman (BBN), having built the ARPANET switches and now building the SATNET software, could easily produce the necessary patches to glue the programmes together in the same machine.

Indeed, this is what they were under contract with DARPA to provide. By embedding each new network into the ARPANET, a seamless internetworked capability was possible, but with no realistic possibility of unleashing the entrepreneurial networking spirit that has manifest itself in modern day Internet developments. A new approach was in order.

The Packet Radio (PRNET) programme had not yet gotten underway so there was ample opportunity to change the approach there. In addition, up until then, the SATNET programme was only an equipment development activity. No commitments had been obtained for the use of actual satellites or ground stations to access them. Indeed, since there was no domestic satellite industry in the U.S. then, the only two viable alternatives were the use of Intelsat or military satellites. The time for a change in strategy, if it was to be made, was then.

INTERNET ARCHITECTURE

The authors created architecture for interconnecting independent networks that could then be federated into a seamless whole without changing any of the underlying networks. This was the genesis of the Internet, as we know it today.

In order to work properly, the architecture required a global addressing mechanism (or Internet address) to enable computers on any network to reference and communicate with computers on any other network in the federation. Internet addresses fill essentially the same role as telephone numbers do in telephone networks. The design of the Internet assumed first that the individual networks could not be changed to accommodate new architectural requirements; but this was largely a pragmatic assumption to facilitate progress.

The networks also had varying degrees of reliability and speed. Host computers would have to be able to put disordered packets back into the correct order and discard duplicate packets that had been generated along the way. This was a major change from the virtual circuit-like service provided by ARPANET and by then contemporary commercial data networking services such as Tymnet and Telenet. In these networks, the underlying network took responsibility for keeping all information in order and for re-sending any data that might have been lost. The Internet design made the computers responsible for tending to these network problems.

A key architectural construct was the introduction of gateways (now called routers) between the networks to handle the disparities such as different data rates, packet sizes, error conditions, and interface specifications. The gateways would also check the destination Internet addresses of each packet to determine the gateway to which it should be forwarded.

These functions would be combined with certain end-end functions to produce the reliable communication from source to destination. A draft paper by the authors describing this approach was given at a meeting of the International Network Working Group in 1973 in Sussex, England and the final paper was subsequently published by the Institute for Electrical and Electronics Engineers, the leading professional society for the electrical engineering profession, in its Transactions on Communications in May, 1974.

DARPA contracted with Cerf's group at Stanford to carry out the initial detailed design of the TCP software and, shortly thereafter, with BBN and University College London to build independent implementations of the TCP protocol (as it was then called - it was later split into TCP and IP) for different machines. BBN also had a contract to build a prototype version of the gateway.

These three sites collaborated in the development and testing of the initial protocols on different machines. Cerf, then a professor at Stanford, provided the day-to-day leadership in the initial TCP software design and testing. BBN deployed the gateways between the ARPANET and the PRNET and also with SATNET. During this period, under Kahn's overall leadership at DARPA, the initial feasibility of the Internet Architecture was demonstrated.

The TCP/IP protocol suite was developed and refined over a period of four more years and, in 1980, it was adopted as a standard by the U.S. Department of Defence. On January 1, 1983 the ARPANET converted to TCP/IP as its standard host protocol. Gateways (or routers) were used to pass packets to and from host computers on"local area networks." Refinement and extension of these protocols and many others associated with them continues to this day by way of the Internet Engineering Task Force.

RUNNING THE INTERNET

The Domain Name System

The Internet evolved as an experimental system during the 1970s and early 1980s. It then flourished after the TCP/IP protocols were made mandatory on the ARPANET and other networks in January 1983; these protocols thus became the standard for many other networks as well. Indeed, the Internet grew so rapidly that the existing mechanisms for associating the names of host computers (*e.g.* UCLA, USC-ISI) to Internet addresses (known as IP addresses) were about to be stretched beyond acceptable engineering limits. Most of the applications in the Internet referred to the target computers by name.

These names had to be translated into Internet addresses before the lower level protocols could be activated to support the application. For a time, a group at SRI International in Menlo Park, CA, called the Network Information Center (NIC), maintained a simple, machine-readable list of names and associated Internet addresses which was made available on the net. Hosts on the Internet would simply copy this list, usually daily, so as to maintain a local copy of the table. This list was called the"host.txt" file (since it was simply a text file). The list served the function in the Internet that directory services (*e.g.* 411 or 703-555-1212) do in the US telephone system - the translation of a name into an address.

As the Internet grew, it became harder and harder for the NIC to keep the list current. Anticipating that this problem would only get worse as the network expanded, researchers at USC Information Sciences Institute launched an effort to design a more distributed way of providing this same information. The end result was the Domain Name System (DNS) which allowed hundreds of thousands of"name servers" to maintain small portions of a global database of information associating IP addresses with the names of computers on the Internet.

The naming structure was hierarchical in character. For example, all host computers associated with educational institutions would have names like"stanford.edu" or"ucla.edu". Specific hosts would have names like"cs.ucla.edu" to refer to a computer in the computer science department of UCLA, for example. A special set of computers called"root servers" maintained information about the names and addresses of other servers that contained more detailed name/address associations.

The designers of the DNS also developed seven generic"top level" domains, as follows:

- *Education*: EDU
- *Government*: GOV
- *Military*: MIL
- *International*: INT
- *Network*: NET
- *Organization*: ORG
- *Commercial*: COM

Under this system, for example, the host name"UCLA" became"UCLA.EDU" because it was operated by an educational institution, while the host computer for"BBN" became"BBN.COM" because it was a commercial organization. Top-level domain names also were created for every country: United Kingdom names would end in".UK," while the ending".FR" was created for the names of France.

The Domain Name System (DNS) was and continues to be a major element of the Internet architecture, which contributes to its scalability. It also contributes to controversy over trademarks and general rules for the creation and use of domain names, creation of new top-level domains and the like. At the same time, other resolution schemes exist as well. One of the authors (Kahn) has been involved in the development of a different kind of standard identification and resolution scheme that, for example, is being used as the base technology by book publishers to identify books on the Internet by adapting various identification schemes for use in the Internet environment. For example, International Standard Book Numbers (ISBNs) can be used as part of the identifiers. The identifiers then resolve to state information about the referenced books, such as location information (*e.g.* multiple sites) on the Internet that is used to access the books or to order them. These developments are taking place in parallel with the more traditional means of managing Internet resources. They offer an alternative to the existing Domain Name System with enhanced functionality.

The growth of Web servers and users of the Web has been remarkable, but some people are confused about the relationship between the World Wide Web and the Internet. The Internet is the global information system that includes communication capabilities and many high level applications. The Web is one such application.

The existing connectivity of the Internet made it possible for users and servers all over the world to participate in this activity. Electronic mail is another important application. As of today, over 60 million computers take part in the Internet and about 3.6 million web sites were estimated to be accessible on the net. Virtually every user of the net has access to electronic mail and web browsing capability. E-mail remains a critically important application for most users of the Internet, and these two functions largely dominate the use of the Internet for most users.

INTERNET STANDARDS PROCESS

Internet standards were once the output of research activity sponsored by DARPA. The principal investigators on the internetting research effort essentially determined what technical features of the TCP/IP protocols would become common. The initial work in this area started with the joint effort of the two authors, continued in Cerf's group at Stanford, and soon thereafter was joined by engineers and scientists at BBN and University College London. This informal arrangement has changed with time and details can be found elsewhere.

At present, the standards efforts for Internet are carried out primarily under the auspices of the Internet Society (ISOC). The Internet Engineering

Task Force (IETF) operates under the leadership of its Internet Engineering Steering Group (IESG), which is populated by appointees approved by the Internet Architecture Board (IAB) which is, itself, now part of the Internet Society. The IETF comprises over one hundred working groups categorized and managed by Area Directors specializing in specific categories. There are other bodies with considerable interest in Internet standards or in standards that must interwork with the Internet.

Examples include the International Telecommunications Union Telecommunicationsstandards group (ITU-T), the International Institute of Electrical and Electronic Engineers (IEEE) local area network standards group (IEEE 801), the Organization for International Standardization (ISO), the American National Standards Institute (ANSI), the World Wide Web Consortium (W3C), and many others.

As Internet access and services are provided by existing media such as telephone, cable and broadcast, interactions with standards bodies and legal structures formed to deal with these media will become an increasingly complex matter. The intertwining of interests is simultaneously fascinating and complicated, and has increased the need for thoughtful cooperation among many interested parties.

MANAGING THE INTERNET

Perhaps the least understood aspect of the Internet is its management. In recent years, this subject has become the subject of intense commercial and international interest, involving multiple governments and commercial organizations, and recently congressional hearings. At issue is how the Internet will be managed in the future, and, in the process, what oversight mechanisms will insure that the public interest is adequately served.

In the 1970s, managing the Internet was easy. Since few people knew about the Internet, decisions about almost everything of real policy concern were made in the offices of DARPA. It became clear in the late 1970s, however, that more community involvement in the decision-making processes was essential. In 1979, DARPA formed the Internet Configuration Control Board (ICCB) to insure that knowledgeable members of the technical community discussed critical issues, educated people outside of DARPA about the issues, and helped others to implement the TCP/IP protocols and gateway functions. At the time, there were no companies that offered turnkey solutions to getting on the Internet.

It would be another five years or so before companies like Cisco Systems were formed, and while there were no PCs yet, the only workstations available were specially built and their software was not generally configured for use with external networks; they were certainly considered expensive at the time.

In 1983, the small group of roughly twelve ICCB members was reconstituted (with some substitutions) as the Internet Activities Board (IAB), and about ten"Task Forces" were established under it to address issues in specific technical areas. The attendees at Internet Working Group meetings were invited to become members of as many of the task forces as they wished.

The management of the Domain Name System offers a kind of microcosm of issues now frequently associated with overall management of the Internet's operation and evolution. Someone had to take responsibility for overseeing the system's general operation. In particular, top-level domain names had to be selected, along with persons or organizations to manage each of them. Rules for the allocation of Internet addresses had to be established. DARPA had previously asked the late Jon Postel of the USC Information Sciences Institute to take on numerous functions related to administration of names, addresses and protocol related matters. With time, Postel assumed further responsibilities in this general area on his own, and DARPA, which was supporting the effort, gave its tacit approval. This activity was generally referred to as the Internet Assigned Numbers Authority (IANA). In time, Postel became the arbitrator of all controversial matters concerning names and addresses until his untimely death in October 1998. It is helpful to consider separately the problem of managing the domain name space and the Internet address space. These two vital elements of the Internet architecture have rather different characteristics that colour the management problems they generate. Domain names have semantics that numbers may not imply; and thus a means of determining who can use what names is needed. As a result, speculators on Internet names often claim large numbers of them without intent to use them other than to resell them later. Alternate resolution mechanisms, if widely adopted, could significantly change the landscape here.

The rapid growth of the Internet has triggered the design of a new and larger address space (the so-called IP version 6 address space); today's Internet uses IP version 4. However, little momentum has yet developed to deploy IPv6 widely. Despite concerns to the contrary, the IPv4 address space will not be depleted for some time. Further, the use of Dynamic Host Configuration Protocol (DHCP) to dynamically assign IP addresses has also cut down on demand for dedicated IP addresses. Nevertheless, there is growing recognition in the Internet technical community that expansion of the address space is needed, as is the development of transition schemes that allow interoperation between IPv4 and IPv6 while migrating to IPv6.

In 1998, the Internet Corporation for Assigned Names and Numbers (ICANN) was formed as a private sector, non-profit, organization to oversee the orderly progression in use of Internet names and numbers, as well as certain protocol related matters that required oversight. The birth of this organization, which was selected by the Department of Commerce for this function, has been difficult, embodying as it does many of the inherent conflicts in resolving discrepancies in this arena. However, there is a clear need for an oversight mechanism for Internet domain names and numbers, separate from their day-to-day management. Many questions about Internet management remain. They may also prove difficult to resolve quickly. Of specific concern is what role the U.S. government and indeed governments around the world need to play in its continuing operation and evolution. This is clearly a subject for another time.

ADVANTAGES OF INTERNET

There are many advantages of using the Internet, such as:

Global Audience

Content published on the World Wide Web is immediately available to a global audience of users. This makes the World Wide Web a very cost-effective medium to publish information. Reaching more than 190 countries.

Operates 24 hours and 365 days

You don't need to wait until resources are available to conduct business. From a consumer's perspective as well as a provider's business can be consummated at any time. The fact that the Internet is operational at all times makes it the most efficient business machine to date.

Relatively Inexpensive

It is relatively inexpensive to publish information on the Internet. At a fraction of the cost to publish information by traditional methods, various organizations and individuals can now distribute information to millions of users. It costs only a few thousand dollars to establish an Internet presence and publish content on the Internet.

Product Advertising

You can use the World Wide Web to advertise various products. Before purchasing a product, customers will be able to look up various product specification sheets and find out additional information. You can use the multimedia capabilities of the World Wide Web to make available not only various product specification sheets but also audio files, images, and even video clips of products in action. The beauty of the Web is that it allows customers to explore products in as much detail as they desire. If the client just wants a general overview, he or she can look at the advertising information. For those wanting more in depth information, you can provide white papers and product descriptions for download. The Web allows a business to provide timely information, you can simply place the information on the Web page and it is available immediately for your customers.

Distribute Product Catalogs

The World Wide Web is a very effective medium for distributing product catalogs. In the old days, putting together a product catalog used to be very costly in terms of time and money needed to publish and distribute it. The World Wide Web changes all this by allowing content developers to put together a sales catalog and make it available to millions of users immediately. Furthermore, unlike printed product catalogs that are usually updated around once a month, product catalogs on the World Wide Web can be updated as needed to respond to various changing market conditions.

Online Surveys

Traditional methods of performing surveys are often relatively slow and expensive compared to online surveys conducted on the Internet. For example, in order to fill out various needs of customers or what they would like to see in a future product, it's often necessary to compile a list of address and mail a questionnaire to many customers. The success of such an attempt is not always guaranteed and can be very costly in terms of mailing the questionnaires and entering responses to a databases and analyzing it.

On the other hand, you can use the World Wide Web to automate the whole process. For example, you can set up a CGI script to conduct online surveys. Results of such a survey can be automatically updated to a database. This database can then be used to keep a pulse on various opinions and needs of customers.

Announcements

With the World Wide Web, you can distribute various announcements to millions of users in a timely manner. Because there is virtually no time lag from the time it takes to publish information to making the information available to users, the Web is an ideal medium to publicize announcements. As more people discover the virtues of the Web and get connected to the Internet, the Web will become the medium of choice for many organizations and individuals to publicize various announcements.

Provide Technical Support

You can also use Web site to provide technical support to users. Because Web pages can be updated immediately with new information, various technical support literature can be immediately modified in light of new findings and developments. This can be accomplished without having to distribute changes to all users affected by any changes using traditional mediums of information distribution, which are often quite costly compared to the World Wide Web.

Create Online Discussion Forums

By using applications such as WebBoard, it's possible to set up online discussion forums on the Web.

Obtain Customer Feedback

The interactive nature of the World Wide Web is ideal for obtaining customer feedback. You can easily set up a CGI script to obtain customer feedback about a product or service. Because customer feedback submitted by customers can be read immediately, it's possible to respond to various customer concerns in a timely manner, increasing customer satisfaction and quality of customer service.

Immediate Distribution of Information

When information is added to a Web site, it's immediately available for browsing by millions of Internet users. The World Wide Web is an ideal medium of information distribution because it takes away the time lag associated with publishing content and actually making it available to users

Easy Integration with Internal Information Systems

Internet information systems deployed on the Internet can be easily integrated with internal information systems managed with office productivity applications such as Microsoft Office.

Powerful Content Publishing Tools

A new breed of Internet aware applications will start emerging in software stores by the time you read this. These applications will enable users to develop content for the World Wide Web by simply saving as an HTML file. In addition to software developers making existing applications Internet aware, various new, powerful, and easy-to use Internet content publishing applications are also being developed. These applications will make the task of publishing content on the Internet even easier. Most of these applications are developed for Windows users.

Multimedia

The capability to incorporate multimedia into Web pages is a major advantage of using World Wide Web to publish information. For example, many Web sites use sounds and video clips to make the content easier and more interesting to browse.

Formatting Capabilities

Content published on the World Wide Web can be richly formatted by using various HTML tags and graphic formats. The capability to do this is a major reason for the success of the World Wide Web. In addition to using HTML tags and various multimedia formats in Web pages, various interactive controls can also be added to a web page. This capability allows Web site content developers to create"active" Web sites. For example, before a user sends some information to a Web server for processing, a VBScript or

JavaScript subroutine can be used to verify information typed in by the user. Various formatting capabilities, along with technologies such as Java and VBScript, make the World Wide Web a richly interactive medium that you can use to distribute information to millions of users.

DISADVANTAGES OF INTERNET

Many fear the Internet because of its disadvantages. They claim to not use the Internet because they are afraid of the possible consequences or are simply not interested. People who have yet connected to the Internet claim they are not missing anything. Today's technological society must realise, it is up to them to protect themselves on the Internet.

Children using the Internet has become a big concern. Most parents do not realise the dangers involved when their children log onto the Internet. When children are online, they can easily be lured into something dangerous. When children talk to others online, they do not realise they could actually be talking to a harmful person. In addition, children may also receive pornography online by mistake; therefore, causing concern among parents everywhere.

Whether surfing the Web, reading newsgroups, or using e-mail, children can be exposed to extremely inappropriate material. Pornographic sites tend to make sure they are the first sites to be listed in any search area. Some critics say that parents are responsible for their own children on the Internet because there are available services to protect children. To keep children safe, parents and teachers must be aware of the dangers. They must actively guide and guard their children online.There are a number of tools available today that may help keep the Internet environment safer for children.

Musicians are also concerned with disadvantages to the Net such as, accessibility and freedom. They are upset because the Internet provides their music online at no charge to consumers. File-sharing software, such Kazaa, Emule and may others provides copyrighted songs to all Internet users. The main concern is - the music is free! Musicians feel"they are not getting paid for their work". It is almost impossible to close down all file-sharing services; there are too many of them to count.

Another major disadvantage of the Internet is privacy. Electronic messages sent over the Internet can be easily snooped and tracked, revealing who is talking to whom and what they are talking about. As people surf the Internet, they are constantly giving information to web sites. People should become aware that the collection, selling, or sharing of the information they provide online increases the chances that their information will fall into the wrong hands. When giving personal information on the Internet, people should make sure the Web site is protected with a recognizable security symbol. On the other hand, this does not mean they are fully protected because anyone may obtain a user's information.

Today, not only are humans getting viruses, but computers are also. Computers are mainly getting these viruses from the Internet; yet, viruses may also be transmitted through floppy disks. However, people should mainly be concerned about receiving viruses from the Internet. Some of these dangerous viruses destroy the computer's entire hard drive, meaning that the user can no longer access the computer. Virus protection is highly recommended

In conclusion, today's society is in the middle of a technological boom. People can either choose to take advantage of this era, or simply let it pass them by. The Internet is a very powerful tool. It has many advantages; however, people need to be extremely aware of the disadvantages as well.

11

Intra-Network

For such an extensive and involved subject, which includes so many different technologies, hardware devices and protocols, the definition of networking is actually quite simple. A network is simply a collection of computers or other hardware devices that are connected together, either physically or logically, using special hardware and software to allow them to exchange information and cooperate. Networking is the term that describes the processes involved in designing, implementing, upgrading, managing and otherwise working with networks and network technologies.

Networks are used for an incredible array of different purposes. In fact, the definitions above are so simple for the specific reason that networks can be used so broadly, and can allow such a wide variety of tasks to be accomplished. While most people learning about networking focus on the interconnection of PCs and other"true" computers, you use various types of networks every day. Each time you pick up a phone, use a credit card at a store, get cash from an ATM machine, or even plug in an electrical appliance, you are using some type of network.

In fact, the definition can even be expanded beyond the world of technology altogether: I'm sure you've heard the term"networking" used to describe the process of finding an employer or employee by talking to friends and associates. In this case too, the idea is that independent units are connected together to share information and cooperate.

The widespread networking of personal computers is a relatively new phenomenon. For the first decade or so of their existence, PCs were very much"islands unto themselves", and were rarely connected together. In the early 1990s, PC networking began to grow in popularity as businesses realised the advantages that networking could provide. By the late 1990s, networking in homes with two or more PCs started to really take off as well.

This interconnection of small devices represents, in a way, a return to the"good old days" of mainframe computers. Before computers were small and personal, they were large and centralized machines that were shared by many users operating remote terminals. While having all of the computer power in one place had many disadvantages, one benefit was that all users were connected because they shared the central computer. Individualized PCs took away that advantage, in favour of the benefits of independence. Networking attempts to move computing into the middle ground, providing PC users with the best of both worlds: the independence and flexibility of personal computers, and the connectivity and resource sharing of mainframes. in fact, networking is today considered so vital that it's hard to conceive of an organization with two or more computers that would not want to connect them together!

TYPES OF NETWORKING

The word"networking" strikes fear into legions of otherwise intrepid job hunters. It conjures up one of three images: calling everyone in your address book to see whether anyone knows anyone who may know anyone who may give you an informational interview, attending club meetings with other job hunters or having your friends come up with ideas and contacts instead of advising you to get out there and network. But there is no need to fear because there are many different types of networking techniques you can use to help with your job search and references.

Obviously number three doesn't always work. But the other two aren't so appealing either. Who enjoys calling total strangers and asking them to meet with you when there's nothing in it for them? If they're successful in what they do - and why else would you want to meet with them? - they're likely to be busy doing it.

STRONG-CONTACT NETWORKS

Structured explicitly to pass business referrals among members, they allow only one member per profession. Strong-contact networks are particularly good for developing in-depth relationships because you see the same members week after week and pass referrals as a part of each meeting.

CASUAL-CONTACT NETWORKS

Bring businesspeople together in a less-structured context than strong-contact networks, but for many they are a primary source of referrals; membership is not limited by profession. These groups are good for developing breadth in your network, but deep, long-lasting relationships can be formed as well.

SERVICE ORGANIZATIONS

Associations that exist to provide and support humanitarian efforts and good works in the community and larger venues. They also bring people together in settings that facilitate referral and knowledge networking. Like casual-contact groups, they help you add breadth and diversity to your network.

PROFESSIONAL ASSOCIATIONS

Established to exchange information and ideas among those in a given industry, as well as to promote and support that industry. These networks often include direct competitors, but they also provide contacts in related, non-competing businesses as well.

SOCIAL/BUSINESS ORGANIZATIONS

Combine social activities with business networking and can provide a variety of networking opportunities; many tend to resemble singles bars.

WOMEN'S NETWORKING GROUPS

Still important networking organizations, but are slowly disappearing as women enter the business mainstream, especially as professionals, entrepreneurs, and small-business owners.

ONLINE NETWORKS

A new phenomenon covering a wide range of interests.

TYPES OF COMPUTER NETWORKS

A computer network is two or more computers connected together using a telecommunication system for the purpose of communication and sharing resources". Ask any computer network expert to simplify this definition to you and you will start a debate on how it should not be just two computers but three. Simply put a network is a means of communication between computers. Within a given network, computers can send files, e-mails and other correspondence to each other. Even things like instant messaging, is set up within a computer's network.

LAN

LAN or Local Area Network is the most common kind of network set up. There are two ways to connect a LAN network. The simplest and easiest way is the peer-to-peer connection network. This is when two or more computers are directly connected to each other.

For example if there were four computers in the network, computer 1 would be connected to computer 2, computer 2 would be connected to computer 3 and computer 3 would be connected to computer 4. This means each computer is dependent on the other.

And if there were a network problem with any one computer, all of them would be affected. The other type if the client server connection. This is the type of connection where all the computers in a given network are connected to one central computer. This is a more complicated network but one that is much more efficient that peer-to-peer. A local area network, or LAN, is a network of connected computers in a room, building, or set of buildings. Local area networks have been around since the beginning of computer use. A LAN is defined as a user network whereby data is sent at high rates between people located relatively close to each other. LANs do not usually make use of leased communication lines, but only means of communication that are provided by the installer of the network.

The Internet is a wide area network, or WAN, which is distinct from a LAN. In contrast to the term Internet, local area networks are often called intranets, though sometimes this term refers to a cluster of LANs associated with a particular company or organization but not connected to the larger Internet. A local area network uses a hub or router to connect computers together. The means of communication is the omnipresent Ethernet cable or wireless wi-fi technology. These technologies offer data transfer rates running between 10 to 10000 Mbit/s. Larger, more important LANs have redundant lines or other backup protocols. In networked computers, the most popular communication protocol is TCP/IP. Smaller LANs may be temporary and used between friends to play computer games over the network. Over a network, users can share files, view files, make changes to data on other computers if permitted, play movies or music on multiple computers at once, chat with instant messaging, send e-mails to each other, play games, and so on. All the advantages of the Internet apply, although they only include others on the LAN, and the data transfer rates are high.

Perhaps the most frequently employed use of a LAN is to connect users to the Internet with only one connected router. In modern times, we use broadband cable or DSL modems to connect to the Internet, and it would be clumsy to have a modem associated with every computer, so we simply plug the modem into a router and link the router to computers with Ethernet cables. Configuring a LAN can be intimidating at first, but contemporary operating systems have programmes that do most of the necessary configurations automatically, so setting up a local area network is pretty easy. A local area network (LAN) supplies networking capability to a group of computers in close proximity to each other such as in an office building, a school, or a home. A LAN is useful for sharing resources like files, printers, games or other applications. A LAN in turn often connects to other LANs, and to the Internet or other WAN. Most local area networks are built with relatively inexpensive hardware such as Ethernet cables, network adapters, and hubs. Wireless LAN and other more advanced LAN hardware options also exist.

Examples

The most common type of local area network is an Ethernet LAN. The smallest home LAN can have exactly two computers; a large LAN can accommodate many thousands of computers. Many LANs are divided into logical groups called subnets. An Internet Protocol (IP)"Class A" LAN can in theory accommodate more than 16 million devices organized into subnets.

The High Performance Network

The HPN is used for the exchange of large amounts of operational data. Two Force10 E600 Routers, interconnected via 4-way 10-Gigabit Ethernet aggregated links, provide connectivity between the High Performance Computing Facility (HPCF) and the Data-Handling System (DHS). The HPCF network nodes are connected via 10-Gigabit Ethernet and all DHS nodes via Gigabit Ethernet aggregated links.

The General Purpose Network

The GPN is used for all other traffic. It has at its core two Foundry BigIron RX-16 routers and at the edge seven Foundry Super-X switches. The core routers are interconnected via 4-way 10-Gigabit Ethernet aggregated links and have multiple Gigabit Ethernet uplinks to the edge routers. The core also includes two further Super-X switches that are dual-attached to the RX-16s via 10-Gigabit Ethernet.

The GPN provides connectivity to:

- The HPCF, the DHS and additional servers via Gigabit Ethernet ports in the core.
- The user desktops and laptops via Gigabit Ethernet ports on the edge switches.
- The firewalls (for the Wide Area Network and the Demilitarized Zone (DMZ) via Gigabit Ethernet ports in the core. The DMZ includes ECaccess, web servers, the mail gateway and DNS (Domain Name Servers).

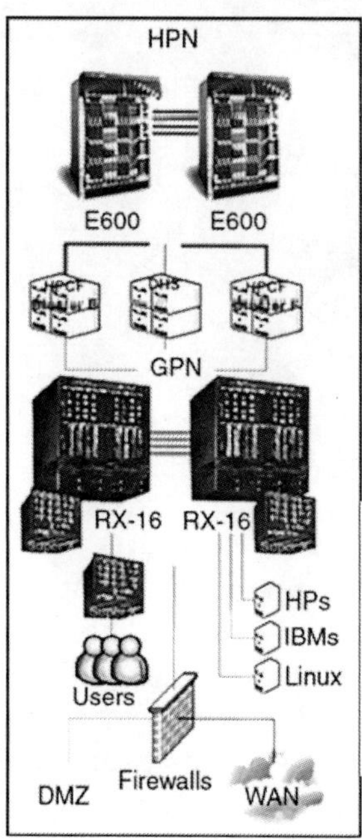

The Hardware

Both the Force10 E600 chassis are populated with 24 10-Gigabit-Ethernet and 144 Gigabit Ethernet ports. For resiliency there are four power supplies, two CPU modules and nine switching fabric modules. Both the RX-16 chassis are populated with 8 10-Gigabit Ethernet ports and 144 Gigabit Ethernet ports. For resiliency there are seven power supplies, two CPU modules and four switching fabric modules. The Super-X chassis each contain up to 156 Gigabit Ethernet ports and dual power-supplies.

WAN

Definition

The wide area network, often referred to as a WAN, is a communications network that makes use of existing technology to connect local computer networks into a larger working network that may cover both national and international locations. This is in contrast to both the local area network and the metropolitan area network, which provides communication within a restricted geographic area. Here is how the wide area network functions, and why it is so important to communications today.

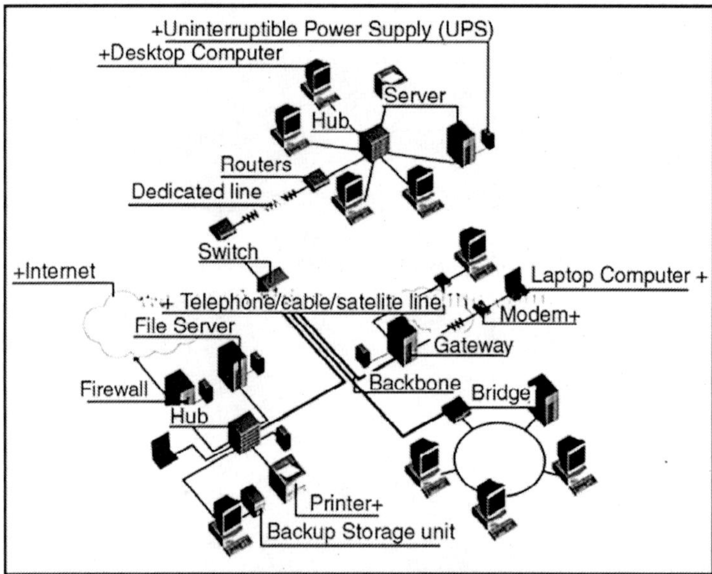

The concept of linking one computer network with another is often desirable, especially for businesses that operate a number of facilities. Beginning with the local area network and going up to the wide area network, this is most easily accomplished by using existing telephony technology. Essentially, fibre optics are used to create the link between networks located in different facilities. Often, this means using standard phone lines, referred to as POTS, or employing PSTN (public switched telephone network)

technology. During the 1990s, a third option, that of ISDN (integrated services digital network) solutions for creation a wide area network gained a great deal of popularity, mainly because the concept made it more cost effective to extend the network beyond national boundaries.

With coverage in a broad area, a wide area network allows companies to make use of common resources in order to operate. For example, many retail drugstores make use of a wide area network as part of their support to customers who fill prescriptions with one of their stores. Once in the common customer database for the pharmacy, the client is free to fill a prescription at any of the company's locations, even while vacationing in another state.

Companies also make good use of the wide area network as well. Internal functions such as sales, production and development, marketing and accounting can also be shared with authorized locations through this sort of broad area network application. The concept of a wide area network as a means of taking individual location based computer networks and using them to create a unified computer network for the entire corporation means that employees can work from just about anywhere. Should one facility be damaged or rendered inaccessible due to natural disaster, employees simply move to another location where they can access the unified network, and keep on working.

OVERVIEW

WAN or Wide Area Network is when several LANs or independent computers are connected to a single, wider network. The Internet is the perfect example of WAN. E-mails, Chat Rooms and IMs all connect to the WAN of the Internet. WAN is much more complex and requires connecting devices or hubs from all over the world.

The term Wide Area Network (WAN) usually refers to a network which covers a large geographical area, and use communications circuits to connect the intermediate nodes. A major factor impacting WAN design and performance is a requirement that they lease communications circuits from telephone companies or other communications carriers. Transmission rates are typically 2 Mbps, 34 Mbps, 45 Mbps, 155 Mbps, 625 Mbps (or sometimes considerably more).

Numerous WANs have been constructed, including public packet networks, large corporate networks, military networks, banking networks, stock brokerage networks, and airline reservation networks. Some WANs are very extensive, spanning the globe, but most do not provide true global coverage. Organizations supporting WANs using the Internet Protocol are known as Network Service Providers (NSPs). These form the core of the Internet. Wide Area Networks, or WANs, connect a geographically diverse group of computers within a state, country, or even across several states or countries. WANs typically are connected by telephone lines, other types of communication lines, or radio waves. Quite often, smaller local area networks (LANs) are linked together to form a WAN. This is accomplished via dedicated private lines, leased from telecommunications firms like Sprint and AT&T, or by Switched Multi-Megabit Data Services (SMDS) technology, developed in 1995 to eliminate the need for a leased line.

WAN technology has been refined over a period of several decades. It first emerged in the mid-twentieth century with the advent of networks like ARPAnet. Developed in 1969 by the Department of Defence, ARPAnet and several other networks eventually evolved into the Internet, the largest WAN in the world. The packet switching technology most commonly used with WANs surfaced in the 1960s, and standard packet switching protocol, known as X.25, was developed in 1976. To increase network speed, packet switching allows for the parceling of data into smaller chunks, known as packets, prior to transmission. These packets can travel independently via alternate routes, and they are reassembled once they reach their target. Although X.25 remained the most popular WAN packet switching protocol for years, other packet switching protocols used with increasing frequency by WAN developers and administrators include the Internet standard, Transmission Control Protocol/ Internet Protocol (TCP/IP), and Frame Relay, used most often by WANs connected via high speed T-1 and T-3 lines.

WANs are used for a variety of purposes. A corporation with offices in several locations may use a WAN to form an intranet. Quite often, the individual offices will use their own LANs for things like internal messaging, data processing functions, and hardware and software sharing. When these LANs are joined together to form a WAN, similar data sharing and messaging capabilities become possible across a much broader geographic area.

Businesses wanting to link up with their suppliers or distributors may create a WAN as a means of establishing an extranet. For example, an extranet could provide a sales representative with electronic access to information in about the time it might take to deliver a product, or the availability of a product. Some WANs bring together various types of communications, such as data, video, and voice. Some organizations, including companies, universities, research centers, hospitals, and libraries, use WANs to connect to the Internet. By connecting the NSP WANs together using links at Internet Packet Interchanges (sometimes called"peering points") a global communication infrastructure is formed. NSPs do not generally handle individual customer accounts (except for the major corporate customers), but instead deal with intermediate organizations whom they can charge for high capacity communications. They generally have an agreement to exchange certain volumes of data at a certain"quality of service" with other NSPs. So practically any NSP can reach any other NSP, but may require the use of one or more other NSP networks to reach the required destination. NSPs vary in terms of the transit delay, transmission rate, and connectivity offered.

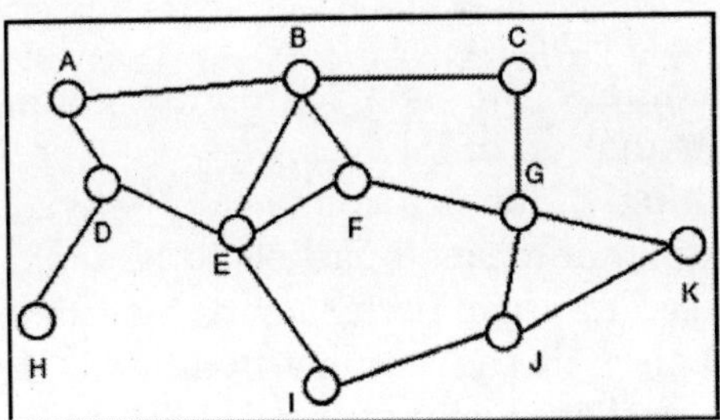

Fig. Typical"mesh" connectivity of a Wide Area Network

A typical network is shown in the figure above. This connects a number of End Systems (ES) (*e.g.* A, C, H, K) and a number of Intermediate Systems (IS) (*e.g.* B, D, E, F, G, I, J) to form a network over which data may be communicated between the End Systems (ES). The characteristics of the transmission facilities lead to an emphasis on efficiency of communications techniques in the design of WANs. Controlling the volume of traffic and avoiding excessive delays is important. Since the topologies of WANs are likely to be more complex than those of LANs, routing algorithms also receive more emphasis. Many WANs also implement sophisticated monitoring procedures to account for which users consume the network resources. This is, in some cases, used to generate billing information to charge individual users.

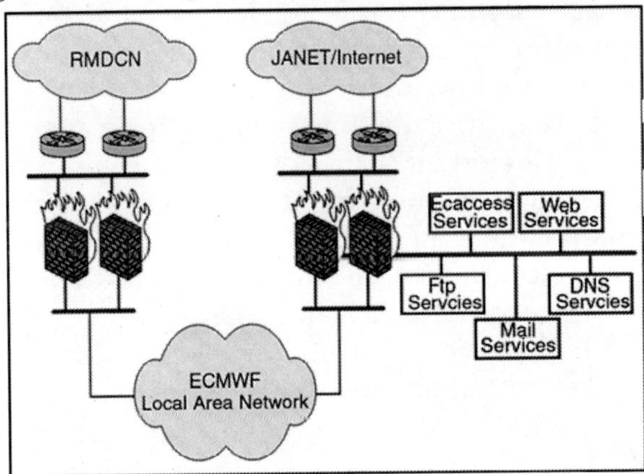

The size of a network is limited due to size and distance constraints.

However networks may be connected over a high-speed communications link (called a WAN link) to link them together and thus becomes a WAN.

WAN links are usually:

- Dial up connection
- Dedicated connection - It is a permanent full time connection. When a dedicated connection is used, the cable is leased rather than a part of the cable bandwidth and the user has exclusive use.
- Switched network - Several users share the same line or the bandwidth of the line.

There are two types of switched networks:

- Circuit switching - This is a temporary connection between two points such as dial-up or ISDN.
- Packet switching - This is a connection between multiple points. It breaks data down into small packets to be sent across the network.

A virtual circuit can improve performance by establishing a set path for data transmission. This will shave some overhead of a packet switching network. A variant of packet switching is called cell-switching where the data is broken into small cells with a fixed length.

WAN CONNECTION TECHNOLOGIES

- X.25: This is a set of protocols developed by the CCITT/ITU which specifies how to connect computer devices over an internet work. These protocols use a great deal of error checking for use over unreliable telephone lines. They establish a virtual communication circuit. It uses a store and forward method which can cause about a half second delay in data reception when two way communications are used. Their speed is about 64Kbps. Normally X.25 is used on packed switching PDNs (Public Data Networks). A line must be leased from the LAN to a PDN to connect to an X.25 network. A PAD (packet assembler/disassembler) or an X.25 interface is used on a computer to connect to the X.25 network. CCITT is an abbreviation for International Telegraph and Telephone Consultative Committee. The ITU is the International Telecommunication Union.
- *Frame Relay*: Devices at both sides of the connection handle Error checking. Frame relay uses frames of varying length and it operates at the data link layer of the OSI model. A permanent virtual circuit (PVC) is established between two points on the network. Frame relay speed is between 56Kbps and 1.544Mbps. Frame relay networks provide a high-speed connection up to 1.544Mbps using variable-length packet switching over digital fibre-optic media. Frame relay does not store data and has less error checking than X.25.
- *Switched Multi-megabit Data Service (SMDS)*: Uses fixed length cell switching and runs at speeds of 1.533 to 45Mbps. It provides no error checking and assumes devices at both ends provide error checking.
- Telephone connections
  - Dial up
  - *Leased lines*: These are dedicated analog lines or digital lines. Dedicated digital lines are called digital data service (DDS) lines. A modem is used to connect to analog lines, and a Channel Service Unit/Data Service Unit or Digital Service Unit(CSU/DSU) is used to connect to digital lines. The DSU connects to the LAN and the CSU connects to the line.

– *T Carrier lines*: Multiplexors are used to allow several channels on one line. The T1 line is basic T Carrier service. The available channels may be used separately for data or voice transmissions or they may be combined for more transmission bandwidth. The 64Kbps data transmission rate is referred to as DS-0 (Digital Signal level 0) and a full T1 line is referred to as DS-1.

Signal	**System**	**Total Kbps**	**Channels lines**	**Number of equivalent T1**
DS-1	T1	1544	24	1
DS-2	T2	6312	96	4
DS-3	T3	44736	672	28
DS-4	T4	274760	4032	3668

– T1 and T3 lines are the most common lines in use today. T1 and T2 lines can use standard copper wire. T3 and T4 lines require fibre-optic cable or other high-speed media. These lines may be leased partially called fractional T1 or fractional T3, which means a customer, can lease a certain number of channels on the line. A CSU/DSU and a bridge or router is required to connect to a T1 line.

– Integrated Services Digital Network (ISDN) - Comes in two types and converts analog signals to digital for transmission. It is a dial up service

- Basic Rate ISDN (BRI) - Two 64Kbps B-channels with one 16Kbps D channel. The D-channel is used tor call control and setup.
- Primary Rate ISDN (PRI) - 23 B-channels and one D channel.

A device resembling a modem (called an ISDN modem) is used to connect to ISDN. The computer and telephone line are plugged into it.

– Switched-56 - A switched line similar to a leased line where customers pay for the time they use the line. Speed is 56Kbps. It is not dedicated and will not work to connect a WAN.

- Asynchronous Transfer Mode (ATM) - May be used over a variety of media with both baseband and broadband systems.

It is used for audio, video, and data. It uses fixed length data packets of 53 8 bit bytes called cell switching. 5 bytes contain header information. The cell contains path information that the packet is to use. It uses hardware devices to perform the switching of the data. Speeds from 155Mbps to 622 Mbps are achieved. Error checking is done at the receiving device, not by ATM. A permanent virtual connection or circuit (PVC) is established.

It may also use a switched virtual circuit (SVC). Service classes:

- Constant bit rate for data.

- Variable bit rate for audio or video.
- Connection less for data.
- Connection oriented for data.

ATM can be embedded in other protocols such as ATM-25, T1, T3, OC-1, OC-3, OC-12, and OC-48.

Some ATM technologies include:

- ATM-25 - 25Mbps speed.
- STS-3 - 155Mbps on fibre or category 5 cable.
- STS-12 - 620 Mbps on fibre cable for campus wide network.
- STS-48 - 2.2 Gbps on fibre cable on a MAN.
- STS-192 - 8.8 Gbps on fibre cable on intercity long distance. Phone companies normally use this.

Synchronous Optical Network (SONET) - A physical layer standard that defines voice, data, and video delivery methods over fibre optic media. It defines data rates in terms of optical carrier (OC) levels. The transmission rate of OC-1 is 51.8 Mbps. Each level runs at a multiple of the first. The OC-5 data rate is 5 times 51.8 Mbps which is 259 Mbps. SONET also defines synchronous transport signals (STS) for copper media which use the same speed scale of OC levels. STS-3 runs at the same speed of OC-3. Mesh or ring topology is used to support SONET. SONET uses multiplexing. The ITU has incorporated SONET into their Synchronous Digital Hierarchy (SDH) recommendations.

NETWORKING TOPOLOGIES

DEFINITION

Network topology refers to the way that your computer network is arranged. The network can have a physical or a logical topology. The physical topology describes the layout of computers and where the workstations are positioned. The logical network topology describes how the information flows through the network. Choosing your physical topology is important because if it is not chosen correctly, this could cause your network to not operate properly. There are several terms that describe the type of physical topology that a network can have. The most common topologies are bus, ring, star, and mesh. In a bus topology, all of the computers are attached to a single cable using terminators. The terminators work to absorb the energy from the signals in the network. The bus topology is easy to install, but it is not reliable because a single default can bring down your network.

In a ring topology, each computer is connected directly to two other computers on the network. As with a bus topology, a single fault can disrupt a ring network. This type of network does have advantages, however, and does not require a network server. In a star topology, each computer is connected using its own separate cable. This set up is more reliable than a bus topology because its design makes it fault tolerant and susceptible to errors.

The information on the network is transmitted from one system to another and the data flows in one single direction. The topology is expensive to maintain and is not reliable because removing one computer can disrupt your entire network. In a mesh topology, a path is present from one computer to another computer in the network. The mesh topology is usually used in internet structure. The mesh topology can be complicated to construct because it has multiple connection between locations. For every computer that you have you will need at least one and a half connections for each one. This contributes to the expensive structure. In choosing a network topology, understand that each one has its advantages and disadvantages. Research each one and see which one fits within your budget and which one fits your network layout. Also consider the amount of maintenance required in each topology. When setting up a network at home, consider a network topology that is simple and easy to maintain. You will also want a topology that is inexpensive to set up. If you are choosing a topology for a business, you will want to consider a topology that is reliable and resistant to errors. Your customers will need a network that is free of downtime; therefore, be sure that your topology is one that withstands disruption.

TYPES OF NETWORKING TOPOLOGIES

BUS TOPOLOGY

A bus topology is a method of transmission on networks that uses a common vehicle for transmissions and thus it is categorized as shared communication. Imagine a bus picking up various people from one stop and dropping of people as it travels and then picking a few more. That is what happens in a bus network exactly. A bus network uses a multi-drop transmission medium, all node on the network share a common bus and thus share communication. This allows only one device to transmit at a time. A distributed access protocol determines which station is to transmit. Data frames contain source and destination addresses, where each station monitors the bus and copies frames addressed to itself.

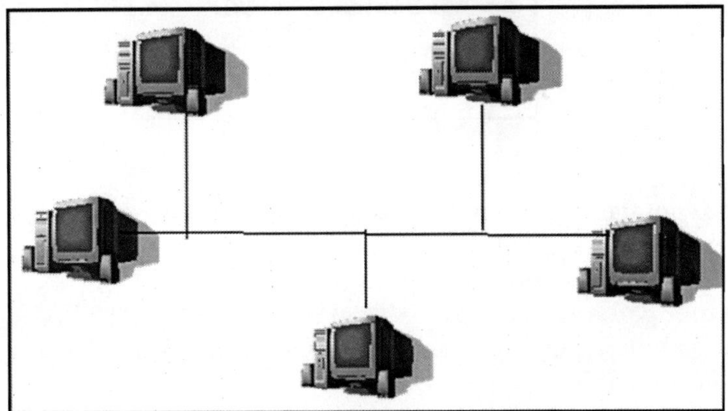

A bus topology connects each computer (nodes) to a single segment trunk (a communication line, typically coax cable, that is referred to as the'bus'. The signal travels from one end of the bus to the other. A terminator is required at each to absorb the signal so as it does not reflect back across the bus.

A media access method called CSMA/MA is used to handle the collision that occur when two signals placed on the wire at the same time. The bus topology is passive. In other words, the computers on the bus simply'listen' for a signal; they are not responsible for moving the signal along.

However in a Bus topology only one device is allowed to transmit at a given point of time. The DAP or the Distribute Access Protocol has the information about which station has to transmit the data. The data that is being transmitted have frames that will have the source name and the network address.

Function of Bus Topology

The bus topology connects each computer on the network into something called the segment trunk. A bus is usually referred to a cable that connects end to end and this is used to transmit the signals from one end to the other end. At every end a terminator is placed so that it understands in which direction the data is traveling and also the terminator is used to absorb the signals.

If the terminator does not absorb the signal then the same signal is reflected back to the bus confusing the whole data flow. The bus is considered to be a passive network because the computers are largely dependant on the signal that is being transmitted.

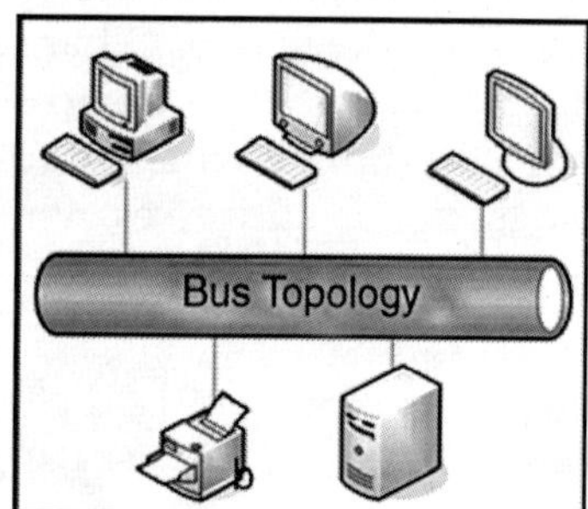

Advantages

The advantage of the Bus network is that if one computer fails in the network the others are still not affected and they continue to work. Bus network is very simple and easy to set up. If there is an urgent need to set up a network and perhaps be used on a short term basis then the Bus network is the best possibility. Bus networks use the least amount of cable to set up making it cost effective.

Limitations

In the bus network you will need a network connection in order to determine if the data is being transferred between two nodes. If the data transfer rate is high then the Bus network does not perform very well because the data travels in a stream and cannot be overloaded. The bus network is a bit challenging when you have to troubleshoot the problems. Bus networks are not suitable as large networks as there are limitations to the number of nodes you can set up for one single cable. As the number of computers increase in the network the data transfer rate goes down accordingly and noticeably.

Conclusion

The bus networks in spite of its limitations is considered to be the easiest and the fastest network that can be set up compared to the other kinds of network. In bus networks there is a collision handling system which ensures that data travels without errors and data is delivered correctly. There is a bus master on the network which ensures that data is flowing in the right direction and order.

All the computers on the bus network however listen for the signals and they do not hold the responsibility to move the signal forward. The signal carries forward on its own. So if one computer is not receiving any signals the signal still carries forward without stopping at the computer that has failed. These days bus networks are less common due to the advancement of networks and there are much lesser complicated networks that are easy to operate and efficient. However even these newer technologies derive their basics from older technologies like the Bus Topology.

RING TOPOLOGY

Definition

A ring topology is a network topology or circuit arrangement in which each network device is attached along the same signal path to two other devices, forming a path in the shape of a ring. Each device in the network that is also referred to as node handles every message that flows through the ring.

Each node in the ring has a unique address. Since in a ring topology there is only one pathway between any two nodes, ring networks are generally disrupted by the failure of a single link.

The redundant topologies are used to eliminate network downtime caused by a single point of failure. All networks need redundancy for enhanced reliability.

Network reliability is achieved through reliable equipment and network designs that are tolerant to failures and faults. The FDDI networks overcome the disruption in the network by sending data on a clockwise and a counterclockwise ring.

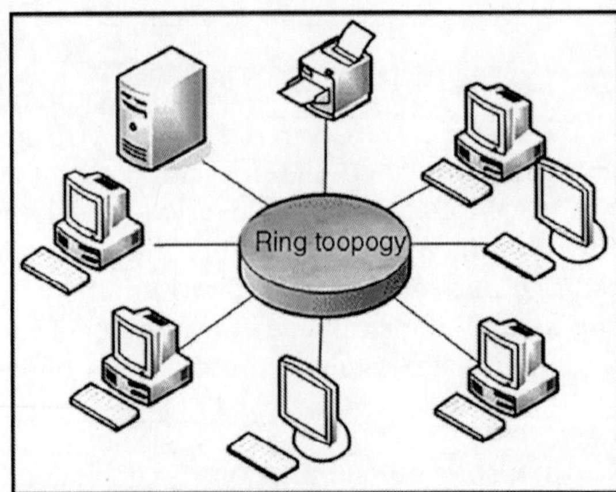

In case there is a break in data flow,the data is wrapped back onto the complementary ring before it reaches the end of the cable thereby maintaining a path to every node within the complementary ring. Ring network connects computers in a circle of point-to-point connections, with no central server, such as a series of desktop computers in an office. Each node handles its own applications and also shares resources over the entire network. If one node becomes inoperative, the other nodes are still able to maintain contact with one another. Such a network is best for decentralized systems in which no priorities are required

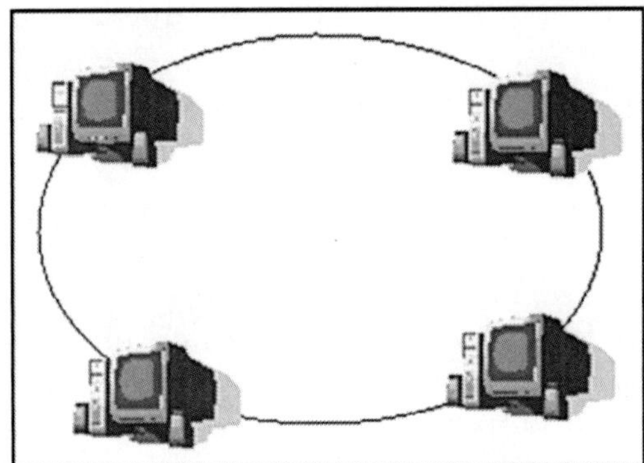

Under the network, a signal is transferred sequentially via a"token" fro one station to the next. When a station wants to transmit, it"grabs" the token, attaches data and an address to it, and then sends it around the ring. The token travels along the ring until it reaches the destination address. The receiving computer acknowledges receipt with a return message to the sender. The sender then releases the token for the token for use by another computer. Each station on the ring has equal access but only one station can talk at a time.

To allow an orderly access to the ring, a single electronic token passes from one computer to the next around the ring as seen in (token ring). A computer can only transmit data when it capture the token.

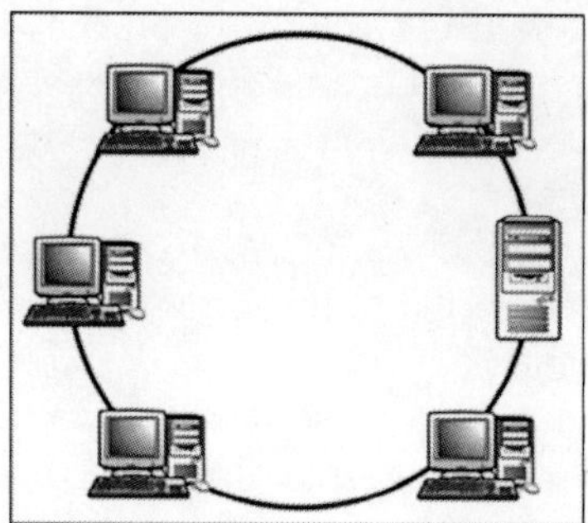

In a true ring topology, if a single computer or section of cable fails, there is an interruption in the signal. The entire network becomes inaccessible. Network disruption can also occur when computers are added or removed from the network, making it an impractical network design in environments where there is constant change to the network.

Ring networks are most commonly wired in a star configuration. In a Token Ring network, a multistation access unit (MSAU) is equivalent to a hub or switch on an Ethernet network. The MSAU performs the token circulation internally. To create the complete ring, the ring in (RI) port on each MSAU is connected to the ring out (RO) port on another MSAU. The last MSAU in the ring is then connected to the first, to complete the ring.

TOKEN RING TOPOLOGY

Unlike Ethernet, Token Ring uses a ring topology whereby the data is sent from one machine to the next and so on around the ring until it ends up back where it started. It also uses a token passing protocol which means that a machine can only use the network when it has control of the Token, this ensures that there are no collisions because only one machine can use the network at any given time.

Figure below shows the basic of a Token Ring Topology. Although 16Mbps is the standard ring speed these days (and Fast Token Ring is being developed) we will consider a 4Mbps Token Ring in this tutorial to explain the basic concepts.

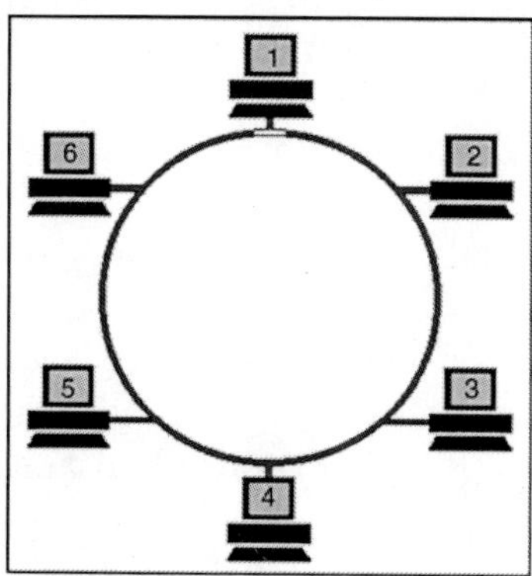

At the start, a free Token is circulating on the ring, this is a data frame which to all intents and purposes is an empty vessel for transporting data. To use the network, a machine first has to capture the free Token and replace the data with its own message.

In the example above, machine wants to send some data to machine, so it first has to capture the free Token. It then writes its data and the recipient's address onto the Token. The packet of data is then sent to machine who reads the address, realises it is not its own, so passes it on to machine Machine does the same and passes the Token on to machine. This time it is the correct address and so number reads the message.

It cannot, however, release a free Token on to the ring, it must first send the message back to number with an acknowledgement to say that it has received the data (represented by the purple flashing screen).

The receipt is then sent to machine who checks the address, realises that it is not its own and so forwards it on to the next machine in the ring, number.Machine does the same and forwards the data to number, who sent the original message. Machin erecognizes the address, reads the acknowledgement from number (represented by the purple flashing screen) and then releases the free Token back on to the ring ready for the next machine to use.

That's the basics of Token Ring and it shows how data is sent, received and acknowledged, but Token Ring also has a built in management and recovery system which makes it very fault tolerant. Below is a brief outline of Token Ring's self maintenance system.

Token Ring Self Maintenance

When a Token Ring network starts up, the machines all take part in a negotiation to decide who will control the ring, or become the'Active Monitor' to give it its proper title. This is won by the machine with the highest MAC address who is participating in the contention procedure, and all other machines become'Standby Monitors'. The job of the Active Monitor is to make sure that none of the machines are causing problems on the network, and to re-establish the ring after a break or an error has occurred. The Active Monitor performs Ring Polling every seven seconds and ring purges when there appears to be a problem.

The ring polling allows all machines on the network to find out who is participating in the ring and to learn the address of their Nearest Active Upstream Neighbour (NAUN). Ring purges reset the ring after an interruption or loss of data is reported.

Each machine knows the address of its Nearest Active Upstream Neighbour. This is an important function in a Token Ring as it updates the information required to re-establish itself when machines enter or leave the ring.

When a machine enters the ring it performs a lobe test to verify that its own connection is working properly, if it passes, it sends a voltage to the hub which operates a relay to insert it into the ring. If a problem occurs anywhere on the ring, the machine that is immediately after the fault will cease to receive signals. If this situation continues for a short period of time it initiates a recovery procedure which assumes that its NAUN is at fault, the outcome of this procedure either removes its neighbour from the ring or it removes itself.

Token Ring Operation using a Hub

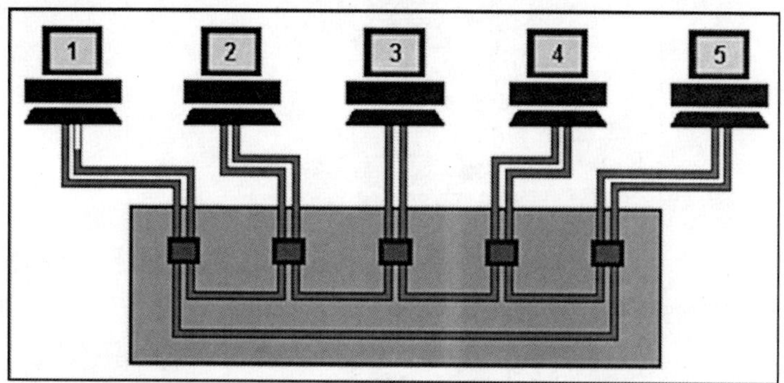

A Token Ring hub simply changes the topology from a physical ring to a star wired ring. The Token still circulates around the network and is still controlled in the same manner, however, using a hub or a switch greatly improves reliability because the hub can automatically bypass any ports that are disconnected or have a cabling fault. Further advancements have been made in recent years with regard to Token Ring technology, such as early Token release and Token Ring switching but as this site is primarily concerned with cabling issues we will not go into any more detail here.

STAR TOPOLOGY

Star topology is the most commonly used physical technology in Ethernets LANS, when installed, the star topology resembles spokes I n a bicycle wheel. The star topology is made up of a central connection point that is a device such as a hub, switch, or router, where all the cabling segments meet.

Each host in the network is connected to the central devices with its own cables although a physical star topology costs more to implement than the physical bus topology, the advantage of star topology make it worth the additional cost. Because each host it connected to the central device with its own cable. When that cable has a problem, only that host is affected, the rest of the network remains operational this benefit is extremely important and is why virtually every newly designed Ethernet a central connection point might be desirable for security or restricted access, but this is also a main disadvantage of a star topology. If the central device fails, the whole network become disconnected.when a star network is expanded to include an additional networking device that is connected for the main networking device, it is called an extended star topology.

Description

A star topology is designed with each node (file server, workstations, and peripherals) connected directly to a central network hub or concentrator as shown in figure below:

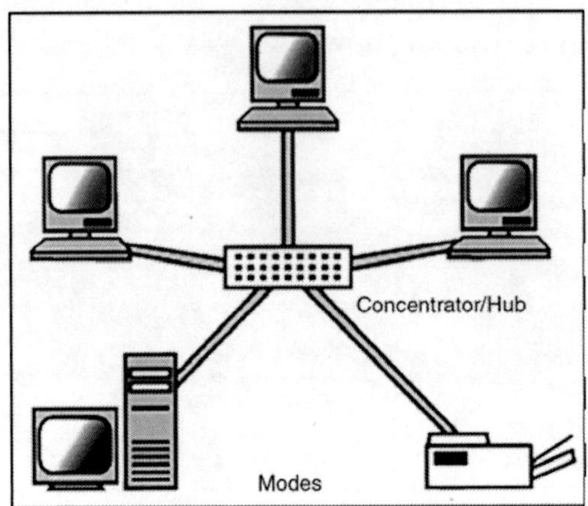

Data on a star network passes through the hub or concentrator before continuing to its destination. The hub or concentrator manages and controls all functions of the network. It also acts as a repeater for the data flow. This configuration is common with twisted pair cable; however, it can also be used with coaxial cable or fibre optic cable. Many businesses and home networks use the star topology. A star network features a central connection point called a"hub" that may be an actual hub or a switch as shown below:

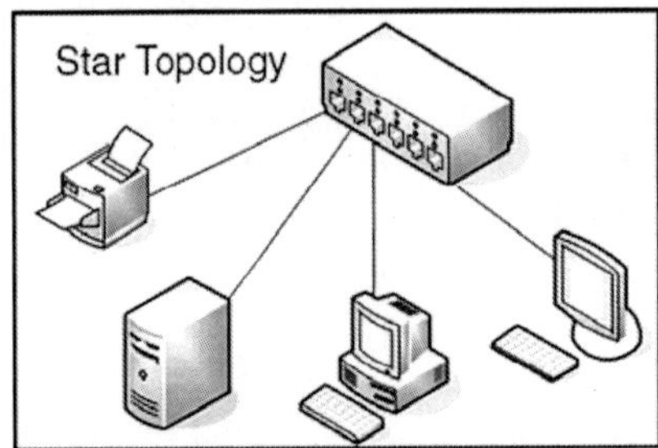

Devices typically connect to the hub with Unshielded Twisted Pair (UTP) Ethernet cables also known as RJ45 cables. Compared to the bus topology, a star network generally requires more cable, but a failure in any star network cable will only take down one computer's network access and not the entire LAN. (If the hub fails, however, the entire network also fails.)

Star topology has the following advantages:

- Easy to manage
- Easy to locate problems (cable/workstations)

- Easier to expand than a bus or ring topology
- Easy to Install and Wire
- No disruptions to the network then connecting or removing devices.
- Easy to detect faults and to remove parts.

Star topology has following disadvantages:

- It is susceptible to a single point of failure be it the server or hub/switch
- With Increased devices and traffic can make the network slow
- Requires more Cable Length.
- If the hub or concentrator fails, nodes attached are disabled.
- More expensive than linear bus topologies because of the cost of the concentrators.

TREE TOPOLOGY

Among all the Network Topologies we can derive that the Tree Topology is a combination of the bus and the Star Topology. The tree like structure allows you to have many servers on the network and you can branch out the network in many ways. This is particularly helpful for colleges, universities and schools so that each of the branches can identify the relevant systems in their own network and yet connect to the big network in some way. A Tree Structure suits best when the network is widely spread and vastly divided into many branches. Like any other topologies, the Tree Topology has its advantages and disadvantages. A Tree Network may not suit small networks and it may be a waste of cable to use it for small networks. Tree Topology has some limitations and the configuration should suit those limitations.

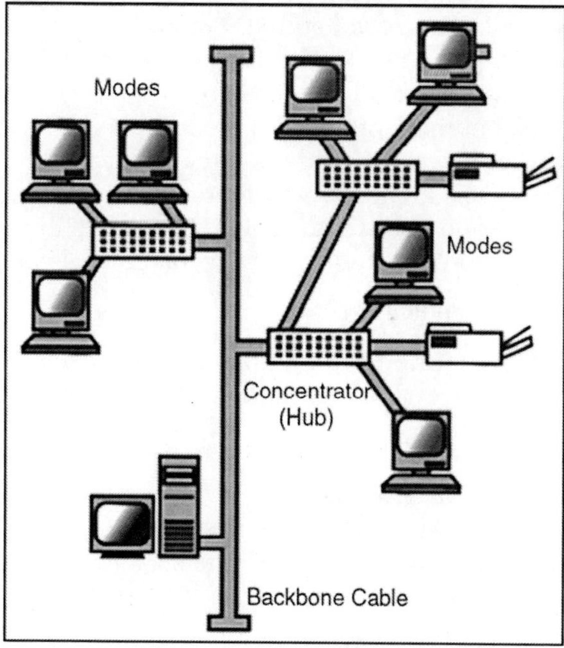

Benefits

A Tree Topology is supported by many network vendors ad even hardware vendors. A point to point connection is possible with Tree Networks. All the computers have access to the larger and their immediate networks. Best topology for branched out networks.

Limitations

In a Network Topology the length of the network depends on the type of cable that is being used. The Tree Topology network is entirely dependant on the trunk which is the main backbone of the network. If that has to fail then the entire network would fail. Since the Tree Topology network is big it is difficult to configure and can get complicated after a certain point. The Tree Topology follows a hierarchical pattern where each level is connected to the next higher level in a symmetrical pattern. Each level in the hierarchy follows a certain pattern in connecting the nodes. Like the top most level might have only one node or two nodes and the following level in the hierarchy might have few more nodes which work on the point to point connectivity and the third level also has asymmetrical node to node pattern and each of these levels are connected to the root level in the hierarchy. Think of a tree that branches out in various directions and all these branches need the roots and the tree trunk to survive. A Tree Structured network is very similar to this and that is why it is called the Tree Topology.

Features

There will be at least three levels of hierarchy in the Tree Network Topology and they all work based on the root node.

The Tree Topology has two kinds of topology integral in it, the star and the linear way of connecting to nodes. The Tree Topology functions by taking into account the total number of nodes present in the network.

It does not matter how many nodes are there on each level. Nodes can be added to any level of the hierarchy and there are no limitations a far as the total number of nodes do not exceed. The higher levels in the hierarchy are expected to perform more functions than the lower levels in the network.

Advantages of a Tree Topology

- Point-to-point wiring for individual segments.
- Supported by several hardware and software venders.

Disadvantages of a Tree Topology

- Overall length of each segment is limited by the type of cabling used.
- If the backbone line breaks, the entire segment goes down.
- More difficult to configure and wire than other topologies.

MESH TOPOLOGY

A type of network setup where each of the computers and network devices are interconnected with one another, allowing for most transmissions to be distributed, even if one of the connections go down. This type of topology is not commonly used for most computer networks as it is difficult and expensive to have redundant connection to every computer. However, this type of topology is commonly used for wireless networks. The mesh topology incorporates a unique network design in which each computer on the network connects to every other, creating a point-to-point connection between every device on the network. The purpose of the mesh design is to provide a high level of redundancy. If one network cable fails, the data always has an alternative path to get to its destination.

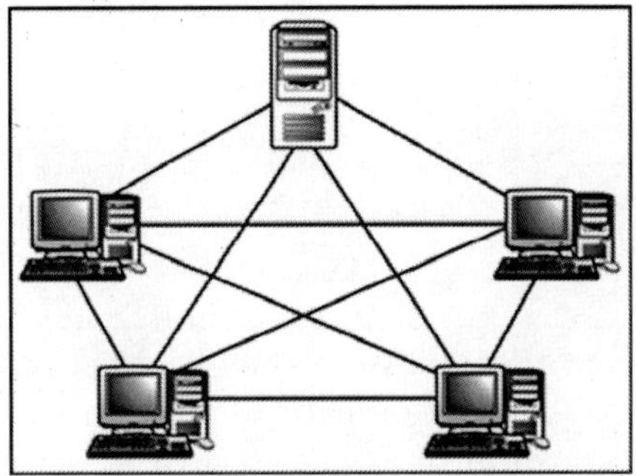

As seen in the above figure, the wiring for a mesh network can be very complicated. Further, the cabling costs associated with the mesh topology can be high, and troubleshooting a failed cable can be tricky. Because of this, the mesh topology is rarely used. A variation on a true mesh topology is the hybrid mesh. It creates a redundant point-to-point network connection between only specific network devices.

Wireless Mesh Networks

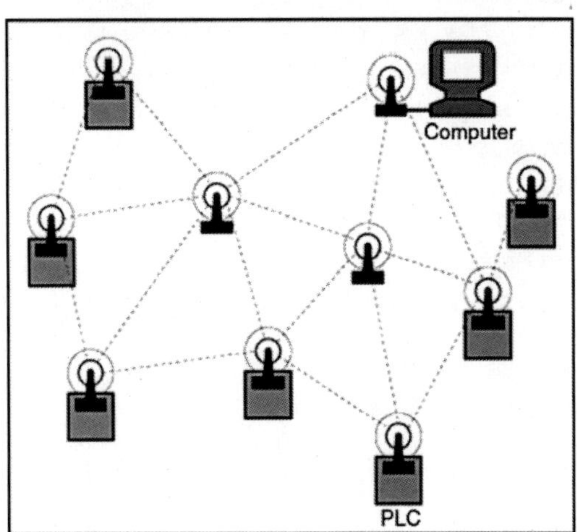

Wireless Mesh Networks work based on the radio frequencies and was originally developed by the army to be able to communicate. The reliability factor is high in any kind of Mesh Network.

There are three types of wireless Mesh Topologies:

1. Fixed Wireless Connections
2. Peer to Peer or Adhoc Networks
3. Node to Node

Fixed Mesh Networks

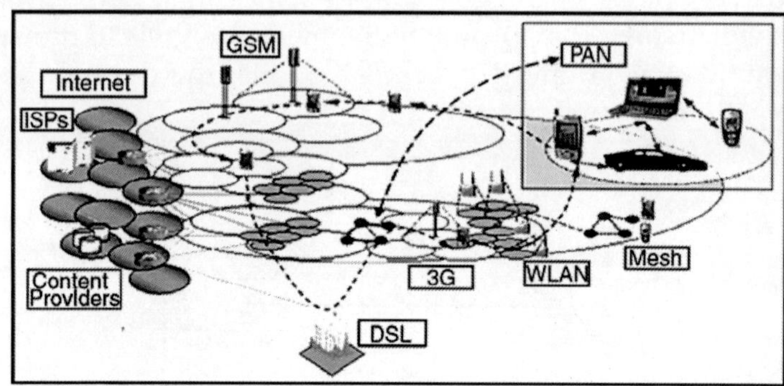

The fixed Mesh Networks will work only in the specified location and they are not mobile networks. They are meant to be used in a limited surrounding with boundaries. The location of nodes in affixed Mesh Network is all pre determined and they are not interchangeable. The fixed Mesh Network does not work on line of sight like the other types of Mesh Networks. The total number of hops in a fixed Mesh Network is usually fixed and also short. There may not be many nodes as this kind of Mesh Networks exist within an office or building. More often than not the data travels ion a specific direction.

Peer to Peer Mobile Networks

In a peer to peer mobile network the individual devices connect to each other using the Mesh Network. The peer does not require connecting to the main node and they can still communicate from one device to another device by taking the shortest possible data transfer route. However many experts believe that in the peer to peer Mesh Networks the problems with scalability in terms of time taken for data transfer is questionable. The device has to know to transmit the data in the most optimal path and the entire data transfer or depends on this single factor. If the device is incapable then the whole purpose of using it in a peer to peer connection is lost.

E-MAIL

DEFINITION

E-mail is simply the shortened form of electronic mail, a protocol for receiving, sending and storing electronic messages. E-mail has gained popularity with the spread of the Internet. In many cases, e-mail has become the preferred method of communication.

Though there is some degree of uncertainty as to when e-mail was invented, the father of the modern version is generally regarded to be American Ray Tomlinson. Before Tomlinson, messages could be sent between users but only those connected to the same computer. They could not be targeted to a particular individual. Tomlinson devised a way to address e-mail to certain users and thus was credited for one of the most important communication inventions in the 20th century.

Tomlinson's idea was to identify the name of the user and the computer at which they were located. As a result, the basic formula for addressing an e-mail was username@usercomputer. This standard has not changed over the years, other than the user computer now commonly being replaced by the name of an e-mail provider. In many cases, this is the same as the user's Internet service provider.

The influence of e-mail cannot be overstated. The United States Postal Service, for example, notes that it handles 212 billion pieces of mail per year. Many sources have nearly that many e-mails being sent back and forth every single day. In other words, e-mail handles more than 300 times the amount of mail of the largest postal system in the world.

In many cases, users receive, send and store e-mail based on one of two standards, SMTP or POP. SMTP stands for simple message transfer protocol. POP stands for Post Office Protocol. Though there is some amount of confusion over what these two protocols mean, the explanation is rather simple. POP is a protocol for storage of e-mail. SMTP is a protocol for sending and receiving.

WORKING WITH E MAIL

In reality, sending your message off into the network cloud is a bit like sending Little Red Riding Hood into the deep dark woods. You never know what might happen. In this diagram, the sender is a human being using their company account to send an e-mail to someone at a different company.

Step A: Sender creates and sends an e-mail

The originating sender creates an e-mail in their Mail User Agent (MUA) and clicks'Send'. The MUA is the application the originating sender uses to compose and read e-mail, such as Eudora, Outlook, etc.

Step B: Sender's MDA/MTA routes the e-mail

The sender's MUA transfers the e-mail to a Mail Delivery Agent (MDA). Frequently, the sender's MTA also handles the responsibilities of an MDA. Several of the most common MTAs do this, including sendmail and qmail (which Kavi uses). The MDA/MTA accepts the e-mail, then routes it to local mailboxes or forwards it if it isn't locally addressed. In our diagram, an MDA forwards the e-mail to an MTA and it enters the first of a series of"network clouds," labeled as a"Company Network" cloud.

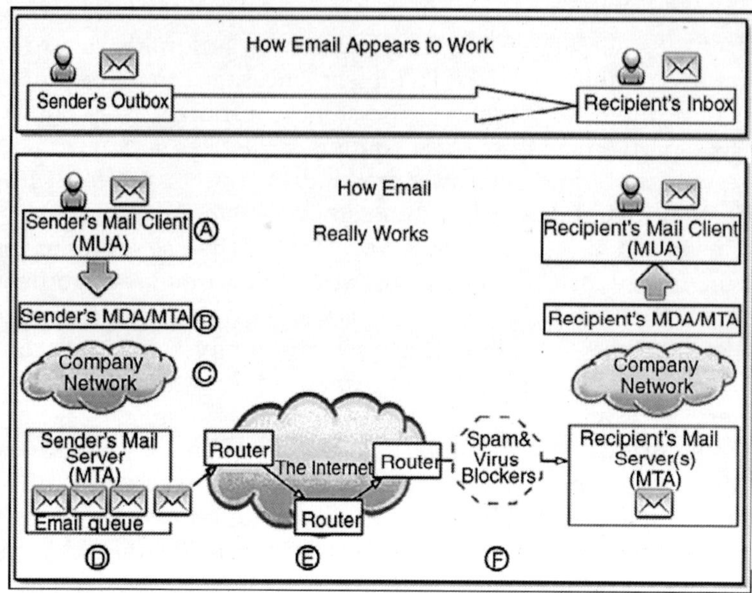

Step C: Network Cloud

An e-mail can encounter a network cloud within a large company or ISP, or the largest network cloud in existence: the Internet. The network cloud may encompass a multitude of mail servers, DNS servers, routers, lions, tigers, bears (wolves!) and other devices and services too numerous to mention. These are prone to be slow when processing an unusually heavy load, temporarily unable to receive an e-mail when taken down for maintenance, and sometimes may not have identified themselves properly to the Internet through the Domain Name System (DNS) so that other MTAs in the network cloud are unable to deliver mail as addressed.

These devices may be protected by firewalls, spam filters and malware detection software that may bounce or even delete an e-mail. When an e-mail is deleted by this kind of software, it tends to fail silently, so the sender is given no information about where or when the delivery failure occurred.

E-mail service providers and other companies that process a large volume of e-mail often have their own, private network clouds. These organizations commonly have multiple mail servers, and route all e-mail through a central gateway server (*i.e.*, mail hub) that redistributes mail to whichever MTA is available. E-mail on these secondary MTAs must usually wait for the primary MTA (*i.e.*, the designated host for that domain) to become available, at which time the secondary mail server will transfer its messages to the primary MTA.

Step D: E-mail Queue

The e-mail in the diagram is addressed to someone at another company, so it enters an e-mail queue with other outgoing e-mail messages. If there is a high volume of mail in the queue-either because there are many messages or the messages are unusually large, or both-the message will be delayed in the queue until the MTA processes the messages ahead of it.

Step E: MTA to MTA Transfer

When transferring an e-mail, the sending MTA handles all aspects of mail delivery until the message has been either accepted or rejected by the receiving MTA.

As the e-mail clears the queue, it enters the Internet network cloud, where it is routed along a host-to-host chain of servers. Each MTA in the Internet network cloud needs to"stop and ask directions" from the Domain Name System (DNS) in order to identify the next MTA in the delivery chain. The exact route depends partly on server availability and mostly on which MTA can be found to accept e-mail for the domain specified in the address. Most e-mail takes a path that is dependent on server availability, so a pair of messages originating from the same host and addressed to the same receiving host could take different paths.

These days, it's mostly spammers that specify any part of the path, deliberately routing their message through a series of relay servers in an attempt to obscure the true origin of the message.

To find the recipient's IP address and mailbox, the MTA must drill down through the Domain Name System (DNS), which consists of a set of servers distributed across the Internet. Beginning with the root nameservers at the top-level domain (.tld), then domain nameservers that handle requests for domains within that.tld, and eventually to nameservers that know about the local domain.

DNS resolution and transfer process

- There are 13 root servers serving the top-level domains (*e.g.*.org.com.edu.gov.net, etc.). These root servers refer requests for a given domain to the root name servers that handle requests for that tld. In practice, this step is seldom necessary.
- The MTA can bypass this step because it has already knows which domain name servers handle requests for these.tlds. It asks the appropriate DNS server which Mail Exchange (MX) servers have knowledge of the subdomain or local host in the e-mail address. The DNS server responds with an MX record: a prioritized list of MX servers for this domain.

An MX server is really an MTA wearing a different hat, just like a person who holds two jobs with different job titles (or three, if the MTA also handles the responsibilities of an MDA). To the DNS server, the server that accepts messages is an MX server. When is transferring messages, it is called an MTA.

- The MTA contacts the MX servers on the MX record in order of priority until it finds the designated host for that address domain.
- The sending MTA asks if the host accepts messages for the recipient's username

Step F: Firewalls, Spam and Virus Filters

The transfer process described in the last step is somewhat simplified. An e-mail may be transferred to more than one MTA within a network cloud and is likely to be passed to at least one firewall before it reaches it's destination.

An e-mail encountering a firewall may be tested by spam and virus filters before it is allowed to pass inside the firewall. These filters test to see if the message qualifies as spam or malware. If the message contains malware, the file is usually quarantined and the sender is notified. If the message is identified as spam, it will probably be deleted without notifying the sender. Spam is difficult to detect because it can assume so many different forms, so spam filters test on a broad set of criteria and tend to misclassify a significant number of messages as spam, particularly messages from mailing lists. When an e-mail from a list or other automated source seems to have vanished somewhere in the network cloud, the culprit is usually a spam filter at the receiver's ISP or company. This explained in greater detail in Virus Scanning and Spam Blocking.

INPUT/OUTPUT INTERFACE

Input and output in IF/Prolog take place using device drivers which are managed on the basis of a driver model. A device driver is responsible for operations for a particular stream type, *e.g.* files, character strings or pipes. Prolog can manage different streams with the same set of generic built-in predicates.

Prolog provides the following built-in devices:

- File is the device for operating system files
- Null is the "bit bucket" device
- Pipe is the device for operating system pipes
- Standard is the device for the standard streams of the Prolog system
- String is the device for input/output using character strings
- Socket is the device for interprocess communication

  The I/O-related COM interfaces which are defined by header files in the oskit/io directory.

Most of these interfaces are fairly generic and can be used in a wide variety of situations. Some of these interfaces, such as the bufio interface, are extensions to other more primitive interfaces, and allow objects to export the same functionality in different forms, permitting clients to select the service that most directly meets their needs thereby reducing interface crossing overhead and increasing overall performance.

MACHINE LANGUAGE

DEFINITION

A language that need not be modified, translated, or interpreted before the processor for which it was designed can use it. The arithmetic and control unit circuits of the processor for which the language is designed can directly sense the operation codes and addresses used in instructions written in machine language. It is also called as the Instructions written in an assembly language or a high-level language must be translated into machine language before a processor can execute them. Sometimes referred to as machine code or object code, machine language is a collection of binary digits or bits that the computer reads and interprets. Machine language is the only language a computer is capable of understanding. Computer designers rather than computer users usually use machine languages.

A system of codes directly understandable by a computer's CPU is termed this CPU's native or machine language. Although *machine code* may seem similar to *assembly language* they are in fact two different types of languages. *Assembly code* consists of both binary numbers and simple words whereas *machine code* is composed only of the two binary digits 0 and 1. Every CPU has its own machine language, although there is considerable overlap between some. If CPU *A* understands the full language of CPU *B* it is said that *A* is compatible with *B*. CPU *B* may not be compatible with CPU *A*, as *A* may know a few codes that *B* does not.

The "words" of a machine language are called *instructions*; each of these gives a basic command to the CPU. A programme is just a long list of instructions that are *executed* by a CPU. Older processors executed instructions one after the other, but newer super scalar processors are capable of executing several instructions at once. Programme flow may be influenced by special *jump* instructions that transfer execution to an instruction other than the following one. Conditional jumps are taken (execution continues at another address) or not (execution continues at the next instruction) depending on some condition. Instructions are simply a pattern of bits — different patterns correspond to different commands to the machine. The more readable rendition of a machine language is called assembly language. Some languages give all their instructions the same number of bits, while the instruction length differs in others. How the patterns are organised depends largely on the specific language. Common to most is the division of an instruction into *fields*, of which one or more specify the exact operation (for example "add"). Other fields may give the type of the operands, their location, or their value directly (operands contained in an instruction are called *immediate*).

ASSEMBLY LANGUAGE

DEFINITION

Assembly language is nothing more than a symbolic representation of machine code, which also allows symbolic designation of memory locations. Thus, an instruction to add the contents of a memory location to an internal CPU register called the accumulator might be add a number instead of a string of binary digits (bits).

No matter how close assembly language is to machine code, the computer still cannot understand it. The assembly-language programme must be translated into machine code by a separate programme called an assembler. The assembler programme recognizes the character strings that make up the symbolic names of the various machine operations, and substitutes the required machine code for each instruction. At the same time, it also calculates the required address in memory for each symbolic name of a memory location, and substitutes those addresses for the names.

The final result is a machine-language programme that can run on its own at any time; the assembler and the assembly-language programme are no longer needed. To help distinguish between the "before" and "after" versions of the programme, the original assembly-language programme is also known as the source code, while the final machine-language programme is designated the object code. If an assembly-language programme needs to be changed or corrected, it is necessary to make the changes to the source code and then re-assemble it to create a new object programme.

OVERVIEW

Although the numbers of the above programme make perfect sense to a computer, they are about as clear as mud to a human. Who would have guessed that they put a dollar sign on the screen? Clearly, entering numbers by hand is a lousy way to write a programme. It doesn't have to be this way, though. A long time ago, someone came up with the idea that computer programmes could be written using words instead of numbers. A special programme called an *assembler* would then take the programmer's words and convert them to numbers that the computer could understand. This new method, called writing a programme in *assembly language*, saved programmers thousands of hours, since they no longer had to look up hard-to-remember numbers in the backs of programming books, but could use simple words instead.

The programme above, written in assembly language, looks like this:

- MOV AX, 47104
- MOV DS, AX
- MOV [3998], 36
- INT 32

When an assembler reads this sample programme, it converts each line of code into one CPU-level instruction. This programme uses two types of instructions, MOV and INT. On Intel processors, the MOV instruction moves data around, while the INT instruction transfers processor control to the device drivers or operating system.

The programme still isn't quite clear, but it is much easier to understand than it was before. The first instruction, MOV AX, 47104, tells the computer to copy the number 47104 into the location AX. The next instruction, MOV DS, AX, tells the computer to copy the number in AX into the location DS. The next instruction, MOV [3998], 36 tells the computer to put the number 36 into memory location 3998. Finally, INT 32 exits the programme by returning to the operating system.

Before we go on, I would like to explain just how this programme works. Inside the CPU are a number of locations, called registers, which can store a number. Some registers, such as AX, are general purpose, and don't do anything special. Other registers, such as DS, control the way the CPU works.

DS just happens to be a *segment register*, and is used to pick which area of memory the CPU can write to. In our programme, we put the number 47104 into DS, which tells the CPU to access the memory on the video card.

The next thing our programme does is to put the number 36 into location 3998 of the video card's memory. Since 36 is the code for the dollar sign, and 3998 is the memory location of the bottom right hand corner of the screen, a dollar sign shows up on the screen a few microseconds later. Finally, our programme tells the CPU to perform what is called an *interrupt*.

An interrupt is used to stop one programme and execute another in its place. In our case, we want interrupt 32, which ends our programme and goes back to MS-DOS, or whatever other programme was used to start our programme.

RUNNING THE PROGRAMME

Let's go ahead and run this programme. First, be sure to print these instructions out, since you will need to refer to them as we go on. Next, click on your start menu, and run the programme called MS-DOS Prompt. A black screen with white text should appear. We are now in MS-DOS, the way computers used to be 20 years ago. MS-DOS was before the days of the mouse, so you must type commands on the keyboard to make the computer do things.

The cursor should move down a line, and you should see the Debug prompt, which is a simple dash. We are now in a programme called *Debug*. Debug is a powerful utility that lets you directly access the registers and memory of your computer for various purposes. In our case, we want to enter our programme into memory and run it, so we'll use Debug's a command, for *assemble*.

Go ahead and type a100 now. The cursor will move down another line, and you will see something like 1073:0100. This is the memory location we are going to enter assembly language instructions at. The first number is the segment, and the second number is the memory location within the segment. Your Debug programme will probably pick a different segment for your programme than mine did, so don't worry if it's different. Another thing to note is that Debug only understands hexadecimal numbers, which are a sort of computer shorthand. Hexadecimal numbers sometimes contain letters as well as well as digits.

Let's go ahead and enter your programme now. Type each of the instructions below into Debug exactly as they appear, and press enter after each one. When you finish entering the last instruction, press enter twice to tell Debug that we are done entering instructions.

```
mov ax,B800
mov ds,ax
mov byte[0F9E],24
int 20
```

As you can see, I've converted all the numbers into hexadecimal, and have made a few other changes so Debug can understand what's going on. If you make a mistake while entering the above programme, press enter twice, type a100, and start entering instructions again at the beginning of the programme. Once you have entered the programme, you can go ahead and run it. Simply type g for *go* and press enter when you are ready to start the programme. You should see a dollar sign in the lower right hand corner of your screen and the words Programme terminated normally. These words are put out by Debug to let you know that the programme ended normally.

HIGH LEVEL LANGUAGES

OVERVIEW

Very early in the development of computers attempts were made to make programming easier by reducing the amount of knowledge of the internal workings of the computer that was needed to write programmes. If programmes could be presented in a language that was more familiar to the person solving the problem, then fewer mistakes would be made. High-level programming languages allow the specification of a problem solution in terms closer to those used by human beings. These languages were designed to make programming far easier, less error-prone and to remove the programmer from having to know the details of the internal structure of a particular computer. These high-level languages were much closer to human language. One of the first of these languages was Fortran II which was introduced in about 1958. In Fortran II our programme above would be written as:

$$C = A + B$$

which is obviously much more readable, quicker to write and less error-prone. As with assembly languages the computer does not understand these high-level languages directly and hence they have to be processed by passing them through a programme called a compiler which translates them into internal machine language before they can be executed.

Another advantage accrues from the use of high-level languages if some international body standardizes the languages. Then each manufacturer produces a compiler to compile programmes that conform to the standard into their own internal machine language. Then it should be easy to take a programme, which conforms to the standard, and implement it on many different computers merely by re-compiling it on the appropriate computer.

This great advantage of portability of programmes has been achieved for several high-level languages and it is now possible to move programmes from one computer to another without too much difficulty. Unfortunately many compiler writers add new features of their own which means that if a programmer uses these features then their programme becomes non-portable. It is well worth becoming familiar with the standard and writing programmes which obey it, so that your programmes are more likely to be portable.

As with assembly language human time is saved at the expense of the compilation time required to translate the programme to internal machine language. The compilation time used in the computer is trivial compared with the human time saved, typically seconds as compared with weeks.

Many high level languages have appeared since Fortran II (and many have also disappeared!), among the most widely used have been:

COBOL	Business applications
FORTRAN	Engineering and Scientific Applications
PASCAL	General use and as a teaching tool
C & C++	General Purpose - currently most popular
PROLOG	Artificial Intelligence
JAVA	General Purpose - gaining popularity rapidly

All these languages are available on a large variety of computers. High-level languages are those programming languages, which are customised and pretty convenient to use. These languages can be operated with several platforms. Some of the high-level languages have relevance even when not associated central processing unit.

CHARACTERISTICS OF HIGH-LEVEL LANGUAGES

In terms of technology, high-level languages are not better than the low-level versions. Rather the computing techniques used in high-level languages are simpler than those applied in low-level programming languages. The term high-level indicates greater degree of abstraction from the so-called computer languages. Unlike low-level programming languages, the high-level languages never come with opcodes. Among the other common features of high-level languages, object-oriented features, string handling schedules and modes for input or outputs of files are worth mentioning.

FUNCTIONS OF HIGH-LEVEL LANGUAGES

The main function of a high-level language is to simplify the use of programming systems to the users. The high-level languages break up the complicated chains of commands into simpler parts. For an efficient computer programming, the codes must be developed in low-level languages. However to make the best possible use of those codes, high-level languages are required.

Over the passage of time, the architectures of computers are becoming more complicated than before. Today's microprocessors require cutting-edge techniques to run the computer systems efficiently. Here comes the role of high-level languages. These programming languages are capable of designing cods that perfectly suit the requirements of modern computing.

DIFFERENT STAGES OF OPERATION

High-level languages operate through different models of programming. Interpreted and compiled are the two programming languages used in the intermediate steps. Intermediate representations and machine code generation are some other steps involved in the operation of high-level languages.

12

Network Communication

COMMUNICATION

In a mobile communication terminal for starting and simultaneously using a plurality of applications, one desired application starts fast to improve the operability when the number of started applications reaches a present limiting number of applications. An application start determining unit searches a list of started applications in response to the instruction of the start of application to obtain the number of started applications, and determines that the application cannot start when the number of started applications reaches a preset limiting number of applications.

An ending-application selecting unit selects, as an ending application to be ended, the application with the low priority from the start applications based on the preset priority of application when the application start determining unit determines that the application cannot start. An application ending unit performs the ending processing of the ending application selected by the ending-application selecting unit and deletes the selected ending application from the list of started applications.

A mobile communication terminal for starting and simultaneously using a plurality of applications, comprising: application start determining means which compares the number of started applications with a preset numerical value that is a maximum number of simultaneously used applications, determines that the application can start when the number of started applications is less than the numerical value, and determines that the application cannot start when the number of started applications reaches the numerical value; ending-priority list creating means which calculates values indicating the using situation of the started applications in response to the determination of the application start determining means that the application cannot start and creates a list of ending priority indicating the order of applications with low influence.

APPLICATIONS

In the case of ending the application; ending-application selecting means which selects the ending application based on the list of ending priority in response to the determination of the application start determining means that the application cannot start and clears the list of ending priority; application ending means which performs the ending processing of the ending application selected by the ending-application selecting means; application starting means which starts the application instructed by a user in response to the determination of the application start determining means that the application starts; and wherein the ending-priority list creating means collects data on evaluation items indicating the using situations including the total time displayed after starting the application, the number of switching times for display operation, and the last display time, obtains the order of started applications every evaluated item, multiplies the order by a weighting coefficient preset every evaluated item and every type of application, adds the multiplied result every application, calculates the values indicating the using situations, sorts the applications in order of the larger values, and creates the list of ending priority.

An application starting control method of a mobile communication terminal for starting and simultaneously using a plurality of applications, comprising the steps of: presetting a numerical value that is a maximum number of simultane-ously used applications; selecting, from started applications, an ending application to be ended based on a priority when the number of simultaneously used applications will exceed the numerical value; newly allowing to start an application after ending the selected ending application; and collecting data for the started applications, including a total time displayed after starting the application, the number of switching times for display operation, and the last display time, determining an order of the respective data for each of the started applications, multiplying each determined order by respective weighting coefficients for each of the started applications, adding the multiplied results for each of the started applications, and creating the priority by sorting the applications based on the added results.

MOBILE NETWORK

A mobile communication terminal for starting and simultaneously using a plurality of applications, comprising: application start determining means which compares the number of started applications with a preset numerical value that is a maximum number of simultaneously used applications, determines that the application can start when the number of started applications is less than the numerical value, and determines that the application cannot start when the number of started applications reaches the numerical value; selecting means which selects an ending application to be ended on the basis of low priority from the started applications, in response to the determination of the application start determining means that the application cannot start; application ending means which performs ending processing of the ending application selected by the ending application selecting means; application starting means which starts the application instructed by a user in response to the determination of the application start determining means that the application can start; and ending-priority list creating means for collecting data on evaluation items indicating the using situations including the total time displayed after starting the application, the number of switching times for display operation, and the last display time, obtaining the order of started applications every evaluated item, multiplying the order by a weighting coefficient preset every evaluated item and every type of application, adding the multiplied result every application, calculating the values indicating the using situations, sorting the applications in order of the larger values, and creating a priority list.

MEMORY

The present invention relates to a mobile communication terminal and an application starting control method thereof. More particularly, the present invention relates to a mobile communication terminal for starting and simultaneously using a plurality of applications and an application starting control method thereof. Recently, one type of mobile phones is sold to start a plurality of applications and simultaneously use a plurality of functions similarly to a personal computer or the like, under the improvement of CPU processing capacity. Such a mobile phone terminal enables a user to send an email while viewing a site screen on the Internet or to check the schedule by a scheduler while having a call.

However, the mobile phone terminal does not have a sufficient memory capacity or power capacity. Therefore, if many applications simultaneously start similarly to the personal computer, a malfunction is caused in the communication function or the started application operation becomes unstable. An unnecessary application must terminate without continuously staying resident in memory when the number of simultaneously-used applications reaches a predetermined limiting number.

Preferably, the unnecessary application automatically ends. As disclosed in the above-mentioned publication, the degree of importance is set to the application so as to use the application with the high degree of importance for a long time when the remaining amount of battery is reduced while a plurality of applications start, and the application with the low degree of importance ends when the remaining amount of battery reduces. However, when the number of applications to be started is over a predetermined number, the application to be ended does not automatically end.

DETAILS

It is an object of the present invention to provide a mobile communication terminal and an application starting control method thereof, for fast starting a desired application and improving the operability by automatically selecting and ending the application to be ended when the number of started applications reaches a predetermined limiting number upon starting the application. According to the present invention, there is provided an application starting control method of a mobile communication terminal for starting and simultane-ously using a plurality of applications, comprising the steps of presetting a limiting number of simultaneously used applications; selecting, from started applications, an ending application to be ended based on the priority when applications over a limiting number are going to be started; and newly allowing to start an application after ending the selected ending application.

The priority may be preset or may be determined based on a using situation of the started application. The selected ending application may be displayed on a screen in response to the selection of the ending application. In this case, the selected ending application is ended in response to the approval operation of a user.

According to the present invention, there is also provided a mobile communication terminal for starting and simultane-ously using a plurality of applications, comprising application start determining means which compares the number of started applications with a preset limiting number of simultaneously used applications, determines that the application can start when the number of started applications is less than the limiting number, and determines that the application cannot start when the number of started applications reaches the limiting number; selecting means which selects an ending application to be ended on the basis of low priority from the started applications in response to the determination of the application start determining means that the application cannot start; application ending means which performs ending processing of the ending application selected by the ending application selecting means; and application starting means which starts the application instructed by a user in response to the determination of the application start determining means that the application can start.

NETWORK APPLICATIONS

The application starting means may start the application instructed by the user in response to the ending processing of the application ending means. The application start determin-ing means may determine whether or not the application starts in response to the instruction to start the application from the user.

The mobile communication terminal may have a list of started applications indicating the started applications. In this case, the application start determining means searches the list of started application to obtain the number of started applications. The application ending means deletes the selected ending application from the list of started applications. The application starting means starts the application determined as the start by the application start determining means and registers the started application to the list of started applications. The mobile communication terminal may further comprises means for receiving the approval of the user before the ending processing of the ending application in response to the selection of the ending application by the ending application selecting means.

According to the present invention, there is also provided a mobile communication terminal for starting and simultaneously using a plurality of applications, comprising application start determining means which compares the number of started applications with a preset limiting number of simultaneously used applications, determines that the application can start when the number of started applications is less than the limiting number, and determines that the application cannot start when the number of started applications reaches the limiting number; ending-priority list creating means which calculates values indicating the using situation of the started applications in response to the determination of the application start determining means that the application cannot start and creates a list of ending priority indicating the order of applications with low influence in the case of ending the application; ending-application selecting means which selects the ending application based on the list of ending priority in response to the determination of the application start determining means that the application cannot start and clears the list of ending priority; application ending means which performs the ending processing of the ending application selected by the ending-application selecting means; and application starting means which starts the application instructed by a user in response to the determination of the application start determining means that the application starts.

The ending-priority list creating means may collect data on evaluation items indicating the using situations including the total time displayed after starting the application, the number of switching times for display operation, and the last display time, place a number to each of started applications in the order of their magnitude every evaluated item, multiply the number by a weighting coefficient preset every evaluated item and every type of application, add the multiplied results every application, calculate the values indicating the using situations, sort the applications in order of the larger values, and create the list of ending priority.

The mobile communication terminal may have a list of started applications indicating the started application. In this case, the application start determining means searches the list of started applications and obtains the number of started applications; the application ending means deletes the selected ending application from the list of started applications, and the application starting means starts the application determined as the start by the application start determining means and registers the started application to the list of started applications. According to the present invention, the limiting number (maximum number) of applications for simultaneous use is set and when the start of a new application amounts to the number of applications over the limiting number, the application for ending is automatically determined and is ended in accordance with the priority from among the using applications. Thus, in case that the number of applications reaches the limiting number, the new application is started quickly and the operability upon starting the application is improved.

WIRELESS COMMUNICATIONS

Wireless communications is a rapidly growing segment of the communications industry, with the potential to provide high-speed high-quality information exchange between portable devices located anywhere in the world. Potential applications enabled by this technology include multimedia Internet-enabled cell phones, smart homes and appliances, automated highway systems, video teleconferencing and distance learning, and autonomous sensor networks, to name just a few. However, supporting these applications using wireless techniques poses a significant technical challenge.

This course will cover advanced topics in wireless communications for voice, data, and multimedia. We begin with a brief overview of current wireless systems and standards. We then characterize the wireless channel, including path loss for different environments, random log-normal shadowing due to signal attenuation, and the flat and frequency-selective properties of multipath fading. Next we examine the fundamental capacity limits of wireless channels and the characteristics of the capacity-achieving transmission strategies. These strategies are typically not practical. Thus, our next focus will be on practical digital modulation techniques and their performance under wireless channel impairments, including flat and frequency selective fading. The next part of the course is spent investigating techniques to improve the speed and performance of wireless links.

We will investigate the design and performance of adaptive modulation and diversity techniques to compensate for flat-fading. Three techniques to combat frequency-selective fading are then examined: adaptive equalization, multicarrier modulation, and spread spectrum. We will also study the multiple access capabilities of spread spectrum with multiuser detection. The course concludes with a brief overview of wireless networks, including multiple and random access techniques, WLANs, cellular system design, and ad-hoc network design.

Applications for these systems, including the evolution of cell phones and PDAs, smart homes and appliances, sensor networks, and automated highways and skyways, will also be discussed. Presenting comprehensive coverage of this fast moving field, Wireless Communications and Mobile Computing provides the R&D communities working in academia and the telecommunications and networking industries with a forum for sharing research and ideas. The convergence of wireless communications and mobile computing is bringing together two areas of immense growth and innovation. This is reflected throughout the journal by strongly focusing on new trends, developments, emerging technologies and new industrial standards. Under the guidance of an international editorial and advisory board drawn from academia and industry, this high quality, peer-reviewed journal, provides leading edge coverage of the opportunities and challenges driving the research and development of mobile communication systems.

All you need to stay ahead:

- High calibre survey papers
- Written by leading experts in the wireless and networking communities.
- Rapid publication times
  Due to electronic review and submission of original research papers
- Special Issues
  Addressing key topics of interest and managed by high profile editors
- An international forum for the sharing of research and ideas
  Key topics presented by leading individuals at the cutting edge of new technologies.

COMPUTER NETWORKS

In computer networks, bandwidth is often used as a synonym for data transfer rate - the amount of data that can be carried from one point to another in a given time period (usually a second). This kind of bandwidth is usually expressed in bits (of data) per second (bps). Occasionally, it's expressed as bytes per second (Bps). A modem that works at 57,600 bps hastwice the bandwidth of a modem that works at 28,800 bps. In general, a link with a high bandwidth is one that may be able to carry enough information to sustain the succession of images in a video presentation. It should be remembered that a real communications path usually consists of a succession of links, each with its own bandwidth. If one of these is much slower than the rest, it is said to be a bandwidth bottleneck.

In electronic communication, bandwidth is the width of the range (orband) of frequencies that an electronic signal uses on a given transmission medium. In this usage, bandwidth is expressed in terms of the difference between the highest-frequency signal component and the lowest-frequency signal component. Since the frequency of a signal is measured in hertz (the number of cycles of change per second), a given bandwidth is the difference in hertz between the highest frequency the signal uses and the lowest frequency it uses. A typical voice signal has a bandwidth of approximately three kilohertz (3 kHz); an analog television (TV) broadcast video signal has a bandwidth of six megahertz (6 MHz) -- some 2,000 times as wide as the voice signal.

BANDWIDTH MONITOR PRO

- Do you ever wonder how much bandwidth you are using?
- How fast you are downloading or uploading?
- Or if you're closing in on your monthly transfer limit?
- If so Bandwidth Monitor Pro is the utility for you!

Detailed Logging

Supports logging of all your network adapters at once with separate statistics for each adapter. You can go back and check your daily, weekly, monthly, yearly or total transfer.

Always Control

With the small transfer graph placed in the system tray you always have control of your bandwidth usage.

Highly Customizable

Bandwidth Monitor Pro can be customized to display the information you want. You can also change the graph type and colours.

Advanced Alert System

- You can set up rules with various actions and conditions.
- Lets say that you have a monthly transfer limit of 30GB.
- You can then set up Bandwidth Monitor Pro to alert you when your approaching that limit.

MOBILE INTERNET WML

WML (Wireless Markup Language) is the new web language for making sites on mobile phones. Over the past few months new WAP (Wireless Applications Protocol) phones have become extremely popular and many large websites have created special 'mobile' versions of their site. Many people predict that, over the next few years, WAP sites will become even morepopular and e-commerce over mobile phones will be widely available.

USING WML

Although you might not have any plans immediately for creating a WAP version of your site, it is always a good idea to get involved in new technology. All you need to do is make a small site (even one page) which tells people a bit about your website. In the future you can develop the site further with things like e-mail and information for people to get directly off their phones. The main sites which will benefit from WAP are ones providing a service like e-mail, live sports scores or a calendar service etc. But there are many other uses. For example, a site giving music reviews could put their reviews on a WAP site. People could then read the reviews on their mobile phone while browsing through the CDs in a shop.

HAVING WAP PHONE

To create a WAP site you don't need a WAP enabled phone. You can get a WAP simulator for a PC. This is a piece of software which will give you a WAP phone on your desktop.

You can then type in the URLs of WAP sites and can view them on your PC. You can get a very good free WAP simulator from YourWAP

COMPARING SITES

WAP sites are not like standard web sites at all. As an example, you are looking at part of the Gowansnet web site. As you can see, sites written in WML are monochrome, very limited and there is very little screen space. Because of this you must be very careful when you are designing a WAP site as it is nothing like a web site.

BEGINNING WAP SITE

After reading the introduction you should understand about WAP sites, WML and what you can do with them so I will go straight into how to create a site. Note that you should really either have a WAP phone or a WAP simulator so that you can view your site and a knowledge of HTML is useful.

Finding A WML Host

Unfortunately WML cannot be run on all web hosts. For WML content to be run, a web host must make some changes to the configuration of their web server. If your host cannot do this for you, you can try WAPHosts.net. They can provide you with a server which will support WML.

Declaring A WML Document

Cards

Instead of having pages, WAP sites have cards. These are what is displayed on the screen at one time, just like a page. More than one card can be inserted in each WML document. To declare a card, insert the following:

```
<card id="index" title="My WAP Site"
newcontext="true">
```

This will make a card with the ID index (used for linking) and will display the text: My WAP Site at the top of the screen.

Closing Tags

Unlike with HTML, it is extremely important to close WML tags. If you do not, a page will certainly not work. You must close both the <card> and <wml> tags:

```
</card>
</wml>
```

ADDING TEXT

In the last part I showed you how to create the basic file which will contain your WAP site. In this part I am going to show you how to insert text and how to format it.

The <p> Tag

Just like in HTML the <p> tag is used to show where a paragraph begins and ends. Unlike HTML, though, all text on a WML page must be inside these tags. You are not allowed to nest these tags either. One important thing to remember about WML is that, unlike HTML where a page will still display even if there is bad code, a WAP phone will just reject a page if there is and code it doesn't understand.

As with HTML you use the tags as follows:

```
<p>
information
</p>
```

Aligning Text

Aligning text in WML is nearly exactly the same as in HTML, except you can't use the centre tag. All aligning must be done using the following <p> tags:

Centre:

```
<p align="centre">
```

Right:

```
<p align="right">
```

The
 Tag

In WML (as mentioned earlier) all tags must be closed. This causes problems when using old HTML tags (like <Br>) which have no closing tag. To get around this, some tags have had a/ put on the end e.g.

```
<Br/>
```

This, like in HTML will make a line break.

Text

In WML there is actually no font tag (as you can only display text in the phone's default font in black). To show text all you need to do is put it in between the <p> and </p> tags. Here is an example of a full WML document:

```
<?xml version="1.0"?>
<!DOCTYPE wml PUBLIC "-//WAPFORUM//DTD WML 1.1/        /
EN" "http://www.wapforum.org/DTD/wml_1.1.xml">
<wml>
<card id="index" title="My WAP Site"
newcontext="true">
<p align="centre">
```

Welcome to my new WAP site. You can view this on your mobile phone anywhere in the world!
 It is amazing!

```
</p>
</card>
</wml>
```

HYPERLINKS & IMAGES

In part 3 I showed you how to create a basic WAP site with one page and some text. This week I will show you how you can make this better by adding extra parts, linking to them (and other sites) and how to add images to your site.

More Cards

As I explained in the second part of this tutorial, WAP sites have cards instead of pages. They are really the same as pages except they can all be written in one file. To add another card, all you need to do is put in another <card> tag with a different ID to the others. For example:

```
<card title="About Me" id="about">
 information
</card>
```

would be added below the first card but before the </wml> tag.

Linking

There are three ways to link to another WAP site, file or card. Just like in HTML these can either be the full path to a file or a relative link.

To link to a WAP site you use the following:

```
<a href="http://gowansnet.waphosts.net/">
 Gowansnet</a>
```

in your text. To link to another file on your site you would use:

```
<a href="links.wml">My Links</a>
```

and to link to another card in the same page you use:

```
<a href="#about">About Me</a>
```

For suppliers, the thought of a uniform operating environment was disconcerting. Consumer lock-in was woven tightly into the fabric of the industry. Individual consumers, particularly those with UNIX system experience, envisioned standardized environments, but had no way to pull the market in their direction. However, for one category of consumer - governments- the standardization of the UNIX system was both desirable and within reach.

Governments have clout and are the largest consumers of information technology products and services in the world. Driven by the need to improve commonality, both US and European governments endorsed a shift to the UNIX system. The Institute of Electrical and Electronic Engineers POSIX family of standards, along with standards from ISO, ANSI and others, led the way.

Consortia such as the X/Open Company (merged with the Open Software Foundation in 1995 to form The Open Group) hammered out draft standards to accelerate the process. In 1994, the definitive specification of what constitutes a UNIX system was finalized through X/Open Company's consensus process. The Single UNIX Specification was born-not from a theoretical, ivory tower approach, but by analyzing the applications that were in use in businesses across the world.

With the active support of government and commercial buyers alike, vendors began to converge on products that implement the Single UNIX Specification, and now all major vendors have products labeled UNIX 95, which indicates that the vendor guarantees that the product conforms to the Single UNIX Specification.

Vendors continue to add value to the UNIX system, particularly in areas of new technology, however that value will always be built upon a single, consensus standard. Meanwhile, the functionality of the UNIX system was established and the mid-life crisis was resolved. Suppliers today provide UNIX systems that are built upon a single, consensus standard. It is also important to remember that even when variance among UNIX systems was at its worst, IT professionals agreed that migration among UNIX system variants was far easier than migration among the proprietary alternatives.

TextProcessing and Word Processing

Almost every computer user needs a method of preparing documents. In the world of personal computers, word processing is the norm: editing and manipulating text in a ``What-You-See-Is-What-You-Get'' (WYSIWYG) environment and producing printed copies of the text, complete with graphics, tables, and ornamentation.

Commercial word processors from Corel, Applix, and Star Division are available in the UNIX world, but text processing, which is quite different conceptually, is more common. In text processing systems, text is entered in a page-description language, which describes how the text should be formatted. Rather than enter text within a special word processing environment, you can modify text with any editor, like vi or emacs. Once you finish entering the source text (in the typesetting language), a separate programme converts the source to a format suitable for printing. This is somewhat analogous to programming in a language like C, and ``compiling'' the document into printable form.

Many text processing systems are available for Linux. One is groff, the GNU version of the classic troff text formatter originally developed by Bell Labs and still used on many UNIX systems worldwide. Another modern text processing system is TeX, developed by Donald Knuth of computer science fame. Dialects of TeX, like LaTeX, are also available. Text processors like TeX and groff differ mostly in the syntax of their formatting languages. The choice of one formatting system over another is based upon what utilities are available to satisfy your needs, as well as personal taste.

Many people consider groff's formatting language to be a bit obscure and use find TeX more readable. However, groff produces ASCII output which can be viewed on a terminal more easily, while TeX is intended primarily for output to a printing device. Various add-on programmes are required to produce ASCII output from TeX formatted documents, or convert TeX input to groff format.

Another programme is texinfo, an extension to TeX which is used for software documentation developed by the Free Software Foundation. texinfo can produce printed output, or an online-browsable hypertext ``Info'' document from a single source file. Info files are the main format of documentation used in GNU software like emacs. Text processors are used widely in the computing community for producing papers, theses, magazine articles, and books. (This book is produced using LaTeX.) The ability to process source language as a text file opens the door to many extensions of the text processor itself. Because a source document is not stored in an obscure format that only one word processor can read, programmers can write parsers and translators for the formatting language, and thus extend the system. What does a formatting language look like? In general, a formatted source file consists mostly of the text itself, with control codes to produce effects like font and margin changes, and list formatting.

Programming Languages and Utilities

Linux provides a complete UNIX programming environment which includes all of the standard libraries, programming tools, compilers, and debuggers which you would expect of other UNIX systems.

Standards like POSIX.1 are supported, which allows software written for Linux to be easily ported to other systems. Professional UNIX programmers and system administrators use Linux to develop software at home, then transfer the software to UNIX systems at work.

This not only saves a great deal of time and money, but also lets you work in the comfort of your own home. (One of the authors uses his system to develop and test X Window System applications at home, which can be directly compiled on workstations elsewhere.) Computer Science students learn UNIX programming and explore other aspects of the system, like kernel architecture.

With Linux, you have access to the complete set of libraries and programming utilities and the complete kernel and library source code. Within the UNIX software world, systems and applications are often programmed in C or C++. The standard C and C++ compiler for Linux is GNU gcc, which is an advanced, modern compiler that supports C++, including AT&T 3.0 features, as well as Objective-C, another object-oriented dialect of C. Besides

C and C++, other compiled and interpreted programming languages have been ported to Linux, like Smalltalk, FORTRAN, Java, Pascal, LISP, Scheme, and Ada (if you're masochistic enough to programme in Ada, we aren't going to stop you).

In addition, various assemblers for writing protected-mode 80386 code are available, as are UNIX hacking favorites like Perl (the script language to end all script languages) and Tcl/Tk (a shell-like command processing system which has support for developing simple X Window System applications). The advanced gdb debugger can step through a programme one line of source code at a time, or examine a core dump to find the cause of a crash.

The gprof profiling utility provides performance statistics for your programme, telling you where your programme spends most of its execution time. As mentioned above, the emacs text editor provides interactive editing and compilation environments for various programming languages. Other tools include GNU make and imake, which manage compilation of large applications, and RCS, a system for source code locking and revision control.

Finally, Linux supports dynamically linked, shared libraries (DLLs), which result in much smaller binaries. The common subroutine code is linked at run-time. These DLLs let you override function definitions with your own code. For example, if you wish to write your own version of the malloc() library routine, the linker will use your new routine instead of the one in the libraries.

X Window System

The X Window System, or simply X, is a standard graphical user interface (GUI) for UNIX machines and is a powerful environment which supports many applications. Using the X Window System, you can have multiple terminal windows on the screen at once, each having a different login session. A pointing device like a mouse is often used with X, although it isn't required. Many X-specific applications have been written, including games, graphics and programming utilities, and documentation tools. Linux and X make your system a bona fide workstation. With TCP/IP networking, your Linux machine can display X applications running on other machines.

The X Window System was originally developed at the Massachusetts Institute of Technology and is freely distributable. Many commercial vendors have distributed proprietary enhancements to the original X Window System as well. The version of X for Linux is XFree86, a port of X11R6 which is freely distributable. XFree86 supports a wide range of video hardware, including VGA, Super VGA, and accelerated video adaptors. XFree86 is a complete distribution of the X Windows System software, and contains the X server itself, many applications and utilities, programming libraries, and documents.

Standard X applications include xterm, a terminal emulator used for most text-based applications within a window, xdm, which handles logins, xclock, a simple clock display, xman, a X-based manual page reader, and xmore. The many X applications available for Linux are too numerous to mention here, but their number includes spreadsheets, word processors, graphics programmes, and web browsers like the Netscape Navigator. Many other applications are available separately. Theoretically, any application written for X should compile cleanly under Linux.

The interface of the X Window System is controlled largely by the window manager. This user-friendly programme is in charge of the placement of windows, the user interface for resizing and moving them, changing windows to icons, and the appearance of window frames, among other tasks. XFree86 includes twm, the classic MIT window manager, and advanced window managers like the Open Look Virtual Window Manager (olvwm) are available. Popular among Linux users is fvwm--a small window manager that requires less than half the memory of twm.

It provides a 3-dimensional appearance for windows and a virtual desktop. The user moves the mouse to the edge of the screen, and the desktop shifts as though the display were much larger than it really is. fvwm is greatly customizable and allows access to functions from the keyboard as well as mouse. Many Linux distributions use fvwm as the standard window manager. A version of fvwm called fvwm95-2 offers Microsoft Windows 95-like look and feel. The XFree86 distribution includes programming libraries for wily programmers who wish to develop X applications. Widget sets like Athena, Open Look, and Xaw3D are supported. All of the standard fonts, bitmaps, manual pages, and documentation are included. PEX (a programming interface for 3-dimensional graphics) is also supported.

Many X application programmers use the proprietary Motif widget set for development. Several vendors sell single and multiple user licenses for binary versions of Motif. Because Motif itself is relatively expensive, not many Linux users own it. However, binaries statically linked with Motif routines can be freely distributed. If you write a programme using Motif, you may provide a binary so users without the Motif libraries can use the programme.

A major caveat to using the X Window System is its hardware requirements. A 80386-based CPU with 4 megabytes of RAM is capable of running X, but 16 megabytes or more of physical RAM is needed for comfortable use. A faster processor is nice to have as well, but having enough physical RAM is much more important. In addition, to achieve really slick video performance, we recommend getting an accelerated video card, like a VESA Local Bus (VLB) S3 chipset card. Performance ratings in excess of 300,000 xstones have been achieved with Linux and XFree86. Using adequate hardware, you'll find that running X and Linux is as fast, or faster, than running X on other UNIX workstations.

Networking

Would you like to communicate with the world? Linux supports two primary UNIX networking protocols: TCP/IP and UUCP. TCP/IP (Transmission Control Protocol/Internet Protocol) is the networking paradigm which allows systems all over the world to communicate on a single network, the Internet. With Linux, TCP/IP, and a connection to the Internet, you can communicate with users and machines via electronic mail, Usenet news, and FTP file transfer.

Most TCP/IP networks use Ethernet as the physical network transport. Linux supports many popular Ethernet cards and interfaces for personal computers, including pocket and PCMCIA Ethernet adaptors.

However, because not everyone has an Ethernet connection at home, Linux also supports SLIP (Serial Line Internet Protocol) and PPP (Point-to-Point Protocol), which provide Internet access via modem. Many businesses and universities provide SLIP and PPP servers. In fact, if your Linux system has an Ethernet connection to the Internet and a modem, your system can become a SLIP or PPP server for other hosts.

NFS (Network File System) lets your system seamlessly share file systems with other machines on the network. FTP (File Transfer Protocol) lets you transfer files with other machines. sendmail sends and receives electronic mail via the SMTP protocol; C-News and INN are NNTP based new systems; and telnet,rlogin, and rsh let you log in and execute commands on other machines on the network. finger lets you get information about other Internet users.

The full range of mail and news readers is available for Linux, including elm, pine, rn, nn, and tin. Whatever your preference, you can configure a Linux system to send and receive electronic mail and news from all over the world. The system provides a standard UNIX socket programming interface.

Virtually any programme that uses TCP/IP can be ported to Linux. The Linux X server also supports TCP/IP, and applications running on other systems may use the display of your local system.

UUCP (UNIX-to-UNIX Copy) is an older mechanism to transfer files, electronic mail, and electronic news between UNIX machines. Historically, UUCP machines are connected over telephone lines via modem, but UUCP is able to transfer data over a TCP/IP network as well. If you do not have access to a TCP/IP network or a SLIP or PPP server, you can configure your system to send and receive files and electronic mail using UUCP.

Several conventions have sprung up around the development effort. Anyone who wishes to have their code included in the ``official'' kernel, mails it to Linus Torvalds. He will test and include the code in the kernel as long as it doesn't break things or go against the overall design of the system. The system itself is designed using an open-ended, feature-minded approach. The number of new features and critical changes to the system has recently diminished, and the general rule is that a new version of the kernel will be released every few weeks. Of course, this is a rough figure. New release criteria include the number of bugs to be fixed, feedback from users testing pre-release versions of the code, and the amount of sleep Linus Torvalds has had this week. Suffice it to say that not every bug is fixed, nor is every problem ironed out between releases. As long as the revision appears to be free of critical or recurring bugs, it is considered to be stable, and the new version is released. The thrust behind Linux development is not to release perfect, bug-free code: it is to develop a free UNIX implementation. Linux is for the developers, more than anyone else.

Anyone who has a new feature or software application generally makes it available in an alpha version--that is, a test version, for those brave users who want to hash out problems in the initial code. Because the Linux community is largely based on the Internet, alpha software is usually uploaded to one or more Linux FTP sites and a message is posted to one of the Linux Usenet newsgroups about how to obtain and test the code. Users who download and test alpha software can then mail results, bug fixes, and questions to the author. After the initial bugs have been fixed, the code enters a beta test stage, in which it is usually considered stable but not complete. It works, but not all of the features may be present. The software may also go directly to a final stage, in which the software is considered complete and usable.

Keep in mind that these are only conventions--not rules. Some developers may feel so confident of their software that they decide it isn't necessary to release alpha or test versions. It is always up to the developer to make these decisions. You might be amazed at how such an unstructured system of volunteers who programme and debug a complete UNIX system gets anything done at all. As it turns out, this is one of the most efficient and motivated development efforts ever employed. The entire Linux kernel is written from scratch, without code from proprietary sources. It takes a huge amount of work to port all the free software under the sun to Linux. Libraries are written and ported, file systems are developed, and hardware drivers are written for many popular devices--all due to the work of volunteers.

Linux software is generally released as a distribution, a set of prepackaged software which comprises an entire system. It would be difficult for most users to build a complete system from the ground up, starting with the kernel, adding utilities, and installing all of the necessary software by hand. Instead, many software distributions are available which include everything necessary to install and run a complete system. There is no single, standard distribution--there are many, and each has its own advantages and disadvantages. We describe installation of the various Linux distributions starting on.

Of course, you may copy Linux from a friend who already has the software, or share the purchase cost with someone else. If you plan to install Linux on a large number of machines, you need only purchase a single copy of the software--Linux is not distributed with a ``single machine'' license. The value of commercial UNIX implementations should not be demeaned. In addition to the price of the software itself, one often pays for documentation, support, and quality assurance. These are very important factors for large institutions, but personal computer users may not require these benefits. In any case, many businesses and universities have found that running Linux in a lab of inexpensive personal computers is preferable to running a commercial version of UNIX in a lab of workstations.

Linux can provide workstation functionality on a personal computer at a fraction of the cost. Linux systems have travelled the high seas of the North Pacific, and manage telecommuni-cations and data analysis for an oceanographic research vessel. Linux systems are used at research stations in Antarctica. Several hospitals maintain patient records on Linux systems. Other free or inexpensive implementations of UNIX are available for the 80386 and 80486.

One of the best known is 386BSD, an implementation of BSD UNIX for the 80386. The 386BSD package is comparable to Linux in many ways, but which one is better depends on your needs and expectations. The only strong distinction we can make is that Linux is developed openly, and any volunteer can aid in the development process, while 386BSD is developed by a closed team of programmers. Because of this, serious philosophical and design differences exist between the two projects. The goal of Linux is to develop a complete UNIX system from scratch (and have a lot of fun in the process), and the goal of 386BSD is in part to modify the existing BSD code for use on the 80386.

NetBSD is another port of the BSD NET/2 distribution to several machines, including the 80386. NetBSD has a slightly more open development structure, and is comparable to 386BSD in many respects.

Another project of note is HURD, an effort by the Free Software Foundation to develop and distribute a free version of UNIX for many platforms. Contact the Free Software Foundation (the address is given in Appendix C) for more information about this project. At the time of this writing, HURD is still under development.

NETWORK TOOLS

VeriCenter remotely manages your network infrastructure, including routers, hubs, and switches, for the highest reliability and optimized performance. When a problem is detected and isolated, VeriCenter takes the steps necessary to coordinate with hardware vendors and carrier partners for problem resolution. At all times, you're able to access critical information about your network through our secure Web-based Customer Portal. Our services are designed to provide you with complete management of critical network devices within your environment, using the tools and expertise of our Network Operations Centre (NOC). Every productive data network is made up of two intergral parts - infrastructure (communications environment) and active elements, which utilise the communications environment. The infrastructure can be made up of a structured cabling system based on melicke or optical lines, wireless transfer system etc. The quality and performance of the infrastructure directly affects the resulting attributes and output of the data network.

With the rapid development of Internet applications and technology, more and more emphasis is being put on securing access to data networks and on protection of the actual data with systems against misuse or attack. There is an evident trend of integrating various security functions into basic network elements, such as switches, routers etc.

The convergence trend for data and telephony into one communications infrastructure has brought the need to secure the necessary quality of service (QoS) for operations sensitive to the quality of the data network (IP telephony, video-conferencing). A modern data network is capable of working with several classes of operations and each of these classes is capable of securing the necessary quality of service. Since it was established, GiTy has been oriented to the most up-to-date technologies, which guarantee the maximum possible output for data networks and their long technological lifetime. Key components of data networks developed by us are products from the foremost technological manufacturers, such as Siemon, Cisco Systems, Enterasys Network, 3COM, Allied Telesyn and Crossbeam.

Data networks developed by us provide users with high performance, the maximum level of security and the tools needed for management of the quality of services for individual applications.

One way of conserving this network traffic is to slice the network up into smaller segments. These segments are connected to a bridge. Bridges are smarter than hubs and repeaters. They also use software to help get the job done. Bridges are able to read MAC addresses, which are also known as hardware addresses that are burned onto the NIC inside every computer on the network, of each data packet the is circulated on the network segments connected on the bridge. It is by learning which MAC addresses are live on the network that the bridge is able to control traffic that is local to a particular segment and keep it from spreading to other network segments that are being serviced by another bridge. A bridge device filters data traffic at a network boundary. Bridges reduce the amount of traffic on a LAN by dividing it into two segments. Bridges operate at the data link layer (Layer 2) of the OSI model. Bridges inspect incoming traffic and decide whether to forward or discard it. An Ethernet bridge, for example, inspects each incoming Ethernet frame - including the source and destination MAC addresses, and sometimes the frame size - in making individual forwarding decisions.

Bridges serve a similar function as switches, that also operate at Layer. Traditional bridges, though, support one network boundary, whereas switches usually offer four or more hardware ports. Switches are sometimes called "multi-port bridges" for this reason. Computer networks serve the purpose of connecting many different computers or terminals to each other, host computers, printers, file servers etc. so that expensive computing assets, programmes, files and other data may be shared among many users. A large network may typically contain one or more gateways, routers and bridges operating in conjunction with one or more network segments.

A segment is section of a network connected to a group of machines which may communicate with each other via repeater operations without having to traverse a bridge or router. Bridges and routers are useful in that they allow connections of multiple segments such that more computers may communicate with each other than would otherwise be possible given the limited bandwidth of the media.

13

Webs of Influence on English Language

TEACHING ENGLISH LANGUAGE LEARNERS WITH COMPUTERS

Active communication with others is key to human learning. This straightforward premise currently undergirds much theory and research in student learning in general, and in second language and literacy learning in particular. Both of these academic areas have long acknowledged communication's central role in successful learning with the exact intricacies of instructional conversations and the forms these take having been the focus of close analysis. In this examination of computer-supported classroom discourse, specific forms of instructional conversation employed by a veteran elementary teacher of beginning-level English language learners (ELLs) are examined. The focal teacher orchestrates instructional conversations around computers with children whose immediate needs are to learn the English language, specifically the "language of school" and the concomitant social complexities implied in order to participate in mainstream instructional activity.

With these goals shaping language and literacy activity, their ESOL (English for speakers of other languages) teacher makes use of the computer to capture, motivate, and anchor learner attention to, and render comprehensible the target language they hear and see on and around the computer screen. The anatomy of the activity she orchestrates around the computer and the language she uses to support it—labeled here as triadic scaffolds—are the focus of analysis. Forms and functions of triadic discourse (teacher, learner, computer) are examined for their potential unique role in second language and literacy instruction.

Computer technology is being widely used in classrooms as a means of supporting instruction. Concurrently, much attention in the education research community has focused on instructional technologies generally and more particularly on the critical role of contexts of use; that is, the situational features and verbal instructional dynamics that can accompany computer use. This analysis examines the communicative dynamics of an experienced English for speakers of other languages (ESOL) teacher working with her students around computers. My interest here is to present particular patterns of instructional discourse that are at once (a) making distinct referential use of the physical features of the computer and (b) accomplishing second language and literacy activity in ways that make good pedagogical sense.

In this case, the guiding notion of good pedagogical sense is rooted in what Gee (2000) points to as critical elements of effective literacy instruction: a "judicious mixture" of (a) learner involvement in their language and literacy learning ("immersion in a community of practice"); and (b) instructional language ("overt focusing and scaffolding...[to] focus learners on the most fruitful sorts of patterns in their experience") that supports learner acquisition of a community's practices. This analysis of instructional conversations around computers is an attempt to closely detail and explicate such mixtures in action.

THE LANGUAGE OF SCHOOL

The number of children in U.S. schools for whom English is their second language is nearing five million and growing. While ELLs are expected to master the English language, they are also expected to learnacademic content in the very language they are in the process of learning. In short, their instructional needs are multiple and complex. Language is, after all, essential to virtually all aspects of daily life. It is key to improving one's lot and imagining different worlds. Likewise, schools are brimming with language: lectures, directions, advice, admonitions, facts, fantasies, and dissings. It would be difficult to disagree with the notion that something as critical and pervasive as language should be featured and so treated in schools.

Yet the trend has traditionally been for language to be treated as a given, a prerequisite—not as essential to all learning. Moreover, "organizational structures in schools give or deny students access to an apprenticeship to the discourses of academic success". Nonetheless, children need language that provides access to the practices of their various communities.

A characteristic of at-risk learners—both native and non-native speakers of English—is that they may not be communicatively equipped to engage the everyday scripts of school-based activities, activities for which most middle class, "mainstream" students have been prepared since birth. Rather, children come to school versed in the experiences of their homes, their families, and their home culture—cultures comprised of complex ways of knowing and communicating—where what Bloom calls a "theory of mind" is firmly established as a foundation on which children's native communicative repertoire is formed at a young age through social interaction with others.

This is accomplished through observing parents' and peers' ways of understanding, talking about, and being in the world. How a child's home and community understand and communicate about the world and how this is manifest in U.S. school culture can be quite dissimilar. Recent recognition that mastering language use is first and foremost a social process that involves humans relating to one another in effective and productive ways has taken precedence over older notions of language as a body of knowledge that can be broken down into discrete pieces and taught accordingly. When learning the first, or native language children actively learn the ways of knowing, talking about, and doing the world by working out the intentionalities of those around them. Learning a second language can be viewed as comprising similar processes.

The human imperative to work out the intentionalities of others is central to a child's development of a theory of mind—an essential understanding of the self in the world—that accounts for the ways language connects with the immediate social context. With a foundational understanding of language learning as a social/contextual process that benefits from opportunities to interact with others, language teaching professionals typically engage students in activities that make what learners see and hear in the target language salient, referenced, noticeable, and comprehensible, with understanding having relevant consequences: in short, an "authentic need to comprehend and act accordingly" with immediately perceptible consequences.

Correspondingly, instructional activity that has as its goal initiation into the world of school discourses—those ways of talking that have become institutionally sanctioned or "normal"—must be crafted and guided in order to render what gets said and done salient and meaningful to learners. Consequently, the structure of a typical language learning activity might be as follows: A need to engage is established and a context is orchestrated that sets up a particular relationship between aspects of the physical or social environment and learners. The resulting activity—where sight, touch, and speech unite—becomes the locus of learning. Such structured activities make use of "enhanced input," language that has both clear visual referents and whose forms get noticed by students. Language teachers further enhance their aural input through salience-building intonation, prosody, and visual accompaniments of all kinds (gesture, object, facial expression). Such complexes of instructional elements have been variously referred to as "affordances", "optimal samples", and "instructional conversations".

Computers and Language Teaching/Learning

Adding the computer into the instructional mix affords many opportunities for this sort of language learning activity. Learning what language sounds like, looks like, and means can be supported and enhanced through teacher and student talk about what they see on the computer screen (e.g., an instructor verbally directing a child's sizing and placement of an image). Thus, specific verbal instructional strategies known widely as teaching "scaffolds" can be facilitated by virtue of the physical properties of the computer. Wood, Bruner, & Ross's definition of scaffolding is instructive in this regard. Their four-component definition of instructional scaffolds can be readily applied to what the presence of the computer accomplishes in the instructional conversation: a) what appears on the screen can be viewed as reducing the size of the task so the child can complete it; b) what appears on the screen and what changes to it are possible can be viewed as keeping the child's attention in the moment; c) what appears on the screen can facilitate making salient relevant features; and d) what the teacher says and does in reaction to what appears on the screen can be viewed as modeling ways to accomplish.

Each of these four key characteristics of scaffolding involves more than the language used per se. Each involves strategic instructional moves that, as a complex whole, are at the heart of the craft of teaching. The presence of the computer potentially amplifies such moves. Indeed, recent research on computer-supported learning contexts indicates that these interactional routines can provide the kinds of stimulation and anchoring of language so central to the language learning process.

Second language and literacy learning contexts that promote and sustain the social construction and negotiation of meaning-making are widely considered as optimal.

In light of such optimal contexts, Meskill, Mossop, and Bates propose specific physical features of computers that are especially supportive of joint meaning-making and instructional conversations. Features such as publicness, instability, anchored referents, and the anarchic nature of computers can be viewed as enabling acquisition-oriented activity when skilled language professionals take instructional advantage of them.

A language educator can make use of the visual representations of a word or picture on the computer screen (a public, anchored referent), to communicatively reinforce word, phrase, and sentence-level meaning. Further, she can direct learners to manipulate what they see on the screen (publicness, anchored referents, instability) thereby reinforcing the aural/visual aspects of the language she is teaching. If a student wishes to exercise her own volition by changing what is on the screen independent of the teacher's directives (anarchy), this also becomes a rich venue for immediate, referenced target language learning. From this perspective, computer screens can serve to anchor attention to forms and functions in immediate, highly tangible, and communicatively authentic ways.

The following analysis focuses on the computer-supported instructional scaffolding of an ESOL teaching professional as she uses computers to teach beginning-level English language learners the language and literacy they need to participate in the everyday academic activities of their school. Special focus of these instructional sequences is given to the interplay between the teacher's utterances, the features of the machine, children's responses, and what these together accomplish instructionally.

Context

"Mrs. M" has taught English to non-native speakers in the same mid-size, post-industrial city school district for over 30 years; the majority of that tenure has been as the sole elementary ESOL specialist in the district. As such, she has traveled between the district's elementary schools to teach groups of mostly low socioeconomic status (SES) English language learners (ELLs). Over the years, this role has come to include serving as the main liaison between schools and ELL families as well as the wider immigrant community. She regularly sees that children receive the medical and social services support they need; this can mean "pounding on doors. Making sure kids get to the dentist even when I've got to drive them. That they've got a winter coat to wear to school" (interview with Mrs. M).

Mrs. M's main objective during her 30 years as an ESOL professional has been to do everything in her power to ensure that her English language learners are equipped with the linguistic and cultural skills they need to actively participate and succeed in school. She sadly describes how the ELL children she has worked with over the years have been subjected to gross misunderstanding, racial abuses, and all out anger on the part of their classroom teachers and other school personnel. This is mainly due, she observes, to school personnel perceptions that ELLs' lack of responsiveness is "rude and disrespectful when these kids aren't understanding or that they don't know how to respond."

To these ends, she works intensively with her students on basic oral and written literacy, content area language and accompanying concepts, and the appropriate verbal and non-verbal ways of "doing school" that will gain them access to the academic/school discourse that surrounds them. This is her stated way of combating the negative reactions her students tend to experience: She immediately teaches them comprehension and responsiveness techniques they need to appear cooperative, to fit in. She accomplishes her multiple instructional goals through modeling, guidance, and investment-building that are profoundly respectful and caring.

Each elementary school in the district uses the ESOL "pullout" approach to ELL instruction. Children leave their regular classrooms to come to Mrs. M's room daily for 45-minutes of intensive ESOL instruction. The remainder of their day they spend in the mainstream classroom from which they are "pulled out" and where they receive little or no linguistic/instructional support.

Mrs. M's class sessions are held in a small private room. The room is bright and cheerful with posters on the wall. There is a table where the teacher plus 4-8 students can work together. Two computers line the wall to the side of the worktable. As soon as the children enter the room, Mrs. M engages them in level-appropriate conversation about their clothes, the weather, their health, the class they just came from, their family, and the like.

After these informal yet always instructional conversations, Mrs. M's sessions typically consist of group table work that focuses and prepares students to successfully engage in subsequent language and literacy activities that she orchestrates around the computers. Like most language instructors, Mrs. M makes use of software not designed specifically for ELLs. Instead, she uses native-speaker software that aligns with the theme of the class's current work and that can be used in ways that support learners practicing target language around the machines through interaction with their teacher and peers. She uses content-rich games, simulations, and productivity tools to complement her instruction. Sample themes of these activities are the alphabet, colors, animals, shapes, geography, and food. These topics steer focal academic vocabulary and each activity consistently integrates the five language skills: listening, speaking, reading, writing, and pronunciation.

Data Collection and Analysis

Mrs. M's sessions with two groups of ELLs were audio recorded with field notes made of non-verbal components of the activity over the course of 3 months. In addition to a 1 1/2 hour culminating interview, all informal conversation with Mrs. M before, during, and after class sessions was also recorded. Transcripts of Mrs. M's classes and her comments about them were successively coded on a number of emerging dimensions. Through processes of review, revision of codes, and re-review, labels were assigned to verbal and non-verbal actions on Mrs. M's part that formed part of the triadic scaffolds seen as predominating her work with ELL children around the computers.

The construct triadic scaffold grew out of observing a preponderance of similar verbal routines around the computer coupled with the fact that these routines appeared to most accurately characterize Mrs. M's approach to exploiting computers for their overall attention-getting and maintaining quality as well as the continuous opportunities they afford for language and literacy learning. Descriptions of these verbal strategies and what these were intended to accomplish were checked against interview data with Mrs. M as were the labels for the roles played by the computer. These data collection and analysis activities comprise an attempt to capture the special computer-supported techniques this one very experienced teacher employs to coax and support children's English language and literacy learning.

Triadic Scaffolds

Data consist of transcripts of classroom interaction and interviews with the participating teacher. Three coders, one of whom was the author and all of whom were language-teaching professionals, examined, discussed, and independently coded classroom and interview transcripts. Coders initially employed Meskill, Mossop, and Bates' (1999) unique features of electronic texts (publicness, anchored referents, instability, and anarchy) in their attempts to make sense of the role of the computer in these instructional conversations. In addition, commonly favored second language teaching strategies (modeling, echoing, recasting, and the like) also served to guide analysis.

Through discussion and negotiation of, and ultimately agreement on, terminology, select classroom data came to be coded by a set of (a) teaching strategies (both verbal and nonverbal, global and local); (b) the role of the computer in the instructional scaffold; and (c) what these combined (teacher + computer features) strategies appear to accomplish and what the teacher reports them as accomplishing. Due to their tripartite nature, these verbal instructional strategies came to be characterized as triadic scaffolds—three dimensions of an utterance that at once aims to teach language, is fashioned to be instructional, and references the computer in a sociolinguistically and instructional way.

Triadic scaffolds are thus comprised of and were coded as follows:

1. S—a teacher verbal strategy
2. C—contribution of the computer
3. A—what the strategy accomplishes

Those instances of strategies reported effective by the teacher—those that appeared to accomplish her aims—are clusters of verbal routines (including gesture) that clearly connect with learner investment in language and literacy learning with the computer. Two excerpts containing triadic scaffolds—one from each of the two pull-out classes observed—are explicated below. The first involves two second graders and the use of an alphabet game to reinforce pronunciation, vocabulary, spelling, and listening. The second involves three fourth graders and the use of an animal game to reinforce vocabulary, pronunciation, spelling, and listening. In both cases, the aim is less what the design of the computer software might dictate, and more the thematic focus and conversational opportunities for language and literacy work that its use affords. Illustrative triadic scaffolds are in bold with their components explicated in boxed, bolded text.

Four second-graders are transitioning from table-work to computer-work. They have been preparing for the computer time by reviewing the English alphabet and sound-letter correspondence. They work in pairs with an application called Alphabet Express, software designed for beginning readers whose native language is English. In the following, the pair of boys, Joe and Sam, work under Mrs. M's guidance. Mrs. M's stated instructional aim here is to teach listening, speaking, vocabulary, reading, and pronunciation simultaneously through talk and activity around the computer screen.

Two trios (one girls, one boys) are working at the computers using The Animal Game, a colorful software application designed for native speakers of English to learn the names and families of animals. Cathy, Fiona, and Rachel work together under Mrs. M's guidance.

In this brief excerpt, Rachel is watching the others, waiting her turn. Learners had previously reviewed animal names and their pronunciation during table work. Again, Mrs. M's stated aim is to work on listening, speaking, vocabulary, and reading simultaneously in an authentic context. The trios have been taking turns playing an identification game. The computer used by one trio is not playing sound.

Highlighted and labeled instances of triadic scaffolds are typical of the routines Mrs. M uses to teach language and literacy skills to beginning-level ELLs as they are use the computer. In these two cases, children are newcomers and as such speak and understand very little English. It is important to note that as they advance, so too will the complexity of the language Mrs. M uses in these scaffolds.

Typical teacher verbal strategies with these beginning-level learners such as directing, questioning, echoing, and focusing accomplish language learning goals; the computer serves to physically support and motivate attention while at the same time providing referents for the language in use. In all cases, talk and action are immediately perceived (public), situationally cued (anchored), and subject to both the machine's instability and to learners' individual or collective volition (anarchy). Children's responses to these scaffolds are continually evidenced in their attentiveness to the activity at hand, their continual nonverbal responses to the verbal scaffolds (pointing, moving the mouse, nodding, keying, smiling, etc.), as well as their verbal responses which, for beginning level language learners are both an accomplishment and a clear indication of successful progress in acquiring the language. Moreover, Mrs. M reports that she hears her students using the language that they learn while using the computer in other school contexts: "They use what they learn with me on the computers all the time. I hear them. Their teachers hear them. It's great."

In the first sample triadic scaffold above, Mrs. M uses the verbal strategy of directing ("What's this? Do you remember? Ohh the what? Sam, what is it called?") with the accomplishments of getting the children situated to use the computers, the sociolinguistic accomplishment of learners responding to aural directives and questions in English that are representative of school talk, and focus on the sound/m/ in mouse. The computer serves to provide an immediate, visual, anchored referent and thereby anchors the children's attention on what the teacher is saying, what they ought to be doing, and the literacy material they see on the computer screen. In the second triadic scaffold, Mrs. M uses an echoing strategy to reinforce the language these children need to acquire ("It's his turn").

The children learn the basic language of turn taking, making requests, giving and responding to directives ("The train"), and, almost incidentally, the pronunciation and spelling rules of the words on the screen. In this instance, the computer motivates and anchors the children's attention to these interactions while guiding them to affect the right outcome on the computer screen. She comments, "They get so involved with what I say and what they're doing on the screen that their comprehending becomes really easy for even the most basic beginners. They get it so quickly so I see them saying the same things I say within a couple of days."

With the older students in the second excerpt, the instability of the machine (it will not play sound, but may offer other options) focuses learners on attending to the language of problem solving being modeled by their teacher: "You really can't play without sound. You know what we'll play another game." This is high level language that Mrs. M is making accessible by virtue of the instability of the machine and their collective actions in response to that instability. Likewise, in the final triadic scaffold, Mrs. M provides the aural component for the learners' decision-making process while focusing the girls' attention on the information on the screen and the procedures required by the animal game. We can observe Mrs. M again using the language of directing to model and reinforce the language of school with the computer anchoring and motivating the children's language and literacy learning. The children consequently learn the language of goal setting and problem solving as modeled by Mrs. M and made possible by the instability and unpredictable nature of the machine and, again almost incidentally, the names and pronunciation of jungle animals.

In spite of the often "directed" feel to this teacher's talk, these interactions are eminently social in nature with children fully involved and responsive. The children's careful attending to what gets said and done is clearly evident; their acquisition of the language that gets used and scaffolded is likewise apparent. This is in contrast to the rest of their day in the mainstream classroom where there is little support for neither comprehension nor opportunity to participate. In Mrs. M's class learners actively participate in the conversation by moving the cursor around the screen and clicking the mouse as a form of response while Mrs. M models and forces meaning out of language that is directly related to sight, action, and the immediate social milieu. Each bit of talk is anchored to what is seen on the screen and to the social process of manipulating it and moving forward. She reports, "I am amazed at what I, whatever vocabulary, whatever activity I do with them, how it could be reinforced so easily now."

The forward movement evident in the activity requires collective collaboration in order to not stall. What is seen, said, and done to keep things moving along is, therefore, consistently relevant and salient—precisely what the language acquisition process thrives on. The children moreover enjoy a certain degree of control over the interactions as they are the ones holding the mouse, controlling the keyboard, and thereby directing the action. Opportunities for action are inherent when learners have physical/decisional control over what appears and happens on computer screens. With the language routines they learn in order to participate successfully in this kind of cooperative work, moreover, they are equipped to access the academic discourse that makes up the bulk of their school day as well as participate where they may not have before.

Skilled language teaching professionals consistently use what anchors they have available to exploit the aural-visual-action interface. This type of scaffolding—scaffolding that is particular to second language and literacy instructional activity—has characteristics that mark it as unique from the traditional sense of the term. Scaffolding in the Wood, Bruner, and Ross (1976) sense describes verbal moves on the part of an instructor that, while initially controlled by her, gradually guides responsibility over to the learner. In second language and literacy instruction, scaffolding has a three-fold purpose. Language teachers not only scaffold learning in the traditional sense of cueing, supporting, and sustaining thought, but employ the added dimension of tailoring learner attention to both the forms of talk and accompanying visual referents to which that language corresponds in the immediate physical and social environment.

Such calculated instruction requires continual use of an internal syllabus for each individual learner so that scaffolds can be implemented to give "support to the edge of a child's competence". In the case of children who also need to learn the language of school, a dimension of scaffolding becomes the modeling of school discourse and how it enjoins the ways school gets done. As composites, then, the triadic scaffolds used by Mrs. M reflect Gee's judicious mixture in that (a) learners are directly mentored into a community of practice; (b) their learning is overtly scaffolded by a skilled mentor; and (c) learners' attention is deliberately focused on "fruitful patterns" (the English language they need to learn).

While Lemke (1995) sees a monologic, controlling tendency in technology, he paradoxically also sees technology as a means of breaking old patterns of social reproduction. For, as new technologies become more widely available, the univocal transmission of voice through one teacher, or one school administration will become less sustainable. However much the presence of technology may imply equilibrium, the issue of traditional modes of social reproduction in schools that appears to be going on in these classroom conversations must also be addressed.

If we turn to the broader context of these children's learning and the social/pedagogical imperatives expressed by the teacher, we can see that her aim is to strengthen her students' voices and participation and thereby avert what might otherwise end up being an "ESL ghetto". Her aims are continually informed by immediate practical matters of survival for these children in a context where understanding the language of school is socioacademically crucial. Mrs. M is consequently ever watchful of the tenuous relationship between children's development of school-based language and literacy and their development of a theory of mind in their second language so that they have less risk of joining the ranks labeled "left behind": "These kids need to feel like they can do school, that they can participate like everyone else. I try to help them with that, with the English they need."

Some have suggested that having children use computers as tools for learning increases motivation in children who are less likely to be motivated by school. Mrs. M's ELLs are no exception. Indeed, she reported several anecdotes where children who otherwise "removed" themselves from the school community by keeping their heads down on their desks, crying, acting out, and behaving in ways that revealed strong disconnections with school, became highly motivated and animated when the computer was turned on.

I became most excited when we had this little boy John... John was unreachable. He was just, he was a first grader, very little bit of English. I couldn't get John to color. I couldn't get him to even get excited about using markers. Nothing turned John on. He had his head down on the desk most of the day—in his regular classroom and with me. And I was surprised by that, because I had other first graders and we did lots of little fun projects and the other six year olds were joining in, but not John. Then finally we put him next to the computer and Well! He sat up! I couldn't believe it. He had a smile on his face, and he started, I mean his eyes were bright! And I thought my god look at this kid, he wanted to interact, he wanted to do something. That was a real turning point.

John wanted to type his name, this is a kid I couldn't get a pencil in his hand, he was so lethargic, wouldn't hold a pencil. And here he's typing his name. It was amazing to me.

Such incidents parallel those of Elliot & Hall who found that explicit modeling of self-regulating behaviors around computer tasks contributed to better performance of at-risk preschoolers. Indeed the kinds of ongoing scaffolding provided by Mrs. M and those explicitly modeled and encouraged in the Elliot and Hall study are quite similar; both make use of the special features of the computer to anchor and support such strategies. Through this kind of activity, children learn to respond appropriately to oral directives and suggestions, to understand the language and rules of turn taking, and to follow the steps of solving a problem. In both cases, the computer context served to capture and maintain learner attention in ways unlikely to occur offline.

The kinds of verbal routines that are used to regulate and model regulation, what Wootton terms forms of "successive guidance," constitute the major material that initiates children into the discourse communities in which, if they are to be successful in school, they must fully participate. Technologies represent potential contexts where active participation of learners, in conjunction with caring teachers, can be orchestrated and orchestrated well. Studies of learning with and around computers consistently point to a teacher's planning, orchestration, and moment-by-moment support of learning as being critical to successful instructional activity. Nowhere is this more the case than with non-native English speaking children from diverse backgrounds for whom the social norms and accompanying discourses of school are new and challenging.

This experienced instructor exploits the machines in her classroom to stimulate children's enthusiasm for learning while exploiting the computers' special language and literacy affordances in ways that model, guide, and initiate learners into ways of doing school. Mrs. M's talk is dense with triadic scaffolds. Cross referencing what appears on the screen with her comments and directives is continual. On a moment-by-moment basis, we can observe her capitalizing on the physicality of the computer to orchestrate language and literacy learning. She exploits the computer for its capacity to draw and maintain learner focus, stimulate problem-solving, anchor discourse, and encourage learner-directed talk and action.

Oftentimes a lack of understanding on the part of educators concerning English language learners places their education in jeopardy. A key conceptual obstacle to understanding these students' needs is the folk assumptions that the language and complexities of "doing school" are inherently obvious. This folk model can spell disaster for those whose cultural/familial backgrounds do not mirror nor prepare children for these complexities. "The verbal abilities that children who fail in school lack are not just some general set of such abilities, but rather specific verbal abilities tied to specific school-based practices and school-based genres of oral and written language". Indeed, such cross-cultural situations can become exacerbated when unequal power relations are also at work. In school, those in power, teachers, use talk that reflects an "implicit model of literate discourse" that too often neither considers nor accommodates learners who have yet to be initiated into this specific genre of communication. Deconstructing the obvious is the ESOL specialist's first line strategy: Undertaking careful analysis of what children need to know in a given context. Her second is to orchestrate instructional activity that apprentices her students to learning language that can help them navigate and participate.

This seasoned teacher's instruction with computers and ELLs employs specific strategies that exploit the physical features of the medium to assist children in learning the language that will help them navigate these contexts. She uses the public feature to anchor language and attention to language. She makes use of the unstable feature to model problem solving and the language through which it can take place, and the anarchic feature to encourage learner volition and autonomy.

For Mrs. M's ELLs, these instructional sequences are just the beginning of their guided immersion into the world of the cognitive academic language they must master to participate in the mainstream, a process that risks derailing if the foundational language of doing school is not first mastered and used to access institutional streams of meaning. At first blush, what Mrs. M does with her learners may look like social reproduction of mainstream discourse structures, and indeed to some extent it is. However, equipped with the language that gains them access to, and acceptance at school, these children may be better poised to claim their identities and participate in the (re)shaping of schools than were they not so equipped. As active participants they are positioned to construct their contexts of being and learning, a process that benefits from inclusion as opposed to exclusion.

Technology represents no magic bullet for the problems of schooling. Indeed, empirical studies of programs of excellence for ELL children continue to point to excellent teachers as the prevailing influence on school success and that exemplary uses of technologies with elementary students are typically driven by constructivist models of teaching and learning. This examination of Mrs. M's teaching reaffirms the critical role of caring, thoughtful educators in meeting the widely varying needs of ever-changing populations of school age children while illustrating ways that computers can be thoughtfully integrated into language and literacy instruction. Delineated strategies and routines for giving and guiding the voice of at-risk English Language Learners as they use computers can serve as a basis for future empirical work on computer supported learning dynamics as well as points for modeling and discussion in professional development in computer-assisted language learning (CALL).

TEACHING ENGLISH LANGUAGE LEARNERS

Support materials for this title may be accessed through www.ablongman.com

Technology and Teaching English Language Learners is a professional text designed with the goal of equipping future language teachers with the tools technology provides for the English as a Second Language (ESL) learning classroom. The book is broken into eight chapters with a preface and index. The chapters cover subjects including communicative language teaching, content-based instruction for ESL students, using technology for oral language skills, using technology for teaching reading and writing, teaching thinking skills, culture in the classroom, and assessment. Each chapter deals with the issues surrounding these topics and their connection with technology.

The book uses an interactive style that introduces a question/answer format to relate the key issues within the text. For example, a sample question reads, "How does technology support language as communication in authentic settings?" Each section begins with a question like this one and is followed by a short answer to the question. Then examples and implications for the topic are shown. Each chapter ends with a summary of key ideas, a learning activities section for students to complete, resources for technologies, and resources for teacher development.

The text supports the teaching method of communicative language learning. There is a chapter devoted to the history and development of this method citing such authors as Nunan and Brown. It also shows how to use technology when using the communicative approach in the classroom. This text is best used for CALL training for educators going into ESL classrooms. Professors using this text will find it presents many practical issues and ideas they will probably be addressing with their students; and students will find this text one they may want as part of their professional library due to the resources it provides in the field of educational technology.

There are many strengths associated with this text. One hat is helpful to those unfamiliar to the technology field is the use of visuals and illustrations that show Web sites and activities mentioned in the text. If the text mentions a Web site specifically, a picture of the site may be shown to clarify and illustrate. This is helpful not only to those who may not be familiar with the technical language or examples, but also for visual learners who learn best by seeing what they read. Another strength of this text is the resource list at the end of each chapter. This section gives Web sites, software programs, and other important sources that teachers may find helpful to implement the ideas presented in the chapter. The resource list may also be an incentive for those studying from this text to keep it as a resource for their classrooms. The text is also useful due to the fact that examples are presented from a variety of ESL levels. Those in the K-12 field will find helpful examples as will those involved in the adult ESL field.

Another strong point in this text is the presentation of how technology will affect classrooms in the future. This is helpful because teachers need to be aware of the changes that may affect them in the future. Also, teachers may like that the text has learning activities associated with each chapter at the end of the chapters. They may assign these as activities for use in or out of class to help students make meaningful connections to the text. These activities are already designed for group work, which will also benefit teachers looking to save time during lesson planning. There are a few drawbacks to these activities, but these will be discussed separately.

Finally, the text presents a variety of cross-cultural/inter-cultural issues related to ESL (and second langauge learning in general) and shows how technology can play a part in resolving challenges brought up by such issues in the classroom. For example, the text addresses, "How can technology be used to facilitate respect for cultural differences within an ELL class?" The text then gives an example of how prejudice may be overcome by the development of projects involving the World Wide Web. The accesss of students to perspectives from students all over the world is an important factor for teachers to keep in mind as technology, and the Internet more specifically, becomes a prominent pedagogical resource in the majority of classrooms. The incorporation of terms from both the technology and ESL fields can make the reading difficult for some. Although it is apparent that the authors wanted their book to be an accessible souce for non-experts, it sometimes falls short of this goal with the extended use of technical terms and wordy sentences. A second problematic issue is that some of the suggestions may be unrealistic for many classroom teachers. For example, the book suggests that students be assigned teleconferencing to enhance their speaking skills. This is an excellent way for teachers to incorporate technology with the communicative approach.

Unfortunately, many teachers do not have access to the technology needed for such an advanced activity, thus making it a less viable option. Another example shows how teachers have used international projects accomplished via the World Wide Web to teach language skills. Although in this case the technology is available to many, time and organizational management of this type of project may make it unusable for some, especially those with large classrooms. Although, this attribute has a weak side it is commendable that the book offers a variety of options for the use of technology and some of the examples do have alternate activities from which teachers can choose.

Finally, the learning activities at the end of each chapter may be difficult for some students to perform. For example students to use examples from their classrooms and have knowledge of school policy in their region. This may be difficult for students who are not currently teaching or international students in MATESOL programs who would be unfamiliar with current regional policy. Thus, teachers using this text would need to take these issues into account and plan accordingly, either to avoid those exercises, or have the information available for the students to access.

Overall, this text provides many insights into the use of technology to enable language learners to acquire English to their full capacity. With its much strength teachers can take technology to a whole new height of usefulness in their classrooms. And, for those unfamiliar with technology, this book presents them with basic information about the tools that can make their classroom not only a technology friendly place, but a learning friendly place as well.

THE MEDIUM OF NETSPEAK

SPEECH OR WRITING

The Internet is an electronic, global, and interactive medium, and each of these properties has consequences for the kind of language found there. The most fundamental influence arises out of the electronic character of the channel. Most obviously, a user's communicative options are constrained by the nature of the hardware needed in order to gain Internet access. Thus, a set of characters on a keyboard determines productive linguistic capacity (the type of information that can be sent); and the size and configuration of the screen determines receptive linguistic capacity (the type of information that can be seen). Both sender and receiver are additionally constrained linguistically by the properties of the Internet software and hardware linking them. There are, accordingly, certain traditional linguistic activities that this medium can facilitate very well, and others that it cannot handle at all. There are also certain linguistic activities which an electronic medium allows that no other medium can achieve. How do users respond to these new pressures, and compensate linguistically?

It is important to know what the various limitations and facilitations are. A well-established axiom of communication states that users should know the strengths as well as the restrictions of their chosen medium, in relation to the uses they subject it to and the purposes they have in mind. People have strong expectations of the Internet, and established users evidently have strong feelings about how it should be used to achieve its purposes. However, it is not a straightforward relationship. The evolution of Netspeak illustrates a real tension which exists between the nature of the medium and the aims and expectations of its users. The heart of the matter seems to be its relationship to spoken and written language. Several writers have called Internet language 'written speech'; and *Wired Style* advises: 'Write the way people talk. '

The authors of a detailed study of an asynchronous chatgroup, Davis and Brewer, say that 'electronic discourse is writing that very often reads as if it were being spoken–that is, as if the sender were writing talking'. But to what extent is it possible to 'write speech', given a keyboard restricted to the letters of the alphabet, numerals, and a sprinkling of other symbols, and a medium which–as we shall see–disallows some critical features of conversational speech? Moreover, as the world is composed of many different types of people who talk in many different ways, what kind of speech is it, exactly, that the new style guides want us to be writing down? The language of geeks has had a strong influence on Netspeak hitherto, its jargon appealing to a relatively young and computer-literate population. But what will happen to Netspeak as the user-base broadens, and people with a wider range of language preferences come online? 'Write the way people talk' sounds sensible enough, until we have to answer the question: which people?

Before we can answer these questions, we need to be clear about the nature of spoken and written language, and of the factors which differentiate them–factors which have received a great deal of attention in linguistics. Speech is typically time-bound, spontaneous, face-to-face, socially interactive, loosely structured, immediately revisable, and prosodically rich. Writing is typically space-bound, contrived, visually decontextualized, factually communicative, elaborately structured, repeatedly revisable, and graphically rich. How does Netspeak stand, with reference to these characteristics?

What makes Netspeak so interesting, as a form of communication, is the way it relies on characteristics belonging to both sides of the speech/writing divide. At one extreme is the Web, which in many of its functions (e.g.

databasing, reference publishing, archiving, advertising) is no different from traditional situations which use writing; indeed, most varieties of written language can now be found on the Web with little stylistic change other than an adaptation to the electronic medium. Legal, religious, literary, scientific, journalistic, and other texts will all be found there, just as they would in their non-electronic form. Any attempt to identify the stylistic distinctiveness of Web pages will need to deal with the same sort of visual and graphic matters as any other variety of written expression. Here therefore we find a use of language which displays the general properties of writing: for example, Web page-writers typically have no idea who their readers are going to be, and in their guessing, targeting, and feedback-requesting they display the same behaviour as any paper-bound author or organization might. At the same time, some of the Web's functions (e.g. e-sales) do bring it much closer to the kind of interaction more typical of speech, with a consequential effect on the kind of language used, and many sites now have interactive facilities attached, in the form of e-mail and chatgroup facilities.

In contrast to the Web, the situations of e-mail, chatgroups, and virtual worlds, though expressed through the medium of writing, display several of the core properties of speech. They are time-governed, expecting or demanding an immediate response; they are transient, in the sense that messages may be immediately deleted (as in e-mails) or be lost to attention as they scroll off the screen (as in chatgroups); and their utterances display much of the urgency and energetic force which is characteristic of face-to-face conversation. The situations are not all equally 'spoken' in character. We 'write' e-mails, not 'speak' them. But chatgroups are for 'chat', and people certainly 'speak' to each other there–as do people involved in virtual worlds. Player X 'says' something to player Y, as in this sequence from one study:

Plate raises his hand and shouts ... Fork sighs loudly.... Plate says 'Nope'

These are 'speech acts', in a literal sense. The whole thrust of the metalanguage in these situations is spoken in character.

But there are several major differences between Netspeak and face-to-face conversation, even in those electronic situations which are most speech-like. The first is a function of the technology–the lack of simultaneous feedback. Messages sent via a computer are complete and unidirectional. When we send a message to someone, wetype itakeystro keat a time, but it does not arrive on that person's screen a keystroke at a time–in the manner of the old teleprinters. The message does not leave our computer until we 'send' it, and that means the whole of a message is transmitted at once, and arrives on the recipient's screen at once. There is no way that a recipient can react to our message while it is being typed, for the obvious reason that recipients do not know they are getting any messages at all until the text arrives on their screens.

Correspondingly, there is no way for a participant to get a sense of how successful a message is, while it is being written– whether it has been understood, or whether it needs repair. There is no technical way of allowing the receiver to send the electronic equivalent of a simultaneous nod, an *uh-uh,* or any of the other audio-visual reactions which play such a critical role in face-to-face interaction. Messages cannot overlap. As a result, recipients are committed to experiencing a waiting period before the text appears–on their screen there is nothing, and then there is something, an 'off–on' system which well suits the binary computer world but which is far removed from the complex realities of everyday conversation. The same circumstances apply even in two-way protocols, such as the systems which split a screen to allow the messages from two participants to be seen side-by-side; it may appear from the layout as if such dialogues are providing simultaneous feedback, but it is not really there, because of the temporal delay.

The second big difference between Netspeak and face-to-face conversation also results from the technology: the rhythm of an Internet interaction is very much slower than that found in a speech situation, and disallows some of conversation's most salient properties. With e-mails and asynchronous chatgroups, a response to a stimulus may take anything from seconds to months, the rhythm of the exchange very much depending on such factors as the recipient's computer (e.g. whether it announces the instant arrival of a message), the user's personality and habits (e.g. whether messages are replied to at regular times or randomly), and the circumstances of the interlocutors (e.g. their computer access). The time-delay (usually referred to as *lag*) is a central factor in many situations: there is an inherent uncertainty in knowing the length of the gap between the moment of posting a message and the moment of receiving a reaction.

Because of lag, the rhythm of an interaction– even in the fastest Netspeaken counters, insynchro nouschat groups and virtual worlds–lacks the pace and predictability of that found in telephonic or face-to-face conversation. Even if a participant types a reply immediately, there may be a delay before that message reaches the other members' screens, due to several factors, such as bandwidth processing problems, traffic density on the host computer, or some problem in the sender's or receiver's equipment.

All lags cause problems, but some are much worse than others. A low lag is of the order of 2–3 seconds, a delay which most participants tolerate–though even here some people find their tolerances tested, for 2–3 seconds is significantly greater than that found in most conversational exchanges. Anything over 5 seconds will certainly generate frustration, often prompting people to make remarks about the lag itself–references might be made to the 'lag monster' or to 'lag wars'. The frustration is on both sides of the communication chain. From the sender's point of view, the right moment to speak may be missed, as the point to which the intended contribution related may have scrolled off the screen and be fast receding from the group's communal memory.

And from the recipient's point of view, the lack of an expected reaction is ambiguous, as there is no way of knowing whether the delay is due to transmission problems or to some 'attitude' on the sender's part. Unexpected silence in a telephone conversation carries a similar ambiguity, but at least there we have well-established turn-taking manoeuvres which can bring immediate clarification ('Hello?', 'Are you still there?'). The linguistic strategies which underpin our conversational exchanges are much less reliable in chatgroups. Colin may never get a reaction to his reply to Jane because Jane may never have received it (for technical reasons), may not have noticed it (because there are so many other remarks coming in at the same time), may have been distracted by some other conversation (real or online), may not have been present at her terminal to see the message (for all kinds of reasons), or simply decided not to respond. Equally, she may have replied, and it is *her* message which has got delayed or lost. When responses are disrupted by delays, there is little anyone can do to sort such things out.

The larger the number of participants involved in an interaction, the worse the situation becomes. Delays in a conversation between two people are annoying and ambiguous, but the level of disruption is usually manageable, because each person has only one interlocutor to worry about. If a simple e-mail situation is affected by serious delay, feedback via phone or fax is easily providable. But when an electronic interaction involves several people, such as in chatgroups, virtual worlds, and e-mails which are copied repeatedly, lag produces a very different situation, because it interferes with another core feature of traditional face-to-face interaction, the conversational *turn*. Turn-taking is so fundamental to conversation that most people are not conscious of its significance as a means of enabling interactions to be successful.

But it is a conversational fact of life that people follow the routine of taking turns, when they talk, and avoid talking at once or interrupting each other randomly or excessively. Moreover, they expect certain 'adjacency-pairs' to take place: questions to be followed by answers, and not the other way round; similarly, a piece of information to be followed by an acknowledgement, or a complaint to be followed by an excuse or apology. These elementary strategies, learned at a very early age, provide a normal conversation with its skeleton.

When there are long lags, the conversational situation becomes so unusual that its ability to cope with a topic can be destroyed. This is because the turn-taking, as seen on a screen, is dictated by the software, and not by the participants: in a chatgroup, for instance, even if one did start to send a reaction to someone else's utterance before it was finished, the reaction would take its turn in a non overlapping series of utterances on the screen, dependent only on the point at which the send signal was received at the host server. Messages are posted to a receiver's screen linearly, in the order in which they are received by the system. In a multi-user environment, messages are coming in from various sources all the time, and with different lags.

Because of the way packets of information are sent electronically through different global routes, between sender and receiver, it is even possible for turn-taking reversals to take place, and all kinds of unpredictable overlaps. The time-frames of the participants do not coincide. Lucy asks a question; Sue receives it and sends an answer, but on Ben's screen the answer is received before the question. Or, Lucy sends a question, Sue replies, and Lucy sends another question; but on Ben's screen the second question arrives before Sue's reply to the first. Or Lucy, not yet having received Sue's reply, reformulates her question and sends it again; Sue replies to both; Ben then receives the sequence in the order Q1, R2, Q2, R1.

The situation may be further complicated if Sue (or anyone) decides to give answers to two questions from different participants, sending them together. The possibilities for confusion, onceorderlyturn-taking is sodisrupt ableandadj acency-pairs are so interruptable, are enormous. The number of overlapping interactions that a screen may display at any one time increases depending on the number of participants and the random nature of the lags. In a typical scenario, the situation is at best confusing to an outsider, it being extremely difficult to keep track of a topic (a *thread*). What is surprising is that practised participants seem to tolerate (indeed revel in) the anarchy which ensues.

Issues of feedback and turn-taking are ways in which Netspeak interaction differs from conversational speech. But Netspeak is unlike speech also with respect to the formal properties of the medium–properties that are so basic that it becomes extremely difficult for people to live up to the recommendation that they should 'write as they talk'. Chief among these properties is the domain of *prosody* and *paralanguage*–phonological terms which capture the notion of 'it ain't what you say but the way that you say it'–as expressed through vocal variations in pitch (intonation), loudness (stress), speed, rhythm, pause, and tone of voice. As with traditional writing, there have been somewhat desperate efforts to replace it in the form of an exaggerated use of spelling and punctuation, and the use of capitals, spacing, and special symbols for emphasis. Examples include repeated letters (*aaaaahhhhh, hiiiiii, ooops, soooo*), repeated punctuation marks (*no more!!!!!, whohe????,*

(Underbars are also sometimes used for emphasis, as in 'the real answer', but are less widespread, as they have other functions, such as their use as space-fillers in addresses to ensure that a compound name is a single electronic string.) These features are indeed capable of a certain expressiveness, but the range of meanings they signal is small, and restricted to gross notions such as extra emphasis, surprise, and puzzlement. Less exaggerated nuances are not capable of being handled in this way, and there is no system in the use of the marks–it seems likely that the number of question-marks or exclamation-marks reflects only the length of time the relevant key is held down. There are signs of other characters or character combinations being used in order to express shades of meaning (e.g. *sure/, \so*), but in the absence of agreed conventions it is difficult to know how to read such symbols, or what the user means by them. As a result, it is no surprise to find participants in chatgroups falling back on literary expressions in an attempt to capture the range of effects and emotions involved, using a graphic convention to distinguish the text from the rest of the conversation, as in these examples:

In virtual worlds, there are commands which allow people to express textually the emotion they feel, often with the addition of synthesized sounds and visual effects. Despite these innovations, users are aware of the ever-present ambiguity when the prosody of speech is lacking, as can be seen in the regular injunctions in usage guides to be careful, especially when engaging in humour or irony.

Related to this is the way Netspeak lacks the facial expressions, gestures, and conventions of body posture and distance (the *kinesics* and *proxemics*) which are socritical in expressing personal opinions and attitudes and in moderating social relationships. The limitation was noted early in the development of Netspeak, and led to the introduction of *smileys* or *emoticons* (a name deriving from Emote, used in MUDs to convey actions:). These are combinations of keyboard characters designed to show an emotional facial expression: they are typed in sequence on a single line, and placed after the final punctuation mark of a sentence. Almost all of them are read sideways. The two basic types express positive attitudes and negative attitudes respectively (the omission of the 'nose' element seems to be solely a function of typing speed or personal taste):

:-) or:):-(or: (

It is plain that they are a potentially helpful but extremely crude way of capturing some of the basic features of facial expression, but their semantic role is limited. They can forestall a gross misperception of a speaker's intent, but an individual smiley still allows a huge number of readings (happiness, joke, sympathy, good mood, delight, amusement, etc.) which can only be disambiguated by referring to the verbal context. Some commentators have even described them as 'futile'.

Without care, moreover, they can lead to their own misunderstanding: adding a smile to an utterance which is plainly angry can increase rather than decrease the force of the 'flame'. It is a common experience that asmile can go down the wrong way: 'And you can wipe that smile off your face, as well!' Those who get into the habit of routinely using smileys can also find themselves in the position of having their unmarked utterances misinterpreted precisely because they have no smiley attached to them. Usage guides warn against overuse.

However, they are not especially frequent; in one study, only 13.4% of 3,000 posts contained them–and some people did not use them at all. Most participants, moreover, made no use of most of the formal possibilities, restricting themselves to just one or two basic types, especially variants of the 'positive' smiley, as in:

dont be silly:) hi:)) that's a pain:)))))

It should be noted, too, that smileys have other roles than disambiguation. Sometimes they seem to be doing little more than expressing rapport. Often, their presence seems to have purely pragmatic force–acting as a warning to the recipient (s) that the sender is worried about the effect a sentence might have. David Sanderson makes this point in his dictionary, when he recommends:

You might include a smiley as a reminder of the ongoing context of the conversation, to indicate that your words don't stand on their own. A smiley can point out to the other participants of the conversation that they need to understand you and your personality in order to understand what you've said.

What is interesting to the linguist, of course, is why these novelties have turned up now. Written language has always been ambiguous, in its omission of facial expression, and in its inability to express all the intonational and other prosodic features of speech. Why did no one ever introduce smileys there? The answer must be something to do with the immediacy of Net interaction, its closeness to speech. In traditional writing, there is time to develop phrasing which makes personal attitudes clear; that is why the formal conventions of letter-writing developed.

And when they are missing, something needs to replace them. A rapidly constructed Net message, lacking the usual courtesies, can easily appear abrupt or rude. A smiley defuses the situation. (Incidentally, the same problems can arise with faxes, especially quickly handwritten ones, though as yet smiley-type conventions have not made an impact there.)

Whatever their function, and despite their limited use, smileys are one of the most distinctive features of e-mail and chatgroup language. But they are not the only mechanism devised to get round the absence of kinesic and proxemic features. Verbal glosses are also used, often within angle brackets, as in the prosodic examples above:

This convention is widely used in virtual worlds for all kinds of kinesic effects, such as and. Abbreviated words are also found in some groups, notably = 'grin', used to react to a message thought to be funny, or to convey teasing. The convention has developed a small system of its own: bigger smiles are symbolized by,, etc., and a range of acronyms based on the letter have been devised, such as = 'very big grin', <gd&r> = 'grinning, ducking and running' (as a music-hall performer might do after a bad joke). </gd&r>

These features of Netspeak have evolved as a way of avoiding the ambiguities and misperceptions which come when written language is made to carry the burden of speech. They are brave efforts, but on the whole Netspeak lacks any true ability to signal meaning through kinesic and proxemic features, and this, along with the unavailability of prosodic features, places it at a considerable remove from spoken language. Absent also are other linguistic features typical of conversational speech, and these make it even more difficult for language to be used on the Internet in a truly conversational way. These limitations arise out of the current dependence of the medium on typing speed and ability (see chapter 8 for future possibilities). The fact of the matter is that even the fastest typist comes nowhere near the spontaneity and speed of speech, which in conversation routinely runs at 5 or 6 syllables a second.

Even apparently spontaneous Internet messages can involve elements of preplanning, pausing to think while writing, and mental checking before sending, which are simply not options in most everyday conversation. Some features of spoken language are often present in Internet writing, as we shall see below, such as short constructions, phrasal repetition, and a looser sentence construction. But studies of e-mail and chatgroup interactions have shown that they generally lack the very features of spoken language which indicate most spontaneity–notably, the use of reaction signals (*m, mhm, uh-huh, yeah...*) and comment clauses (*you know, you see, mind you ...*). Indeed, some writers have identified the lack of these features as one of the reasons why so many Internet interactions are misperceived as abrupt, cold, distant, or antagonistic.

In face-to-face conversation, rapport, warmth, and agreement are regularly conveyed by subtle reaction signals which are injected at salient points by the listener; and the speaker adds softness, sympathy, friendliness, and solidarity by introducing such items as *you know*–there is a world of difference, stylistically, between *I think you're wrong* and *Y'know, I think you're wrong*. But because immediate reaction signals are not possible, and comment clauses are not a natural part of typing (most people are unaware they use them, or how frequently they use them, in everyday speech), these cues are missing from Netspeak. It is possible to do something about comment clauses, and Patricia Wallace is one who recommends their increased use, as a means of improving e-rapport.

Also, informality, and thus warmth, can be improved through the use of colloquial grammar and vocabulary and a readiness to introduce language play. But there is nothing one can do about reaction signals. Addressing someone on the Internet is a bit like having a telephone conversation in which a listener is giving you no reactions at all: it is an uncomfortable and unnatural situation, and in the absence of such feedback one's own language becomes more awkward than it might otherwise be.

Although Netspeak tries to be like speech, in its e-mail, chatgroup, and virtual world incarnations, it remains some distance from it, in respect of several of spoken language's most fundamental properties. One commentator has called it 'metacommunicative minimalism', which he characterizes in this way:

Textual cyberspace filters away all qualities of a personal self save the highly mediated, acutely self-conscious elements that appear in written language. Phatic or metacommunicative cues, the linguistic and paralinguistic signs that maintain cognizance of the social relation between the sender and receiver of a message, are drastically reduced in this medium.

Notwithstanding the way netizens routinely talk about their domain in terms which derive from everyday conversation, in my estimation the actual amount that Netspeak has in common with speech is very limited. The Web is furthest away from it; chatgroup and virtual world interactions are somewhat closer to it; and e-mails sit uncertainly in the middle. The latter three categories are certainly more speech-like than any other variety of traditional writing; but the similarities are balanced, if not outweighed, by the differences. So, if Netspeak does not display the properties we would expect of speech, does it instead display the properties we expect of writing?

Let us consider first the space-bound character of traditional writing–the fact that a piece of text is static and permanent on the page. If something is written down, repeated reference to it will be an encounter with an unchanged text. We would be surprised if, upon returning to a particular page, it had altered its graphic character in some way. Putting it like this, we can see immediately that Netspeak is not by any means like conventional writing. A 'page' on the Web often varies from encounter to encounter (and all have the option of varying, even if page-owners choose not to take it) for several possible reasons: its factual content might have been updated, its advertising sponsor might have changed, or its graphic designer might have added new features.

Nor is the writing that you see necessarily static, given the technical options available which allow text to move around the screen, disappear/ reappear, change colour, and so on. From a user point of view, there are opportunities to 'interfere' with the text in all kinds of ways that are not possible in traditional writing. A page, once downloaded to the user's screen, may have its text cut, added to, revised, annotated, even totally restructured, in ways that nonetheless retain the character of the original. The possibilities are causing not a little anxiety among those concerned about issues of ownership, copyright, and forgery.

The other Internet situations also display differences from traditional writing, with respect to their space-bound presence. E-mails are in principle static and permanent, but routine textual deletion is expected procedure (it is a prominent option in the management system), and it is possible to alter messages electronically with an ease and undetectability which is not possible when people try to alter a traditionally written text. Messages in asynchronic chatgroups tend to be long-term in character; but those in synchronic groups and in virtual worlds are not. In the literature on computer-mediated communication, reference is of tenmade to the *persistence* of a conversational message–the fact that it stays on the screen for a period of time (before the arrival of other messages replaces it or makes it scroll out of sight).

This certainly introduces certain properties to the conversation which are not available in speech. It means, for example, that someone who enters a conversation a couple of turns after an utterance has been made can still see the utterance, reflect upon it, and react to it; the persistence is relatively short-lived, however, compared with that routinely encountered in traditional writing. It also means, for those systems that provide an archiving log of all messages, in the order in which they were received by the server, that it is possible in principle to browse a past conversation, or search for a particular topic, in ways that spontaneous (unrecorded) conversation does not permit; however, in practice none of the systems currently available enable this to be done with ease, time-lags and the other factors described above making it extremely difficult to follow a topical thread in a recorded log.

There are well-established means of finding one's way through a traditional written text: they are called indexes, and they are carefully compiled by indexers, who select and organize relevant information. Indexes of this kind are not likely in interactive Netspeak, because there is so much of it and the subject-matter does not usually warrant it. There has been little research into the question of whether automatic indexing could be adapted so as to provide useful end-products.

The other characteristics of traditional written language also display an uncertain relationship to Netspeak. Is Netspeak contrived, elaborate in its construction, and repeatedly revisable? For the Web, the answer has to be yes, allowing the same range of structural complexity as would be seen else where. For chatgroups and virtual worlds, where the pressure is strong to communicate rapidly, the answer has to be no, though the fact that smileys and other graphic conventions have been devised illustrates a certain degree of contrivance. E-mails vary enormously: some people are happy to send messages with no revision at all, not caring if typing errors, spelling mistakes, and other anomalies are included in their messages; others take as many pains to revise their messages as they would in non-Internet settings–or even more, if there is some sensitivity over flaming. Is Netspeak visually decontextualized?

Immediate visual feedback is always absent, as discussed above, so in this respect Netspeak is just like traditional writing. But Web pages often provide visual aids to support text, in the form of photographs, maps, diagrams, animations, and the like; and many virtual-world settings have a visual component built in, with signs of adaptation even in text-only worlds (such as instructions to 'move North' or 'leave through the East door' on a game screen). Is Netspeak factually communicative? For the Web and e-mails, the answer is a strong yes. The other two situations are less clear. Within the reality parameters established by a virtual world, factual information is certainly routinely transmitted, but there is a strong social element always present which greatly affects the kind of language used. Chatgroups vary enormously: the more academic and professional they are, the more likely they are to be factual in aim (though often not in achievement, if reports of the amount of flaming are to be believed); the more social and ludic chatgroups, on the other hand, routinely contain sequences which have negligible factual content.

Finally, is Netspeak graphically rich? Once again, for the Web the answer is yes, its richness having increased along with technological progress, putting into the hands of the ordinary user a range of typographic and colour variation that far exceeds the pen, the typewriter, and the early word processor, and allowing further options not available to conventional publishing, such as animatedtext, hypertext links, and multimedia support (sound, video, film). On the other hand, as typographers and graphic designers have repeatedly pointed out, just because a new visual language is available to everyone does not mean that everyone can use it well. Despite the provision of a wide range of guides to Internet design and desk-top publishing, examples of illegibility, visual confusion, over-ornamentation, and other inadequacies abound.

They are compounded by the limitations of the medium, which cause no problem if respected, but which are often ignored, as when we encounter screenfuls of unbroken text, paragraphs which scroll downwards interminably, or text which scrolls awkwardly off the right-hand side of the screen. The problems of *graphic translatability* are only beginning to be appreciated–that it is not possible to take a paper-based text and put it on a screen without rethinking the graphic presentation and even, sometimes, the content of the message. Add to all this the limitations of the technology. The time it takes to download pages which contain 'fancy graphics' and multimedia elements is a routine cause of frustration, and in interactive situations can exacerbate communicative lag.

Once we take the different Internet situations into account, then the Web is seen to be by far the closest to written language, with chatgroups furthest away, and the other two situations in between. The differences are striking, as later chapters will further illustrate. But on the whole, Netspeak is better seen as written language which has been pulled some way in the direction of speech than as spoken language which has been written down. However, expressing the question in terms of the traditional dichotomy is itself misleading. Netspeak is identical to neither speech nor writing, but selectively and adaptively displays properties of both. Davis and Brewer see it thus, as an eclectic resource: 'Writing in the electronic medium, people adopt conventions of oral and written discourse to their own, individual communicative needs'.

Netspeak is more than an aggregate of spoken and written features. As we shall see in later chapters, it does things that neither of these other mediums do, and must accordingly be seen as a new species of communication. Baron, in a met aphor which take sup the species theme, calls it an 'emerging language centaur–part speech, part writing'. I would have to adopt an aliens metaphor to capture my own vision of Netspeak as something genuinely different in kind—; 'speech + writing + electronically mediated properties'. It is more than just a hybrid of speech and writing, or the result of contact between two long-standing mediums.

Electronic texts, of whatever kind, are simply not the same as other kinds of texts. According to Marilyn Deegan, they display fluidity, simultaneity (being available on an indefinite number of machines), and nondegradability in copying; they transcend the traditional limitations on textual dissemination; and they have permeable boundaries (because of the way one text may be integrated within others or display links to others).

Several of these properties have consequences for language, and these combine with those associated with speech and writing to make Netspeak a genuine 'third medium'.

NETSPEAK MAXIMS

How should we further characterize Netspeak, viewed as a novel medium combining spoken, written, and electronic properties? One method is to continue with the comparative approach used above. Several linguists and philosophers of language have investigated what counts as a 'normal' kind of conversation.

The philosopher H. P. Grice is one, well known in pragmatics research for his four maxims of conversation that underlie the efficient co-operative use of language. They can be expressed as follows:

The maxim of Quality

Try to make your contribution one that is true, specifically:

- Do not say what you believe to be false.
- Do not say that for which you lack adequate evidence.
- *The maxim of Relevance*
- Make your contributions relevant.
- *The maxim of Quantity*
- Make your contribution as informative as is required for the current purposes of the exchange.
- Do not make your contribution more informative than is required.
- *The maxim of Manner*
- Be perspicuous, and specifically:
- Avoid obscurity.
- Avoid ambiguity. Be brief.
- Be orderly.

The point of an analysis of this kind is not to suggest that we always behave exactly according to the principles; common experience shows that we do not. But we do seem to tacitly recognize their role as a perspective or orientation within which actual utterances can be judged. For example, people who tell lies or make false claims can be challenged; if they talk too much they can be told (in so many words) to shut up; if they say something irrelevant, they can be asked to stick to the point; and if they fail to make themselves clear, they can be requested to say it again. The fact that we do all of these things indicates that we are bearing these maxims in mind.

Moreover, if someone makes a remark that seems to flout these maxims, we instinctively look for ways to make sense of what has been said. If Joe asks 'Where's Uncle Kevin?' and Jill replies 'I expect there's a dilapidated blue bicycle outside The Swan', we do not criticize her for breaking all four maxims at once.

Rather, we take it for granted that she is co-operating in the conversation, and that (a) she has good grounds from past experience for knowing that a bicycle will be outside The Swan at this time; (b) she knows the mention of a bicycle is relevant, because Uncle Kevin rides one; (c) she knows its attributes include being dilapidated and blue, and feels that the mention of both makes for a more vivid or jocular sentence than one which uses just one adjective or no adjective at all; and (d) she knows that Joe knows all this, so that her answer will be perfectly clear. In such ways, and by making such assumptions, we are able to make sense of all kinds of superficially bizarre contributions to conversations.

It is not so easy to work out what is going on in the Internet world. Part of the difficulty arises out of the anonymity inherent in the electronic medium. This is not the first medium to allow spoken interaction between individuals who wish to remain anonymous, of course, as we know from the history of telephone and amateur radio; but it is certainly unprecedented in the scale and range of situations in which people can hide their identity, especially in chatgroups and virtual worlds.

These situations routinely contain individuals who are talking to each other under nicknames (*nicks*), which may be an assumed first-name, a fantasy description (*topdude, sexstar*), or a mythical character or role (*rockman, elfslayer*). In e-mails, the personal identity element (the part of the address found before the @) may be any of these, or simply a number or code, it then being up to the sender to decide what authentic signature the text of the e-mail will contain.

The lexical structure and character of the names themselves is an important feature of Netspeak, of course; but there are other consequences for the type of language used. Operating behind a false persona seems to make people less inhibited: they may feel emboldened to talk more and in different ways from their real-world linguistic repertoire. They must also expect to receive messages from others who are likewise less inhibited, and be prepared for negative outcomes. There are obviously inherent risks in talking to someone we do not know, and instances of harassment, insulting or aggressive language, and subterfuge are legion.

Questions about identity–of a kind which would be totally redundant in face-to-face settings–are also a feature of initial chatgroup encounters. Certain kinds of information are asked for and given, notably about location, age, and gender (not usually about race or socio-economic status). Gender is so sensitive an issue that it has given rise to the terms *Morf* (= 'male or female'), an online query addressed to someone who uses a gender-ambiguous name (e.g. *Chris, Hilary, Jan*) and *Sorg* (= 'straight or gay'). People seem to become particularly anxious if they do not know the sex and sexual preference of the person they are talking to.

Multiple and often conflicting notions of truth therefore coexist in Internet situations, ranging from outright lying through mutually aware pretence to playful trickery. As Patricia Wallace puts it, referring to the absence of prosodic and kinesic clues in Netspeak: 'The fact that it is so easy to lie and get away with it– as long as we can live with our own deceptions and the harm they may cause others–is a significant feature of the Internet. ' It is of course possible to live out a lie or fantasy logically and consistently, and it is on this principle that the games in virtual worlds operate and the nicknamed people in chatgroups interact.

But it is by no means easy to maintain a consistent presence through language in a world where multiple interactions are taking place under pressure, where participants are often changing their names and identities, and where the co-operative principle can be arbitrarily jettisoned. Putting this another way, when you see an Internet utterance, you often do not know how to take it, because you do not know what set of conversational principles it is obeying. Here are two such circumstances, both of which undermine the maxim of quality.

A *spoof* is any message whose origin is suspect; the sending of such messages, *spoofing,* is commonplace in some Internet situations. Unattributed utterances may be introduced into a virtualworlds conversation, for example. Normally, each conversational turn is preceded by the name of the player, along the lines of *Mole says, 'I'm hungry.'* But it is possible for a player to interpolate an utterance with no name preceding, such as: *An angry lion appears in the doorway.* Spoof utterances may also be inserted by the software, and not by any of the participants. When a spoof is noticed, the players may condemn it, question it, or play about with it.

The result can be a fresh element of fun injected into a game which is palling, with everybody knowing what is going on and willingly participating. Equally, because spoofing can confuse other players, and severely disrupt a game which is proceeding well, the various guides to manners in virtual worlds tend to be critical of it, and discourage it. Some groups insist on displaying the identity of the spoofer, such as by making the sender add his/her nick afterwards: *1,000 linguists have converged on Parliament–Doc.* Because there is no way of knowing whether the content of a spoof is going to be true (with reference to the rest of the conversation) or false, such utterances introduce an element of anarchy into the co-operative ethos of conversation.

A similar problem arises with *trolling,* the sending of a message (a *troll*) specifically intended to cause irritation to others, such as the members of a chatgroup. It is an innocent-sounding question or statement, delivereddeadpan, andusuallyshort, thoughsometrolls are verbose in their apparent cluelessness. For example, somebody who wanted to troll a linguistics group might send the message *I've heard that the Eskimo language has 1,000 words for snow*–then sit back to enjoy the resulting explosions. The term derives from fishing (the trailing of abaited hook to see what bites), though it also captures the resonance of the trolls of Scandinavian mythology–thebridge-guarders who would let people passonly if they answered a question correctly.

On the Internet, the bait is false information, deliberately introduced into a conversation to see who falls for it. People who respond, and correct the misinformation, show that they do not belong to the group, or are newcomers to it (*newbies*); old hands will simply ignore it, or–if they can be bothered–laconically send the response 'nice troll' to the originator, or *YHBT* (= 'you have been trolled') to the responder. Not all chatgroups troll; some insert clues to the existence of a troll into a message that only the cognoscenti recognize; some are very much against the whole process, conscious of the communicative disruption that can result.

The maxim of quantity is also often undermined in Internet situations. At one extreme there is *lurking*–a refusal to communicate. *Lurkers* are people who access a chatgroup and read its messages but do not contribute to the discussion. The motives include newbie reluctance to be involved, academic curiosity (researching some aspect of Internet culture), or voyeurism. Some manuals refer to lurking as 'spying'. *Spamming* refers to the sending of usually unwanted messages of excessive size. The origin of the term lies in a 1970 *Monty Python* sketch in which a cafe waitress describes the available dishes to two customers, and culinary variation is introduced by an increasing reliance on spam–'Well, there's egg and bacon; egg sausage and bacon; egg and spam; egg bacon and spam; egg bacon sausage and spam; spam bacon sausage and spam; spam egg spam spam bacon and spam; spam sausage spam spam bacon spam tomato and spam ...'–the whole interchange being accompanied, as one would expect, by the chanting of the same word from a passing group of Vikings.

In one of those semantic shifts which makes etymology such a fascinating subject, the term was first applied to cases where a single message would be sent to many recipients, as when a company sends out an ad to everyone on a mailing list, producing electronic 'junk-mail'. It later came to be used for the complementary situation–the sending of many messages to one user, as when a group of people electronically lobby a politician or attack a company's policy. Either way, people find themselves having to deal with quantities of unwanted text.

Not all spam is the same, either in intention or effect. Charles Stivale identifies three types common in virtual worlds: playful, pernicious, and ambiguous. *Playful* spamming occurs when visual or audio effects (such as a duck quacking) have been programmed to turn up in the text, unasked-for, at intervals within the game situation.

It can also be found when one character does something aggressively play full to another (a *bonk*–but not in the UK sense, please note), thereby eliciting a vociferous response. In some game situations (especially MOOs), several participants may simultaneously respond to a playful stimulus, producing a sequence of text messages on screen which come in so fast that they can hardly be read. *Pernicious* spamming refers to the Internet equivalent of real-life harassment, often involving sexually explicit language and description of actions, and usually prompting the introduction of control measures of some kind by the group moderators.

Lengthy aggressive utterances (*flaming*–see below) are often involved. *Ambiguous* spamming falls between these extremes. A participant might repeatedly send a message which irritates other players, or cause another player to do something unlooked-for (e.g. *Sting throws Moog out of the plane*) or be sent to another 'room' in the game (such as 'Prison'). The ambiguity lies in the fact that the intention behind the spam may be unclear, and the effect variously unpredictable. What counts as spam is often a matter of taste; as Marvin puts it: 'one participant's spam is another's entertainment'. But in all cases, spamming is a gratuitous addition to the communicative exchange, and thus breaks the maxim of quantity.

Flaming differs from spamming, in that messages (*flames*) are always aggressive, related to a specific topic, and directed at an individual recipient (spamming, by contrast, is often ludic or emotionally neutral, unspecific in content, and aimed at anyone within 'earshot'). It is similar in some ways to the ritual verbal duelling encountered between rival gangs and opposing army generals. However, there is considerable dispute over what counts as a flame, and why people do it. People's sensitivities, tastes, communicative preferences, and styles differ–as they do in everyday conversation, indeed, where it is also not always agreed between two parties whether they are 'arguing' or 'having a discussion', or why an argument has blown up.

Curiously, the two chatgroup parties involved in a flame often do not see their interchange as flaming, though other participants in the group do. Parties who have had their flaming pointed out to them are often surprised at the level of their linguistic aggressiveness–a function, presumably, of flamers finding themselves at a safe and often anonymous electronic distance from each other. Cultural differences intervene, especially when messages are being exchanged internationally, so that an observation which might seem totally innocent to a sender in country A might seem inexplicably rude to a receiver in country B. Also, it often takes time for a series of exchanges to develop from a mild disagreement into an antagonistic interchange, and it can be difficult to identify the point when this happens.

Plainly, an exchange in which participants have stopped talking about their topic and are simply exchanging verbal abuse would be a clear flame; but it is more debatable whether aggressive argument (of the kind common enough in much academic and political debate), continuing to focus on the topic, albeit rudely, is flaming or not. The point has attracted considerable discussion within chatgroups (where flaming behaviour is common, at least by comparison with e-mail). William Millard reports a case where a discussion moved to a different level, involving a dispute over whether a message was a flame or not, thereby attracting the attention of the list moderator, who attempted to control the way the interaction was going:

The message below is not a flame, although the poster claims it is. I have noticed on lists that when anyone uses the word 'flame' in a post hitherto dormant netters gather for the kill from all parts of the known electronic universe. Don't overreact here...

Ironically, such interventions can lead to a further discussion of what constitutes flaming, in which people take strong positions, and end up flaming each other about the topic of flaming–what Millard calls *metaflaming*.

Flaming behaviour, arising as it does out of frustration over the way a conversation is going, would seem more to contravene Grice's maxim of manner than of quantity. Its presence in Netspeak should not be underestimated. Millard, focusing on academic lists, identifies several factors in Internet writing which account for it. In addition to the metacommunicative minimalism of the medium, referred to above, there is also: the customary economic constraints on connection time (and thus on personal patience), the delayed response of the audience, or the uncertainties ensuing from the consciousness that Internet communities are new enough to lack clear social protocols–as well as the general underlying tension between conceptions of language as a transparent medium for serious work or a dense material for ludic performance –all of which, he concludes, 'implies that online academic writing as a genre is conducive to anxiety, wrath, and vendetta'.

The point goes well beyond the academic. Some groups have even gone so far as to experiment with flame filters, which search a message for potential inflammatory words or phrases (e.g. *get + lost/real/with it/life; you + noun*) and automatically exclude them. But the investigation of the formal linguistic equivalents of this particular genre of communicative competence is too rudimentary for such procedures to be reliable–both in what they exclude and fail to exclude. Rather more useful are such features as the 'scribble' comm and (used on the virtual community known as The Well = 'Whole Earth' Lectronic Link'), which allows senders to delete what they have sent, inserting in its place.

The maxim of manner is also seriously challenged by the way some Internet situations operate. Will contributions be orderly and brief, avoiding obscurity and ambiguity? Brevity is certainly a recognized desideratum in all Netspeak interactions, in terms of sentence length, the number of sentences in a turn, or the amount of text on a screen. Style manuals repeatedly exhort users to be brief; and while there are several signs of brevity in the different Internet situations, it takes only a short exposure to the Web to find many instances where the principle is honoured more in the breach than the observance.

Also, Web page designers constantly talk about the importance of 'clear navigation' around a page, between pages in a site, and between sites, with the aim of providing unproblematic access to sites, clear screen layouts, and smoothly functioning selection options (for searching, help, further information, etc). But the inevitable amateurishness of many Webpages (the cost of designing a high-quality Website can be considerable) means that the manner maxim is repeatedly broken.

In synchronous chat groups, the challenge is much more fundamental; there is an extraordinary degree of disorder, chiefly due to the number of participants all speaking at once, which makes a transcript of an interaction extremely difficult to follow. An interesting question is the extent to which obscurity and ambiguity is more likely in Netspeak because of the dependency of the medium upon typed input. Typing, not a natural behaviour, imposes a strong pressure on the sender to be selective in what is said, especially if one is not a very fast or competent typist. And selectivity in expression must lead to all kinds of inclarity.

Fourthly, the maxim of relevance–that contributions should clearly relate to the purpose of the exchange–is also undermined in some Internet situations. What is the purpose of an Internet exchange, one might well ask? In some cases, it is possible to define the purpose quite easily–a search for information on a specific topic on the Web, for example, or the desire to score points in a fantasy game. In others, several purposes can be present simultaneously, such as an e-mail which combines informational, social, and ludic functions. But in many cases, it is not easy to work out what the purpose of the exchange is. People often seem to post messages not in a spirit of real communication but just to demonstrate their electronic presence to other members of a group, to 'leave their mark' for the world to see (in the spirit of graffiti), or to use the medium to help themselves think something out.

The extreme situation is found in many chatgroups, where from the amount of topic-shifting we might well conclude that no subject-matter could ever be irrelevant. Informal conversation has long been recognized for its relative randomness of subject-matter; but identifying the threads of subject-matter in a spoken dialogue is simplicity itself compared with the nature of the exchanges in such chatgroups, where several topics are being discussed at once, participants are interpolating comments about the way the conversation is going, and irrelevant utterances are being routinely introduced (as in the case of spoofing) for ludic or other reasons. The notion of relevance is usually related to an ideational or content-based function of language; but here we seem to have a situation where content is not privileged, and where factors of a social kind are given precedence.

The social function of much Internet communication has been a major theme of the literature in recent years, especially with reference to the concept of a 'virtual community'. This notion has been not a little contentious, with some considering it an empty phrase, and others trying to give it a meaningful definition. Certainly, the mere fact of having engaged in an Internet activity does not produce in a user the sort of sense of identity and belonging which accompanies the term *community*. On the other hand, some Internet situations do promote such a sense of belonging, which comes from 'the experience of sharing with unseen others a space of communication'.

Underlying this view is a broader issue, to do with the way the Internet has come to be used in practice. To summarize a complexdebate (in a netshell, perhaps): the Internet is not as global a medium as it might at first appear to be. While in principle much has been made of its ability to transcend the limitations of physical environments, cultural differences, and time-zones, thereby allowing people from anywhere to communicate with people anywhere else about anything at all, in practice the types of communication which take place are much more restricted and parochial. Most Internet interactions are not global in character; we are not talking to millions when we construct our Web pages, send an e-mail, join a chatgroup, or enter a virtual world. Derek Foster, summarizing a paper on computer-mediated communication (CMC) by Garth Graham, comments: 'The interactivity of CMC is about human connections. It is about talking. It serves individuals and communities, not mass audiences. ' Howard Rheingold describes the Internet as an 'ecosystem' of subcultures. And Patricia Wallace identifies purpose as much more important than geography:

Though I like the 'global village' metaphor, the Internet is not really like that most of the time. With respect to human interaction, it is more like a huge collection of distinct neighborhoods where people with common interests can share information, work together, tell stories, joke around, debate politics, help each other out, or play games.

Internet users are evidently wanting to talk to others who belong to their interest group (subculture, elite, niche ...) or whom they would like to influence so that they become part of their interest group. Indicative is the way group members typically use such labels as 'guests', 'outsiders', and 'foreigners' when referring to visitors to their forum. The more light-hearted accounts go even further. Andy Ihnatko, for example, characterizes the situation in this way: 'the true purpose of language is to reenforce the divisions between society's tribes, or at least to make things difficult enough to understand so that the riff-raff keeps out.

The new language of the Internet, spoken by a great number of rather insular types who like to keep interpersonal contact to a bare minimum to begin with, is no exception. ' Sociological analysis now seems to be moving away from the view that the kind of reduced social cues described earlier disallow the development of complexsocial and personal relationships on the Net. Just because we use a restricted set of graphic characters does not stop people constructing a new social world, and some have argued that cyberspace in certain conditions permits considerable levels of sophistication.

Interesting linguistic questions follow. If real Internet communities are relatively small-scale, they will demonstrate their solidarity by evolving (consciously or unconsciously) measures of identity, some of which will be nonlinguistic (e.g. shared knowledge, a particular morality) and some linguistic in character. The linguistic features will take time to evolve, especially in a medium where technological facilities change so quickly and where some degree of nonconformity is commonplace among users, but eventually they will provide the community with an occupational dialect which newcomers will have to learn if they wish to join it.

Linguistic idiosyncrasies belonging to individual chatgroups and MUDs have often been noted, at least as anecdotal observations. One of the aims of what one day might be called Internet sociolinguistics (or dialectology) will be to determine just how systematic such features are and how many such dialects can be distinguished. However, it is also likely, given the constraints that come from everyone using a broadly similar computer technology and having a broadly similar set of motivations, that there will be a set of shared linguistic features, found regardless of the Internet situation.

THE LANGUAGE OF E-MAIL

STRUCTURAL ELEMENTS

At one level, it is extremely easy to define the linguistic identity of e-mail as a variety of language; at another level, it is surprisingly difficult. The easy part lies in the fixed discourse structure of the message–a structure dictated by the mailer software which has become increasingly standardized over the past twenty years. Just in the same way as we can analyse the functionally distinct elements that constitute a newspaper article (in terms of headline, body copy, illustration, caption, etc.) or a scientific paper (in terms of title, authorship, abstract, introduction, methodology, etc.), so we can seeine-mail safixedsequence of discourse elements. They will be so familiar to likely readers of this book that they need only the briefest of expositions. The difficult part, to which the bulk of this chapter relates, lies in the range of opinions about the purpose of e-mail, as a communicative medium, and about the kind of language which is the most appropriate and effective to achieve that purpose.

With over 800 million people using e-mail by 2000, and 100 million or so being sent each day, a consensus seems unlikely, especially when age, sex, and cultural differences are taken into account. At the same time, it ought at least to be possible to identify what the parameters of disagreement are, to develop a sense of the range of linguistic features which any characterization of e-mail would have to include.

An individual e-mail consists of a series of functional elements, for which terminology varies somewhat, all of which are similar in purpose to those found intraditional letters and memos. 'Compose' screens typically display a bipartite structure, with a preformatted upper area (the *header* or *heading*) and a lower area for the main text (the *body* or *message*). In some systems, if we choose to attach a file to the e-mail, a third space becomes available, in which an icon representing the attachment is located.

HEADERS

The underlying format of the header contains four core elements (different systems vary in the extent to which they display all four, and the order in which they display them):

- Thee-address (or addresses) to which the message is being sent (following *To:*), typed in full manually or inserted automatically by typing a prompt which calls up a character-string from an address-book (either the full e-address or a more memorable short form, or nickname); this is an obligatory element;
- The e-address from which the message has been sent (following *From:*), inserted automatically; this is also an obligatory element;
- A brief description of the topic of the message (following *Subject:*), inserted manually; this is an optional element, but the software will query its absence (e.g. 'This message has no subject. Are you sure you want to send it?'), and it is considered efficient practice to include it;
- The date and time at which the message is sent (following *Date:*), inserted automatically by the software.

The fact that these are core elements is supported by the information electronically recorded once a message is sent. These are the chief elements represented in the Outboxand Sent folders, under the headings *To, Subject,* and *Sent* (often, along with an indication of the server account employed).

When a message is received, they are the chief elements represented in one's Inbox (with *From* replacing *To* and *Received* replacing *Sent*).In addition, several optional elements are available within the header area:

- A space for addresses which are to receive a copy of the message (following *Cc:*, which stands etymologically for *carbon copy,* but which is often glossed as *courtesy copy*), inserted manually or automatically; here too, short and full forms of an address are available, the latter usually being placed within angle brackets; the message's prime recipient is informed that these copies have been sent;
- A space for addresses which also receive a copy of the message (following *Bcc:*, for *blind carbon copy*), but without the prime recipient's knowledge;
- A space in which a symbol (such as a paper-clip) appears if an attachment has been added to the message; this also appears along with the summary in the Outboxand Sent folders, and appears on the recipient's screen;
- A space in which a symbol (such as an exclamation mark) appears if a priority is to be given to the message when it is received (it does not have anything to do with the speed at which the message will be electronically transmitted); low, normal, and high priorities are usually recognized.

There is very limited scope for usage variation, within headers, because so much of the information is dictated by the software. The conventions of e-address structure (the registered two-part designation on either side of the @ symbol) are fixed, and if not followed exactly, the message will either not be accepted by the sender's software or will be returned ('bounced back') by the server to which the sender is connected (it may also disappear into cyberspace and never be seen again). The same considerations affect copies of messages– though e-mail manuals additionally raise the pragmatic question of the decision-making behind copied messages.

The sending of time wasting, unnecessary copies is criticized, and caution is expressed over the use of blind copies–for instance, if people other than the intended recipients learn of their existence, the motives of the writer may be questioned. If there are several main or copy recipients, the question of the order in which their addresses are listed may be relevant: in strongly hierarchical institutions, senior people may expect to see their names at the front of a list. A principle of alphabetical order is often advocated to avoid provoking unintended misinterpretation. So is the avoidance of excessive use of the priority feature: if every message is marked urgent, the convention ceases to be meaningful.

The language of the subject line, however, has received a great deal of attention. Because it is the first thing that the recipient receives, along with the sender's name, it is a critical element in the decision-making over what priority to assign to it or whether to open it at all (in the case of someone who receives many e-mails every day). A great deal of junk-mail, if not automatically filtered out, is known to be junk only because of the subject description.

Subjects such as 'Free Your Life Forever', 'Win $31,000,000 dollars and a PTC ruiser!', and 'Confidentiality Assured!' can be confidently categorized as junk (though I am not thereby denying its interest tosome), as can most messages whose subject is in capital sthroughout ('Do you have the Yen to be a Millionaire?'

'Don't go to sleep without reading this') or which have certain words emphasized ('Technology for You', 'For Serious Marketers only!'). For messages which do not fall within this category, other considerations apply. Because there is a limit on the number of characters to be displayed in the recipient's Inbox summary, lengthy subject descriptions will be truncated, often intriguingly, such as 'New edition of the Cambridge Encyclopedia and … ', and may be so unclear as to be informationally empty.

Clear, brief, relevant, and concrete subject descriptions are recommended in the various guides, with the most important bit of information put at the beginning of the line. Deliberately misleading subject lines (as sometimes encountered in e-mail from advertisers) are considered a breach of netiquette.

It is also important for correspondents to make continued use of a subject description, once it is chosen, to enable groups of related messages (a *thread*) to be placed together, especially if messages are forwarded. Even an apparently simple switch such as 'My review' (in the sender's subject line) to 'Your review' (in the subject line of the receiver's response) can be the source of difficulty–not immediately, but in due course, if the whole correspondence relating to this topic needs to be gathered together, for the first message will (typically) be sorted under M and the second under Y. Electronic filters require exact matches.

Similarly, subject lines need to be very specific, otherwise they will not be easy to retrieve at a later date: among the messages in my folder are some with the subject 'Your message', 'Reply to letter', and 'Re: visit', none of which are going to be helpful should occasion to search out a specific thread of messages arise. 'Writing a subject line with *real oomph*' is the heading in one usage manual, and as long as a reasonably broad notion of oomphiness is permitted, I have no problem with that.

Although the header is formally distinct from the message area below, it is not always functionally separate. It is possible to disregard the identity function of the subject line, and use it as an introductory element in the message itself. An e-mail from my daughter, enclosing a promised message, consisted of the following subject:

here it is...

The body of the message then began:

... all in one piece.

Another example had, as subject, 'friday nights gonna be alright', which was followed by the opening sentence, 'on the 10th that is'. This dependence of the body copy on the subject line is also sometimes seen in advertising mail, where the subject may be expressed as a question ('Do you want to ...?') to which the opening sentence of the body gives the answer ('Yes, you do!'). A further variation is a message which contains a greeting in the subject line: an example was 'Dear Mr Pinter', which the body copy then continued conventionally.

Greetings and Farewells

Turning now to the body of the e-mail, this too can be viewed in terms of obligatory and optional elements. The obligatory item is, patently, a message of some sort. What is interesting is the extent to which it is preceded by a *greeting* (or *salutation, opening*) and followed by a *farewell* (or *signature, closing*). Several types of e-mail have no greeting at all. They include first messages from people who do not know the recipient, and are therefore typical in the case of public announcements and junk-mail.

Some messages include an automatically derived 'Dear X' or 'Hi, X' in their openings, of ten with bizarre results. Automatic junk-greetings in my case have included 'Hi, Professor D', 'Hello, Crystal', and 'Dear Mr Wales'. Automatic acknowledgements, indicating that a message has been received by a system, or that the recipient is away from the office, do not usually greet, though the range of auto responses received by my son include:

Dear BEN CRYSTAL Dear b. crystal@restofaddress. com Dear bcrystal

Within institutions, e-mails can be mainly used for the sending out of information and instructions to all members of staff, in the manner of a traditional memo, so that a personalized greeting is unnecessary. A general enquiry posted to a group of recipients (in the manner of an asynchronous chatgroup), where the aim is to obtain information for the benefit of all, is also unlikely to be opened with a greeting (unless it is of the 'Dear all', 'Dear List Member' type) and just as unlikely to generate personalized responses.

Between people who know each other, greetingless messages are usually promptly sent responses, where the responder sees the message as the second part of a two-part interaction (an *adjacencypair*), for which an introductory greeting is inappropriate. For example:

Arriving message: David, will 7.30 be OK for the talk? Colin Response message: Fine

where the following would be unlikely:

Response message: *Colin, Fine.

or, even less so:

Response message: *Dear Colin, Fine.

The longer the delay in responding, the more likely the response will contain a greeting, if only an apology for the time-lag.

By contrast, two-thirds of a sample of 500 e-mails in my Deleted folder from people who know me contained an introductory greeting. They express a wide range of effects, from most formal to most informal, and indicate several kinds of social relationship and intimacy. They could be classified in many ways, but an important variable is the use of an initial endearment (*+Dear* messages were twice as common as*–Dear* messages).

–Dear

General word: *Hi, Hello again, Hi there!, Bonjour*

General word plus ID: *Hi from Pete, Goodday from Oz*

Intimate name alone: *David, david, Dave, DC, Dad*

Combination of general word and intimate name: *Hi David, Hey D, Hello David, Hello DC, Good morning David, Howdy David, Hi dad*

Formal name: *Professor Crystal, Professor*

[but never (yet): General word and formal name: **Hi, Professor Crystal,* **Hello Professor*]

+Dear

With intimate name: *Dear David, Dear Dave*

With whole name: *Dear David Crystal, Annwyl David Crystal* [Welsh: 'Dear']

With title and surname: *Dear Professor Crystal, Dear Dr Crystal, Dear Mr Crystal, Estimado profesor Crystal*

By far the most frequent individual greeting formula was *Dear David,* followed by *David,* then *Hi David,* confirming the general view about the medium as a means of informal interaction between people who know each other. On the other hand, such a range of greetings defies easy generalization.

Another factor is the location of the name, once it is used. The majority of my messages place the greeting at the head of the message body, usually spaced away from the maintext as in a traditional letter. This is always the case in *+Dear* openings. With informal*–Dear* openings, however, the location varies. It is most often spaced and separate (in a ratio of 3:1, in my corpus). When it is on the same line, it is usually the first word, but is sometimes placed later, especially in replies (*Thanks, David; OK David; Thanks for your message, David*), which to my intuition is more informal than an initial placement. It is unusual for an inserted name to appear much later in the opening paragraph, or in later paragraphs– though occasionally one finds instances of 'rapport renewal', such as (from a third paragraph):

Sorry to put you to this bother, David, but ...

This is no different from what is done in traditional informal letterwriting.

Farewells display fewer possibilities for variation, but the same points of principle arise. Two elements are available: a pre-closing formula (of the *Best wishes* type) and the identification (ID) of the sender. Most interpersonal messages (80%, in my case) end with both elements present, and the influence of traditional letter writing is evident in the overwhelming tendency to place each element on a separate line, usually spaced away from the message body. The remaining 20% give a name, and dispense with the formula. I have only one instance in my files of a closing formula which was not followed by a name–the sender perhaps thinking that it was not needed, given its presence in the header (alternatively, it might have been the result of forgetfulness, or have been mysteriously lost in transmission).

The usual range of formulae, known from traditional letter-writing, is employed, with the same range of functions (affection, gratitude, expectation, communicative intent, and so on): *Lots of love, Thanks for everything, See you soon, Let me know if this isn't clear,* etc.

The informality of the medium is reflected in the relative absence of the *Yours sincerely* type (turning up in only 5% of my messages, though it seems to be increasing). There seems to be no difference between old and young in their predilection for formulae, though preferences vary dramatically, as we would expect. (I cannot see myself ever using the *ta ta babe* used by one of my children to her friend.)

IDs can be manually or automatically inserted. The manual ones are of three kinds: first name, initial letter (s), and first name followed by surname (or vice versa in languages where the ordering conventiondiffers). Titles, qualifications, and other 'letters after the name' may be present, depending on the formality of the message; and there may also be a status or origin identifier on a separate line (e.g. *Course Organizer, Personnel Department*). In informal interaction, it is common to see the use of initialisms–either the initial letter of just the first name, or of both the first name and surname– even between people who do not know each other well. One reason for this is the bridging option it provides between the message body and a customized signature. In a situation such as the following, (1) may be considered too impersonal, and (2) redundant, whereas (3) combines an element of personal acknowledgement with the full information.

(1)

... so I hope to hear from you soon.

Dr James Smith 333 Some Street, Somewhere, POSTCODE, UK Tel: ...

(2)

... so I hope to hear from you soon.

James Smith

Dr James Smith 333 Some Street, Somewhere, POSTCODE, UK Tel: ...

(3)

... so I hope to hear from you soon.

JS Dr James Smith 333 Some Street, Somewhere, POSTCODE, UK Tel: ...

Automatic signatures are inserted by the mailer software, using text created by the sender and stored in a file. They can be quite complexpieces of writing, though the usage manuals consider lengthy signature files wasteful of time and space. Some consist simply of a person's full name (perhaps with title and qualifications), address, and communication details (phone, fax, e-mail, website). Some add a character note, often framed typographically (commonly within asterisks), such as a slogan, logo, favourite quotation, piece of personal promotion, or even a 'picture' (constructed out of keyboard symbols). For some reason I receive few e-mails from people who go in for slogans and quotations, but when they do occur they all follow the name and are typographically distinguished in some way:

By contrast, most of my son's contacts do add such messages. E-mail guides are circumspect in their advice, noting that the novelty, freshness, or impact of a character note quickly fades, and that ill-chosen items can return to haunt the senders once their interests or status have moved on. 'Cool dude' might have suited John Doe as an office junior, but he may not like to be reminded of his former e-identity now he is a company vice-president. Messages can last a long time, in e-mail archives. And, as Wallace puts it: 'Most of us enter cyberspace ... giving little thought to the online persona–how we come across to the people with whom we interact online. '

The farewell element has two important functions in e-mails, as distinct from traditional letters. First, it acts as a boundary marker, indicating that further scrolling down is unnecessary. There may indeed be additional automatically generated material on the screen, such as an advertisement for a mailserver company, a notice saying that the message has been checked for viruses, or a statement of confidentiality such as the following:

This e-mail is confidential and should not be used by anyone who is not the original intended recipient. If you have received this e-mail in error please inform the sender and delete it from your mail box or any other storage mechanism.

The farewell has come to indicate that no further personalized text is following–and it is this expectation which makes the use of postscripted text unwise. Many e-mail readers do not look beyond the signature. Secondly, the farewell has an extended identity function. Obviously it identifies the sender to the immediate recipient (typically providing information which is not present in the header, especially useful if the e-address is opaque), but it also makes this fuller identification available to others who may eventually see the message, in the case of forwarded or attached mail.

The overriding impression I have, even from such a small sample of material, is of the remarkable amount of variation which is found within the medium. E-mail guidebooks present a much more standardized picture, and in their recommendations reduce the range of options quite considerably. One of them is unequivocal in its support for first-name only: 'Start the message with the person's first name if you're communicating with a person you know on that basis. 'It is equally opposed to what it calls 'outdated or gender-specific forms, such as *Dear Sirs* or *Gentlemen,* from traditional business correspondence'. Similar points are made in relation to farewells.

Forms such as *Yours sincerely* are proscribed; single-word formulae such as *Thanks* or *Best* (or abbreviated forms, as with *THX* or *TTFN,*) are commended.

At the same time, this guide is aware that cultural differences exist: 'Be aware that greetings tend to be more formal and traditional in some parts of the world, such as Japan and Europe' (the authors are writing from a US perspective, hence the unitarian view of Europe). No recognition is given to the possibility that cultural differences of other kinds exist, which should also be allowed for–such as the differences of taste between people of different ages, personalities, professions, and social backgrounds. They immediately feel excluded from the medium. After reading one particularly prescriptive usage manual–prescriptive in its recommendations for informality, that is–a retired teacher commented, 'So e-mail's not for me, then'. Of course it is. It is the manual that needs revision.

As with other domains, allowing a range of linguistic options increases the communicative power of a medium, and usage manuals need to recognize this. In any case, people are voting with their feet: as with traditional spoken or written usage, they will be more influenced in their e-mail practice by the behaviour of their correspondents than by the recommendations of style guides.

As e-mail becomes a routine part of social life, at all levels, it will inevitably be influenced by the linguistic mores of its users. Already many people use it as a more immediate and practical way of sending formal letters and greetings cards (especially when there is a postal strike). In recent months I have received official invitations, letters of agreement, and many other formal communications through this medium, and replied to them in the same way. Some publishers (such as the *Times Higher Education Supplement*) now ask for reviews to be sent primarily as e-mails.

It is likely that the technological benefits of the medium (in terms of speed, forwarding, automatic typesetting, etc.) will eventually be a more important driving force than the fact that it permits a greater degree of informal communication than existed before. My prediction is therefore that e-mail in a few years' time will display a much wider stylistic range than it does at present, as the medium is adapted to suit a broader range of communicative purposes, and the legal issues surrounding the status of certain types of message come to be resolved. The contemporary bias towards informality therefore needs to be kept in perspective.

The body of the message

The content of the many e-mail style books is largely devoted to giving advice about how to write effective message body copy. Virtually identical material can be found in books devoted to older methods, such as letter-writing, typing, and business communication. Although the orientation is electronic, the content is largely traditional, giving advice on eliminating wordiness and cliche, and guidance on grammar (addressing the usual shibboleths, such as whether it is right to use passives, or to end a sentence with a preposition). At times, such books resemble a standard grammar, with tables listing the irregular verbs, frequently misspelled words, and commonly confused words (such as *complement* and *compliment*). Over half of any e-mail guide will be devoted to such matters. The influence of the prescriptive tradition is clear: for example, Flynn and Flynn have a section called 'Bending a few rules to strike an appropriate tone'.

They choose: 'contractions [e.g. *aren't, isn't*] aren't bad', 'feel free to end a sentence with a preposition', '*I, we* and *you* belong in business writing', and 'start your sentence with a coordinating conjunction'. Although this is a reaction *against* traditional prescriptive pedagogy, the effect is nonetheless to reinforce a highly selective view of what language is all about, by focusing on a tiny set of rules to the exclusion of the more general properties of language which characterize the main text of e-mail messages. These properties result from the two chief factors which define the e-mail situation: the limitations imposed by the screen and the associated software; and the dynamic nature of the dialogue between sender and receiver.

A widely held view (dating from the earliest days of e-mailing) is that the body of a message should be entirely visible within a single screen view, without any need for scrolling. Often, this is not a whole screen, because the upper part is needed for a listing of incoming messages. Insofar as people use e-mails for brief and rapid conversational exchanges, fitting a message into a single screen is easily achievable, and in my corpus most people do: 70% of my e-mails fit within the 16-line depth my screen makes available for the first sight of incoming messages. When the messages get longer, and especially when documents of considerable length are sent (as in much business e-communication), the style guides strongly recommend that special attention is paid to the information which appears on the opening screen– providing a strong first paragraph or a summary.

An analogy is often drawn with the 'inverted pyramid' style familiar from newspaper writing– the important information should appear in the opening paragraph, with less important information in the next paragraph, and so on. The analogy is apt. Just as a newspaper editor will often trim an article to fit a space working 'bottom up', by cutting the final paragraph first, then the penultimate, and so on, so an e-mail writer should assume that information located at the end of the message might never be seen, if the reader decided not to scroll down any further. The pressure to provide an executive summary is especially strong in manuals of business communication, but the principle has wider relevance.

The clarity of the message on the screen is a dominant theme of e-mail manuals. Clarity in this context involves both legibility and intelligibility. Legibility chiefly refers to ways of avoiding a screenful of unbroken text. Writers are recommended to use a line-of-white between paragraphs, for example, or to highlight points in a list using a bullet or numbering facility. (The increased use of bullet points is an important stylistic feature of e-mails, having previously been rare in letters and type written documents.) They are advised to use short, simple sentences, long ones being felt to be more difficult toreadon screen. But all questions of legibility have to be considered from two points of view–the reader's as well as the writer's. This is one of the unique features of e-mail communication: there is no guarantee that the message as reproduced on the writer's screen will appear in the same configuration when it reaches the reader's.

A common problem is for the line-length settings to differ, so that a message which sat neatly in 100-character lines at the sender's terminal is reproduced with a highly erratic sequence of long and short line-lengths on the receiving screen, or fails to wrap around at all (requiring an awkward repeated right-scrolling manoeuvre), or is processed so that the end part of each line is simply left out. Many manuals, accordingly, advise writers to keep their line length to 80 characters, to minimize the risk of this happening–or even 70, if message-forwarding is likely, as the tab character which is inserted in front of each line of a forwarded message uses up several characters of space. In addition, any special formatting (such as the use of bold or italic typefaces) may be lost in transmission. And attachments may be unreadable at the other end. No other type of written communication presents us with such potential asymmetry.

The pressure to maintain a message's intelligibility might be thought to be no different from that encountered in any other communicative domain. But the speed and spontaneity with which e-mails can be written and sent makes it more likely that the processes of reflection normally used with written language will not take place. Evidently many people do not read through their message before sending it–often with the unintended consequence that the first reply they receive is a request for clarification. The style manuals differ over the question of just how much editing should take place: on the one hand, they are anxious to maintain their belief in the medium's informality; on the other hand, they are driven by their a ware ness that, the more idiosyncratic behaviour departs from the norms of standard English, the greater the likelihood of unintelligibility.

Most of these manuals, written with a business readership in mind, end up paying lip-service to an informality-induced deviance and coming down hard on the side of the orthodox rules of the standard language. Misspellings, for example, are a natural feature of the body message in an e-mail (not in headers, where senders are usually scrupulous, knowing the consequences of error). They occur, regardless of the educational background of the writer, in any situation where there is fast typing and a lack of editorial revision. For the most part, these errors cause little or no disruption to the communicative process. No-one is likely to be misled by such e-lines as the following:

I'll procede with the practical arrangments. Hav eyou got the tikcets yet?

Noris there adergoing to make a social judgement about the writer's educational ability, on the basis of such data–a contrast with what *would* happen if someone wrote a traditional letter containing such errors. On the other hand, some misspellings can make a reader pause, or make an utterance ambiguous or unintelligible:

Cabwereachyouby8?

The latter examples are rare, in my experience. Of the hundreds of e-mail typing errors I have seen, hardly any really interfere with the meaning. None the less, some manuals are hotly against misspellings of any kind:

For every grammar mistake in an e-mail message there is an average of three spelling mistakes. If you think that you're saving time by not correcting spelling errors, think again. The time saved not checking your spelling is multiplied by the time that it takes for a reader to decipher the misspelled words. Misspelled words jar your reader's concentration by diverting attention away from the idea you are expressing. Not only are misspellings annoying and confusing, they also cause the reader to question your credibility. Misspellings make you look sloppy or, worse yet, incompetent.

And the same anxiety is expressed over punctuation errors–which in e-mails normally refer to omissions: 'Under use of punctuation in e-mail can impede communications.' The attitude doubtless has some force in the context of business communication, where prescriptive attitudes are likely to be strongly present, consciously or unconsciously. But as a principle of general guidance for all e-mail users, it is unreal. Most spelling errors do not distract from the content of a message. Lightly punctuated messages, given the relatively short sentence lengths, pose few problems of ambiguity. Nor, on receiving personalized e-mails, is the credibility of a mis speller or mis punctuator ever seriously questioned, because receivers are fully aware of the situational constraints under which the message was written. They are aware of it because, several times a day, they know they write under the same constraints themselves.

More important, in relation to intelligibility, is the question of a message's coherence, arising out of the inherently dialogic character of e-messaging. Although some e-mails are sent without any expectation of a response, the vast majority does expect a reply– and get one. Accordingly, the communicative unit, as in everyday conversation, is the *exchange*. The chief linguistic evidence for exchanges is the frequency with which response messages begin with an acknowledgement that there has been a previous message: direct feedback expressions, just as in everyday conversation, or elliptical and anaphoric (referring-back) devices, as the square-bracketed queries illustrate in the following selection of opening sentences:

- Yes, I think you're right [about what?]
- No, I won't be there [where?]
- Fine by me [what is?]
- Indeed–couldn't have put it better myself [put what?]
- He'll meet you at the station [who he?]

An explicit acknowledgement of the existence of a previous message is common: excluding replies which have been automatically generated (usually because the recipient is away), 70% of my messages begin with an acknowledgement:

Thanks for your message many thanks for your thoughts Sorry for the delay in replying

Formality varies greatly (*Thank you, Thanks, THX, Ta …*). In my corpus, the majority of the messages *without* any acknowledgement were very short–often one line or one word in length. This is understandable: it would be anomalous to add an acknowledgement which would be longer than the meat of the response. The following seems highly unlikely.

Acknowledgement is also sometimes omitted when the full text of the previous message is reproduced further down the screen, as when use has been made of the 'Reply to Author' option. The opposite situation also occurs, with a reply message consisting solely of an acknowledgement, such as *Thanks.* I have only four examples, so it is difficult to say anything useful about them. Usage manuals differ in their views about this practice: some warm to the fact that a courtesy has been expressed; others castigate it as a time-wasting device.

The length of the text comprising the body of an e-mail is relatively short. A sample of 50 personalized e-mails sent to me averaged 10.9 lines of body copy per message (excluding greetings, farewells, and attachments). There is considerable individual variation: the last 50 of my own e-mails to others averaged 6.56 body lines per message. (I am evidently a briefer respondent than many of my interlocutors.) The vast majority fitted easily into a single screen view. E-mails from institutions (ads, newsletters, business reports, press releases, etc.) were much longer–20 such e-mails showed an average of 30.65 lines per message (though this figure is more difficult to calculate, due to the insertion of all kinds of extraneous matter into the body copy, such as hypertext links). In terms of paragraphs, my incoming personalized e-mails averaged 3.28 paragraphs per message; my outgoing ones averaged 2.0. Institutionalized e-mails were much longer (as we might expect)– an average of 8.35 paragraphs per item.

Paragraph structure is short. Here there is no difference from what is found in institutionalized messages–nor, indeed, in my own outgoing messages, with 78% of my paragraphs being 4 lines or less. (I was surprised to encounter a 22-line paragraph, in one of my e-mails. I now find this difficult to read, and wish I had restructured it before sending.) One difference between personalized and institutionalized messages is that the former use three times as many single-line paragraphs; this seems to reflect the need for length to enable institutions to make their various expository (informational, marketing, etc.) points. Institutional oneline paragraphs tend to be the occasional slogan-like observation to which the writer is giving paragraph prominence (e.g. *There'll never be a bettert imetobuy*). In personalized e-mails, the one-liners tend to be a brief acknowledgement (*See you there, Thanks*), real or rhetorical isolated queries (*What time do you want me to arrive?, Wasn't the concert fine?*), or a response to an individual point (*The Smith book sounds intriguing, The session starts at 12*).

The dialogic character of the body element in an e-mail is made totally explicit when the 'Reply to Author' option is activated, and respondents add reactions which refer directly to the whole of a received message. The process is facilitated by the software, which makes a clear typographic distinction between original message and reaction. After early experiments using indention, standard practice is now to insert a right-pointing angle bracket (sometimes a colon or vertical black line) at the beginning of each line of the original message (including the paragraph-separating lines-of-white), so that (1) becomes (2):

(1) I hope to be there by six, though everything depends on the trains. Will you be coming by train yourself, or are you driving this time? I know Fred is bringing his car.

(2) > I hope to be there by six, though everything depends on the > trains. Will you be coming by train yourself, or are you driving > this time? I know Fred is bringing his car.

The reaction may then be added, in any of three locations: above the whole of the received message, below it, or within it–repeatedly, if necessary.

The procedure is a little like adding notes at the beginning or end of a letter, or in the margins, and returning it to the sender–but with the difference that in e-mail both parties end up with a perfect copy of everything.

All three methods have their advantages and disadvantages. Putting the reply first gets to the point straight away, but the receiver often has to scroll down to be reminded of what the person is reacting to–often necessary, if time has passed since sending the original message. Putting the reply at the end avoids this problem, but forces the receiver to scroll through a message which may be totally familiar–as it would be if it had been sent only a few minutes before. The former option is preferred in many professional settings, where it has become standard practice to reply to a steadily growing chain of e-messages by adding the latest response at the beginning, because when a tailback of messages becomes extensive, it is then very awkward to find a message located at the end and to print it out. In those companies which retain a paper record of their messages, printing out the most recent ones (as opposed to the entire message history) is very much easier if they are at the beginning of a chain, as there is no way of knowing which pages to select for the printer if they are at the end, since e-mail pages are not formatted on-screen in terms of printer pages. 'Print pages 1–2' is an easy instruction; 'Print pages 11–12' requires research. ('Print all', of course, is also an easy option –but at the expense of increasingly bulging filefuls of duplicated pages.)

Some usage manuals disapprove of the within-message reaction. 'Add your reply above or below–*never within*–the original message. 'In fact, within-message commenting is very common, when several points are being made which require individual attention. A within-message reply to (1) above might read:

> I hope to be there by six, though everything depends on the > trains.

I know–remember last time?

> Will you be coming by train yourself, or are you driving this > time?

Car

> I know Fred is bringing his car.

It would not be intelligible to give this sequence of responses at the end of the message:

> I hope to be there by six, though everything depends on the > trains.

> Will you be coming by train yourself, or are you driving this

> time? I know Fred is bringing his car.

I know–remember last time? Car

or at the beginning:

I know–remember last time? Car

> I hope to be there by six, though everything depends on the

> trains. Will you be coming by train yourself, or are you driving

> this time? I know Fred is bringing his car.

To make either intelligible would require major rewriting, with more explicit cross-reference to or paraphrasing of what the sender had said. In business communication, where documents can be very long and reactions to individual points erratically located, guidebook advice to avoid within-message reactions is well taken. A point might easily be missed, and it would be difficult to work out the nature of the overall reply from a sequence of individual, widely separated reactions. In professional correspondence, accordingly, there is a widespread preference for (3) as opposed to (4):

(3)

With reference to your points A, B, and C I think P, Q, and R respectively.

(4)

> Point A Point P

> Point B Point Q

> Point C Point R

But in most interpersonal e-mail, (3) is simply not an option, because of the rewriting (and rethinking) which would be involved.

Message intercalation of the type illustrated by (4) is a unique feature of e-mail language, and a property which could only succeed in an electronic medium. And there is a further refinement. It is possible for recipients to respond to an original message not by adding reactions to selected parts of the original text, as illustrated above, but by editing the original text so that only those parts which require reaction are left. The procedure is, effectively, one of quotation. Thus, for example, I sent the following paragraph (5) to someone, who replied as (6), cutting one of my sentences and pasting it into the new message:

(5)

There are still several loose ends for the Tuesday. We've had a lot of people wanting to contribute, and our original proposals for timing seem to be out. Do you think it would work having two sessions in the afternoon? It would mean cutting down on the tea-break, and maybe even timing dinner a half-hour later than usual. That in turn would push the evening session on a bit, but I don't see any problem there, as everyone is staying the night.

(6)

> Do you think it would work having two sessions in the

> afternoon? Good idea

The longer a sender's paragraphs, the more likely the recipient is to respond in this way. The result has been described as *framing,* because of the way in which the quoted text is demarcated typographically, either through an angle-bracket or a vertical line. Framing is a consequence of the ease with which people can cut and paste from an original message. It is also a feature of chatgroup interactions, where an extended discussion may make use of extensive quotation from several participants, providing the context for a reaction.

Framing has both strengths and weaknesses. It is a convenience, in that a series of points can be responded to rapidly and succinctly, either in the order in which they were made or in some fresh order– much as we can strategically recapitulate a series of points made by an interlocutor in a face-to-face discussion.

Time and memory are saved, as it is no longer necessary to trawl back through an e-mail thread to find the original remarks. And dealing with several points at once (a common strategy in asynchronous chatgroups) saves repeated e-mailing. Reactions to reactions are also possible, with each new reaction retaining its own framing device, so that the page takes on a nested appearance (as shown by the increasing angle brackets):

> B's extract from A's message

> > A'sextractfromB'smessage

> > > B's extract from A's extract ...

On the other hand, everybody knows the difficulties which arise when quotations are being used extensively: meaning can change dramatically when words are quoted out of context, whether innocently or deliberately. Deliberate out-of-context quotation may seem a strange concept to people expecting the e-mail or chatgroup worlds to be inhabited by polite, well-mannered, Gricean individuals.

But analysis of the reasons for flaming in e-interaction shows that misquotation, in order to score a point, is commonly implicated. It may even involve pre-editing of the paste: Tom finds an extract in Dick's message which doesn't quite suit the point he wants to make, so he alters it in some way, and then quotes it as if it were Dick speaking. In the hurly-burly of a chatgroup, nobody (apart perhaps from Dick) is going to take the trouble to check back; and retracing a thread of e-mails to find the relevant point (assuming the relevant items have not been deleted) can be just as laborious. It should also be noted that the option of misquotation is available to both sides: Dick can deliberately edit himself, too.

A framed message is certainly a most unusual object, not like anything else in language use. The stylistic consequences of cutting and pasting text from an earlier message–either our own or someone else's–are also unusual; here, too, there is nothing remotely like it in other domains of writing. Where else would we find so many physically adjacent but semantically unrelated paragraphs of text? In traditional writing, such texts would be penalized for lack of organization and logical progression; but in an e-mail, where the points are taking up different issues in a previous message, such overriding considerations are waived.

The bottom line is that, with e-mail, a new document is created with every transaction. The permanence of e-writing is only a superficial impression. Although a single piece of text may be preserved throughout a thread of messages, via forwarding or replying to author, each screen incarnation gives it a different status and may present it in a different form– either through electronic interference from the software or editorial interference from the new user. Linguistics has yet to devise ways of capturing such dynamic characteristics in its stylistic descriptions.

The issues go well beyond the linguistic. Traditional letter writing, through such features as its choice of notepaper, letterhead typography, style of paragraphing, and signature format, presented a facet of the writer's personality and standing. People can spend ages worrying over these matters– when ordering new notepaper, for example.

In some circumstances–such as the writing of references, job applications, or referee reports–the choices made inevitably affect the receiver's perception of the character of the sender, and influence the outcome in all kinds of unconscious ways. The 'meaning' of a message is much more than these mantic content of its constituent words. But when this kind of material is submitted by e-mail–as it increasingly is–all this extra meaning is lost. Publishers, for example, commonly paste extracts from readers' e-reports on a book proposal into a single document for submission to an editorial board. Instantiating this point, my Cambridge in-house editor remarked:

Inevitably a small part of the 'meaning' as intended by the author of the report is then lost, and some of the authorial control of the text has shifted to me as editor. I now have the power to undertake subtle but acceptable editorial interventions and juxtapositions which would have been barred from me in the era when the physical page was part of the message intended by the author.... Until a year ago [he writes in December 2000] authors of reports remained uncomfortably aware of all this, and there was a nervousness about losing control of format; but then suddenly that bridgehead collapsed, and now anyone will send you more or less anything by e-mail, accepting that an editorial re-formatting will inevitably come into play.

The willing surrender of control over one's written or spoken output is not in itself novel: journalists, for example, have long been used to having their copy altered by senior editors before it appears in print; and one never knows just how much of a radioor television interview will end up being used, or in what way editorial 'cutting and pasting' will affect what one has said. But e-mail permits the extension of such practices to a very wide range of communicative behaviours previously immune to such 'interference', and the consequences have yet to be explored.

Features such as screen structure, message openings and closing, message length, dialogic strategies, and framing are central to the identification of e-mail as a linguistic variety. This is not to deny the presence of other, more local points of stylistic significance, in relation to graphology, grammar, and lexicon, but these are not so critical.

There has been a tendency to highlight the informal features of messages–such as the use of contractions, loose sentence construction, subject ellipsis (*Will let you know*), colloquial abbreviations (*bye, cos, v slow, s/thing*), and 'cool' acronyms (*LOL, CU*)–but these are plainly not indicative of the variety as a whole, as many messages do not use them. Doubtless, given the question/answer basis of many exchanges, an analysis of sentence types will reveal a distinctive bias; for example, the intensity of questioning seems to be greater than in traditional letters, or even in conversation (where rapid-fire questioning of the type illustrated below would be considered a harangue):

Am I asking too much? Does this seem workable to you? Can you get to it, do you think? Do you * want * to get to it?!

Rhetorical questions also seem to be commoner in e-mails than in other varieties of written English, apart from certain types of literary expression. Advertising e-mails are full of them, reflecting a style that is more likely to be heard in commercial broadcasting than in graphic advertising:

How would you like to win ...?

Why wait?

What could be more addictive than both Pokémon and pinball... except for a blend of both? Catch 'em early by pre-ordering for just £22.99.

Have you ever wanted to see ... if it's sunny in San Francisco? if there's new snow at Vail? what traffic is like on Interstate 10 in Phoenix? Well, you can!

The status of a question–whether the sender expects or does not expect a response–is often ambiguous. Self-answering is more common than I recall seeing elsewhere:

Will Mary turn up? I doubt it, after last time. Who knows? Not Jim, anyway.

But these impressions need to be supported by some detailed survey-work before they can be proposed as distinctive features of the variety.

A similar caution needs to be expressed over e-mail graphology. The variety is plainly distinctive at a graphic level, in view of the widespread characterless large bland typeface which provides the default for many mailers: 90% of all my incoming mail uses it. But the fact that an HTML option is also widely available as a sending format means that it is not an obligatory feature of the e-mail situation. Much of the graphological deviance noted in messages is also not universal, being typical of informal Internet exchanges especially among younger (or at least, young at heart) users. I have already referred to misspellings, but examples such as the following hardly fall into that category:

Helllllloooooooo!

There is also a reduced use of capitalization, which may involve either grammar (e.g. sentence-initial) or lexicon (e.g. proper names), or both, as in these examples:

log onto the address below and you will see a mock up of our site the above is an advert I noticed for New Deal an excerpt from a tommy cooper forward igot

The usual range of punctuation expressiveness may be seriously extended:

Yes!!!!!!!! WHAT????? You've got a '"&*! cheek

Smileys are available for use, though they are by no means as frequent as the explanatory literature suggests. Common enough in the exchanges between teenagers, they are almost totally absent in my own incoming mail (apart from two instances from one of my children). Angell and Heslop comment: smileys 'are the equivalent of e-mail slang and should not be used in formal business e-mail messages'. But they do not seem to be much used in nonbusiness circles either. Ingenious keyboard typography may also be used to make material stand out, using asterisks, hyphens, bullets, pipes, and other symbols to create panels, boxes, and borders. Colour is also present, being routinely used to highlight hypertext links (www or @ addresses). The range of typographical options is bound to grow, as technology progresses. MIME (multipurpose internet mail extension) already exists as a standard for sending audio, graphics, and video files as e-mails. But at present, there are few graphic or graphological features that are universally present. Stylistic conformity there may be among particular groups of e-mail users (e.g. undergraduates, teenagers), but in the variety as a whole the potential for significant group differentiation exists.

The uniqueness of e-mail

Writers repeatedly draw analogies between e-mail and other forms of communication, in order to locate it in communicative 'space'. It is: a cross between a conversation and a letter, email is as fast as a telegram and as cheap as a whisper a telegraph, a memo, and a palaver rolled into one faster than a speeding letter, cheaper than a phone call a strange blend of writing and talking

Homer Simpson has it explained to him in this way:

Homer: What's an e-mail? Lenny: It's a computer thing, like, er, an electric letter. Carl: Or a quiet phone call.

From the above analysis, it is clear that e-mails do indeed have elements of the memo about them, notably in their fixed header structure. The informal letter analogy is also appropriate, with the medium's reliance on greetings and farewells, and the use of several informal written features in the message body. The telephone conversation analogy is also proper, given the way a dialogue style can build up over time; and the cheapness of the medium has often been remarked. And some e-mails are highly telegrammatic in style. But e-mail, in the final analysis, is like none of these. The consensus seems to be that it is, formally and functionally, unique.

Functionally, e-mail does not duplicate what other mediums can do. It is better than the telephone in eliminating what has been called 'telephone tag' (in which people repeatedly leave messages with each other to 'call me back'); on the other hand, if an immediate response is essential, and face-to-face communication is impossible, you cannot beat the telephone. E-mail is better than the letter in obtaining a quick response to an enquiry; but not for every kind of message. There is a widespread feeling that letters are better than e-mails for expressing negative content, such as breaking off a relationship or reporting a family death, and that telephone or face-to-face conversation is also better in such cases, where the full range of vocal nuance is needed to do justice to the meaning.

On the other hand, it has been noted that people have a greater tendency to self-disclose on the computer, compared with telephone and face-to-face conversation–a factor which, some think, partly accounts for the growth in e-romances. E-mail has also emerged as a means of communication where nothing was easily available before–such as between professionals whose erratic life-style meant that they were never predictably at the end of a telephone line, between parents and their children at university, or between partners separated by distance, for whom the cheapness of the medium is a godsend.

E-mail has come to be used for some of the purposes traditionally carried out by the letter (e.g. the sending of CVs or job applications, certain types of form-filling), but it has not yet supplanted conventional mail for others (e.g. contractual matters), because of issues to do with privacy, security, and legal tradition. While we may make copies of a will, or of our house deeds, the 'real' documents have a special status which it will be difficult, perhaps impossible, for e-mail to replicate. Certainly, at present, the incompatibilities between software systems (mentioned above) disallow any privileged status for a document where layout is critical, such as a legal document or a commercial advertisement. The limitations of e-mail, as a communicative medium, are in fact still being discovered.

There is no way of controlling an e-mail, once it has been sent; nor is there any way of knowing who will eventually see it or edit it. The e-mail guides are thus very emphatic in their advocacy of caution: 'Don't write anything to or about another that you would not feel comfortable saying face-to-face. ''Watch what you say', says another, 'Big Brother is watching you'– noting that employers and law-enforcement agencies may search your mailboxes.

The exploration of the legal implications is in its infancy. Many issues are known, some extremely serious. There have been complaints about e-bullying (e.g. in e-mail staff reprimands), sexism, sexual harassment, the use of libellous language, and rudeness (often arising out of a misplaced attempt to be funny or ironic).

There can also be ambiguities of an international kind: e-mails which refer to a local time (or date), without making it clear which time-zone is involved; e-mails which write the date in one way, forgetting that the convention is different elsewhere (e.g. 7/3/00 is 7 March in the UK, 3 July in the USA); e-mails which talk about '3 o'clock' without making it clear whether morning or afternoon is intended; e-mails which assume that local abbreviations (e.g. *ABC*) will be universally familiar (whereas it means one thing in the USA and another in Australia); e-mails which assume that a local geographical reference will be known (e.g. *East Coast*); and so on. Many e-mail users are still getting to grips with these matters.

The evolution of e-mail style is in its infancy, and perhaps the only thing we can say for certain is that it will soon no longer be as it currently is. Generalizations about the medium have hitherto been heavily influenced by its technical origins and early years of use. There is an understandable tendency to think of e-mailing solely in terms of informality. It feels temporary, indeed, and this promotes a sense of the carefree. Messages can be easily deleted, which suggests that their content is basically unimportant. Because of its spontaneity, speed, privacy, and leisure value, e-mail offers the option of greater levels of informality than are found elsewhere in traditional writing. But as the medium matures, it is becoming apparent that it is not exclusively an informal medium, and received opinion is going to have to change. Hale and Scanlon observe: 'A well-written electronic missive gets to the point quickly, with evocative words, short grafs, and plenty of white space. Spelling and punctuation are loose and playful. (No-one reads email with red pen in hand.)'

The evidence is growing that an awful lot of people actually do keep such a pen in mind, in educational, business, and other workplace settings, where e-mails are routinely seen as providing a more convenient professionalism (one that can speed up decision-making and build strong daily working relationships) rather than just an opportunity for a chat. Certainly, the spirit of the e-mail style manuals is very much towards being careful, stressing the communicative limitations of the medium. In due course, this emphasis seems likely to gaining round.

The result will be a medium which will port ray a wider range of stylistic expressiveness, from for maltoin formal, just as other mediums have come to do, and where the pressure on users will be to display stylistic consistency, in the same way that this is required in other forms of writing. E-mail will then take its place in the school curriculum, not as a medium to be feared for its linguistic irresponsibility (because it allows radical graphological deviance) but as one which offers a further domain within which children can develop their ability to consolidate their stylistic intuitions and make responsible linguistic choices. E-mail has extended the language's stylistic range in interesting and motivating ways. In my view, it is an opportunity, not a threat, for language education.

Index